Biotherapeutics
PROTIVA

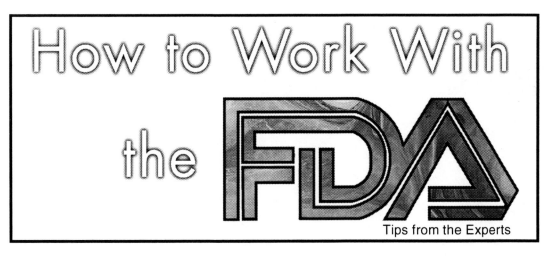

How to Work With the FDA

Tips from the Experts

Wayne L. Pines
Editor

Published by FDLI

Second Reprint 2002

To order additional copies of this publication, or learn more about FDLI please visit our website at www.fdli.org.

FDLI

1000 Vermont Ave., NW, Ste. 200 Washington, DC 20005-4903
Tel: (202) 371-1420   Fax: (202) 371-0649
e-mail: comments@fdli.org
website: www.fdli.org

About the Editor

Wayne L. Pines is an international consultant on regulatory issues, media outreach, and crisis management involving FDA-regulated products. He also conducts training sessions for pharmaceutical, biotechnology and medical device companies on advertising regulation, media and crisis management, and advisory committee preparation. Mr. Pines served for ten years at FDA as Chief of Consumer Education and Information, Chief of Press Relations, and Associate Commissioner for Public Affairs. He has headed the healthcare and regulatory practices at major communications consultancies, and currently is President of Regulatory Services at APCO Associates,- Washington, DC; Managing Director of Communications, Partners & Associates, New York; and Chairman of Therametrix, Inc., a healthcare market research firm in Plymouth Meeting, PA. He also writes a column, "Inside Washington," for WebMD. Mr. Pines is the author of the *FDA Advertising and Promotion Manual*, a legal/regulatory manual published by Thompson Publishing Group. He is co-editor of *A Practical Guide to Food and Drug Law and Regulation*, published by the Food and Drug Law Institute, and *When Lightning Strikes: A How-To Crisis Manual with Classic Case Studies,* published by Washington Business Information. He is a frequent contributor to the FDA regulatory literature. Mr. Pines is a graduate of Rutgers University and resides in Washington, DC.

Table of Contents

Introduction

The Food and Drug Administration (FDA) certainly is the most important consumer protection agency in the world. The products that it regulates account for twenty-five cents of every U.S. consumer dollar. Beyond that, however, the decisions made by FDA and the standards it sets have world-wide repercussions.

Yet to many outsiders, including people who themselves have worked there, the agency can at times be difficult to work with, inscrutable in its processes, and frustrating in its timing. Everyone who has dealt with the agency for any period of time will recognize the truth in this statement.

FDA has launched significant efforts to make its processes more transparent and more efficient, but an overworked staff dealing largely with confidential information whose status has serious medical and financial implications can hardly be expected to be easily understood.

Despite its public visibility, FDA remains a science-based regulatory agency that merits continued support and praise for a job well done. I know of no one who has worked for FDA, or who has worked with it from the outside for any length of time, who does not have the highest respect for the dedicated and sometimes beleaguered people who work for the agency.

FDA also is an agency with a high degree of scientific integrity. The outcome of interaction with FDA ultimately must be, and always should be, determined by the facts and their impact on public health. The process is often frustrating but that fact should be secondary. A new product will not be approved on the basis of process; there must be evidence of its safety and, when appropriate, its effectiveness. Whether a recall is required will be determined by an analysis of the hazard and the public impact, not the process.

By the same token, however, knowing how to meet FDA's requirements, and knowing how to interact with the agency in a productive way, can save time and money, and can therefore lead to a positive outcome. So, process does count in the long run.

This book is largely about process. It is intended to help the reader gain positive outcomes, in a timely and efficient way, by understanding the FDA processes better.

What do you do when FDA seems negatively inclined toward your application? What is the best way to prepare for an advisory committee meeting? When should you request a meeting with FDA, and how do you prepare? What rules of etiquette should one follow in dealing with FDA staff?

These and literally hundreds of other questions are answered by the expert authors.

People who deal with FDA all the time seem to know instinctively about the many "do's and don'ts" involved. There are strategies that work, and some that don't. There are simple steps that companies can take to comply more readily with agency requirements. There are options that sometimes are not considered when things go wrong.

This book attempts to compile all of the above, and more.

The authors were selected because they have practical, day-to-day experience in dealing with FDA. Some have worked there, while others spend their professional lives helping their companies or their clients navigate the agency. All are recognized experts in what they do. All have vast wisdom to share.

Many of the authors are former FDA employees, some of very recent vintage, who agreed to share their insights "from the inside," so to speak. One author, James Morrison, currently is the Ombudsman for the Center for Drug Evaluation and Research. His chapter presents a perspective from the other side.

The authors were asked to avoid simply writing about what the law and regulations say, and about how well-understood FDA processes work; all of this information can be found elsewhere.

Instead, the authors were directed to write in simple language, and to avoid footnotes or legalistic descriptions. They were given latitude to include their own personal experience. They were asked to share their insights into the process. What strategies work? What should be avoided? Are there shortcuts that can save time and money?

In effect, the authors are sharing their hard-gained wisdom and their own intellectual property with the readers. For this, they merit our thanks.

In putting together this book, my thanks go to FDLI's excellent staff, particularly Cathryn Butler, Director of Publications; Costa Bugg, Assistant Director of Publications; and Jean Everard, Administrative Assistant; and to Mary Royals of APCO Associates Inc., for helping to organize the process and especially for contacting authors.

My hope is that this volume will prove to be practical and insightful, and ultimately wise. And if you have a matter before FDA, I hope that this book helps you win.

Wayne L. Pines
APCO Associates Inc.

Kathleen M. Sanzo

Morgan, Lewis & Bockius LLP

How to Get Your Drug Product Approved

I. Introduction

The new drug approval process is a complex, costly, and time-consuming process that can materially affect the value of a company, large or small. A company's ability to obtain approval to market a new drug, generic drug, or an over-the-counter (OTC) drug with the desired drug indications quickly, efficiently, and without over-resourcing is of considerable value to a company and its shareholders. It is critical to strike the proper balance between adequate pre-approval preparation and cooperation with the Food and Drug Administration (FDA) to achieve these objectives. Following are some insights into how the process can be expedited:

II. New Drugs

A. Nonclinical Screening and Testing

- Although not necessary and in some circumstances not advisable, it is possible to discuss nonclinical testing plans with FDA reviewers, especially as it relates to issues of test phasing and timing.

- Although it is helpful to have a broad range of *in vitro* and *in vivo* nonclinical tests completed when preparing to submit an investigational new drug (IND) application, it is important not to unnecessarily delay filing the IND to obtain more nonclinical data because some nonclinical data can be generated during clinical testing. Because patent extension eligibility does not commence until clinical trials begin, it is advisable not to use significant patent time conducting unnecessary or duplicative nonclinical studies that do not add significant value to the initial pharmacology/toxicology database and discussions.

- Make sure that all nonclinical tests to support an IND are conducted according to good laboratory practices (GLPs) to avoid raising questions by FDA or creating an initial impression of lack of sophistication or unreliability of the company.

- If the drug substance has been acquired from another entity (e.g., a company or the National Institutes of Health), it is a critical part of due diligence to ensure that any nonclinical testing meets relevant standards for supporting an IND. Otherwise, the nonclinical tests may need to be repeated. This is especially necessary when using data that may have been generated outside the United States or at more basic research institutions where GLPs may be interpreted differently.

- In addition to Absorption, Distribution, Metabolism and Excretion and animal toxicity data, the nonclinical tests must adequately characterize the drug substance so that FDA will not be concerned about testing the substance on subjects. Consequently, adequate preliminary data on chemistry, manufacturing, and controls (CMC) of the test substance should be developed and provided to FDA.

- Ensure that the investigational substance is made under good manufacturing practices (GMPs), as applicable to small-scale production. It is particularly important for smaller companies or research institutions to understand GMP obligations, to avoid having their data disregarded by FDA.

- Discussion with FDA about the necessary scope of chronic toxicity testing is useful if there is a basis for proposing testing in only one species or testing for a more limited duration (less than twelve months). Similarly, it is useful to discuss with FDA reviewers the proper timing for chronic toxicity and carcinogenicity testing because such testing usually can be delayed to Phase II or later clinical testing (or some comparable point) after some evidence of efficacy has been documented.

- Early in the drug development cycle, consider the regulatory status of the proposed drug product and the type of application necessary. For example, is the drug a biologic-like drug for which a new drug application (NDA) may be submitted, or a biological that will be approved through the biological license application process? Is the drug an orphan product candidate? What effect will that categorization have on whether there will be generic competition for the product? Can the product be approved through a section 505(b)(2) application based on existing published literature or other evidence of safety and efficacy?

- If the product will be approved through a section 505(b)(2) application, it is important to talk with FDA officials early about the scope of any nonclinical testing, bridging studies, and other data requirements. In view of the newness of the FDA's section 505(b)(2) application guidance, detailed discussions with the agency also will be necessary to identify issues relating to exclusivity eligibility.

III. Submission of the IND — Initiation of Clinical Trials

- It is advisable to arrange a pre-IND meeting with FDA if there are serious or novel questions about the proposed test protocol or safety of the drug substance, or if the sponsor intends to conduct expedited development using surrogate endpoints, compressed clinical trials, or fast-track review. Otherwise, it is not necessary to meet with FDA. Also, meetings actually may cause delay, as they provide an opportunity for the identification of minor issues. When a meeting is arranged, it is useful to designate one person from the company to act as the contact point with FDA throughout the IND/NDA review process. The spokesperson most often comes from the company's regulatory affairs department, and less often from the clinical research department.

- At the beginning of the clinical (and sometimes even nonclinical) phase, make sure that the company team is completely familiar with all FDA's applicable guidances and that the team objective is to produce data and ultimately an NDA that facilitates FDA review and approval of the substance.

- The IND should be written sufficiently broadly to allow for modification or expansion of the trials without filing new INDs. There may be commercial reasons, however, for having multiple INDs on the same drug substance (e.g., exploring significantly different indications with different parameters or sharing investigational responsibilities with corporate partners).

- The IND sponsor must consider strategically how much of the detail of the protocol to submit to FDA. The more detail provided, the more specific guidance may be obtained from FDA reviewers, and the more objections or issues may be raised by FDA.

- Important aspects of the clinical protocol to consider prior to submission to or discussion with FDA include:

    (1) primary and secondary objectives of the study;

    (2) target population(s), including pediatric, if appropriate, with subject exclusion and inclusion criteria specified and rationale for the control group(s) identified;

    (3) primary efficacy endpoints or surrogate endpoints, if proposing fast-track review, and protocols intended if these endpoints are not achieved; and

    (4) specific identification of the process, and entity responsible, for any proposed interim analysis to avoid questions about the conditions of such analysis.

- The sponsor should consider whether the product is eligible for orphan drug status and, if so, whether orphan status makes sense for this particular product in view of future brand extensions, exclusivity objectives, and testing issues. Does the appropriate population exist, and is the drug's use in that population medically plausible? What patient or other groups will support the status? If orphan drug designation is a possibility, it should be discussed as early as possible with both the Office of Orphan Drug Products (ODP) and the reviewing division. The reviewing division, for example, may help persuade ODP that the indication is medically plausible.

- The institutional review board (IRB) that monitors a company's clinical trials preferably is resident at the institution at which the trial is taking place. If it is necessary to use a separately-organized IRB that is not affiliated with an institution, ensure that all members are adequate experts, that they represent different perspectives, and that all review processes are properly documented. This will help to avoid questions and additional delays in FDA review.

- Once an FDA reviewing team is assigned to the IND, sponsors should find out as much as possible about each member on the team, either through prior internal experience or through discussions with consultants or other industry officials. The consumer safety officer (CSO)/project manager will be the principal contact for the IND/NDA. It is a good idea to become well acquainted with certain aspects of the CSO: how he/she prefers to discuss issues; how he/she documents agreements; and his/her willingness to discuss issues early, informally, and directly versus only through formal discussion when all agency views have been identified.

- Ordinarily, Phase 2 and 3 protocols will be submitted as amendments to the IND. Phase 2 is intended to begin testing for efficacy and to establish safety parameters in a larger number of patients. If the sponsor intends to request drug approval based on one adequate and well-controlled pivotal trial, the Phase 2 and 3 trials should be larger in patient numbers and multi-center. If only one trial is planned, it is useful to discuss the likelihood of success of the trial with the CSO and medical reviewers, and contingency plans if it does not show sufficient evidence of efficacy.

- During clinical trials, it is critical to closely monitor the studies' progress through the company project leader, the contract research organization (CRO) conducting the studies, or individual investigators. This is especially necessary with respect to reviewing adverse events and conducting adequate trend analysis of them, despite the fact that it often is difficult to know how to characterize an adverse event that occurs when attempting to treat diseases that involve use of multiple medications or that cause multiple organ failure. Similarly, it is difficult to determine the reportability of adverse events that result from clinical trials abroad; FDA generally does not want to receive reports that cannot be analyzed meaningfully. Nonetheless, if the adverse event is life-threatening, it is prudent to discuss it with the reviewing division as soon as possible and reach agreement on its potential relevance.

- IND inspections by FDA are infrequently conducted, unless the research involves gene therapy products.

- Any additional or enhanced CMC data that is developed, or that relates to changes to the formulation being tested, should be submitted on a rolling basis to FDA to avoid delays in review and concern about relevance of the test substance. CMC meetings consistent with FDA's new guidance document should be considered.

- A meeting between sponsor representatives and agency personnel at the end of Phase 2 is important. Such a setting allows companies to meet with the reviewing team, receive initial FDA feedback on clinical trial results, receive agreement as to the proper protocol for Phase 3 studies, resolve any formulation or CMC questions to ensure meaningful data is collected. New Prescription Drug User Fee Act (PDUFA) II requirements mandate that such meetings take place generally within sixty days of the request. For these meetings to be most productive and useful to the sponsor, the sponsor should be well-prepared to present the results of the Phase 2 studies and to discuss the Phase 3 protocol as well as any CMC concerns about product manufacture. Any new *in vitro* or *in vivo* data should be provided also. The sponsor should ensure that FDA promptly prepares minutes of the meeting and that the minutes accurately reflect the agency's comments and/or the parties' agreements on testing issues.

- End of Phase 2/pre-Phase 3 meetings should also be used to discuss the need for or requests of a special protocol assessment for animal carcinogenicity, product stability, and Phase 3 tests. The protocol assessment procedure is in response to PDUFA and results in a binding commitment by FDA to the protocol within 45 days of submission for review. Sponsors should follow closely FDA's new guidelines on the procedure to request protocol review during the initial period of implementation of this program.

- Depending on the indications for the drug and the patient population, as more expansive trials on the product are conducted, the company may receive requests for physician-sponsored or treatment INDs for patients not otherwise eligible for clinical trials. FDA generally does not object to such uses as long as they are not perceived as being company-initiated or used for market seeding purposes. Therefore, careful monitoring of the numbers of such INDs is warranted.

- If, at any time during clinical trials and for any reason, FDA contacts the company to suggest a clinical hold, the company should ask the CSO to identify the problem/deficiencies. Informal discussions about resolution should be undertaken immediately. FDA generally is receptive to, and is helpful in suggesting, methods to resolve asserted deficiencies.

- The FDA reviewing team will communicate with the company project leaders on questions about the IND, and later about the NDA, especially if the application is submitted on a rolling basis. It is important to document internally all telephone conferences with FDA and to confirm them with the agency if substantive agreement on a material issue is reached. Such correspondence may be useful later in the event of changes in team members, disagreements with team members, or controversy or litigation concerning approval of the product or competitive products.

- Similarly, company representatives should understand that all telephone contacts/conferences with FDA will be recorded in writing, and FDA will use such minutes to dispute issues and support litigation. There generally is no "off-the-record" or informal discussion with an FDA team member.

IV. Submission and Review of the NDA

- Although the reviewing team for the NDA is likely to consist of the same or many of the same members from the IND team, there may be new members and additional levels of review. Due diligence on any new members of the team should be conducted. Although it may be evident from the clinical testing period, each reviewing division has its own personality and idiosyncracies with which the sponsor project director must be familiar and understand.

- Assuming that the NDA is accepted for filing, it is useful during the first two months of review to determine from the CSO the priority designation given to the application and, if possible, any review time objectives set internally by the division. In addition, the company should try to ascertain the intended schedule of any pre-approval inspection.

- Depending on the drug, the sponsor may be eligible throughout the NDA review to request various meetings with the reviewing team. These meetings often can be conducted by videoconference, by teleconference, or face-to-face. The preferred communication format should be decided based on the seriousness of potential problems. The meetings may take place near the three-month point (for new chemical entities), toward the end of the review (e.g., to discuss labeling issues or Phase 4 testing commitments), or at any other time there is a significant problem with the sponsor's findings or data. Generally, the sponsor must submit a formal written request for a meeting, even if the meeting is at the suggestion of the agency. In deciding whether to request a meeting, sponsors should determine the objectives of the meeting, keeping in mind the need to choose battles carefully and the need to preserve good will among the reviewers. If a meeting is not necessary, do not request one, even if upper management insists on some form of agency progress report.

- Throughout the NDA review process, it is important to listen closely to FDA reviewers, especially at the mid-review period or the end of the primary review, for any indications of concern, doubt, or need for re-analysis or analysis of different patient populations. Companies often are completely surprised to receive a phone call or information request from the CSO, stating that the agency has identified significant deficiencies and/or cannot approve the NDA, usually due to insufficient evidence of efficacy. Similarly, FDA's comments and questions concerning presentation of the product to an advisory committee often will give a good indication of the agency's view of the efficacy data's strength. When that call comes, it generally is more productive to identify the deficiencies and determine the cost and time to correct them rather than to threaten to go to the Commissioner's office or to sue FDA (which often is the immediate corporate reaction).

- Companies spend much time considering the need for advisory committee review. Agency review deadlines tend to make use of advisory committees the exception rather than the general rule, but it is essential that companies carefully consider: the need for, and possible benefits and risks of, an advisory committee review; whether FDA has indicated a strong position on the need for the review; company time and resources necessary to prepare for such a meeting; and both the positive and negative public relations aspects to committee recommendations. If FDA intends to submit the product to an advisory committee, ample preparation for the meeting is necessary.

- If the proprietary name of the product is critical and has been in use in other markets, the sponsor should communicate with the reviewing division and the Office of Postmarketing Drug Risk Assessment (OPDRA) (previously called the Labeling and Nomenclature Committee (LNC)) early in the NDA review process, or before it starts, to discuss the proposed name. Either the reviewing division or OPDRA can raise concerns about or reject a name. When this occurs, experts should be called on to respond quickly to any concerns (e.g., about doctor/patient confusion) and to prepare a written response. Even if the OPDRA and division approve the name, the decision is not binding on FDA; the agency can demand that the name be changed after commercialization if actual patient, doctor, or pharmacist confusion is reported to FDA.

- Significant time can be required to negotiate final drug labeling with the reviewing division. Because final labeling negotiations generally occur after the approvable letter or complete response on the product has issued, companies who are anxious to complete the approval process sometimes retreat unnecessarily on labeling issues to expedite marketing. Companies should discuss expected labeling with the CSO soon after completion of the Phase 3 trial. Agency questions should be anticipated in order to develop corporate responses before the product launch is looming .

- At the end of the NDA review process, if FDA calls a company to say the agency intends to send a not approvable action letter, the company may be able to negotiate the issue of additional studies or data that must be submitted. Depending on the status of the review, the sponsor may be asked if it wants to withdraw the NDA (and avoid receiving the letter) or agree to extension of the user fee deadline. In almost all cases, it is preferable for a company to agree to the statutory deadline extension and to work with the reviewing team rather than to challenge the decision or lose their place in the review queue.

- One of the last parts of the NDA review process is the division's review of the company's launch marketing materials. There is considerable strategy involved in submitting the materials to the Division of Drug Marketing, Advertising and Communication.

V. Over-the-Counter Drugs

- OTC drugs can be approved through an NDA, NDA supplement for products not used to a material time and extent, or through an OTC monograph (to establish general recognition of safety and efficacy (GRAS/E)). The considerations for working with FDA vary significantly depending on which method of approval is used, and whether the product is being proposed for OTC marketing status initially, as a prescription-to-OTC (Rx-to-OTC) drug switch, or as an "old" or GRAS/E drug substance.

• If the drug is the subject of an Rx-to-OTC switch (through an NDA supplement), it is critical to ensure that FDA agrees that the tests done to support the switch are essential to the approval to support claims for exclusivity. Although FDA will not always agree ahead of time to characterize the tests, and certainly will not raise the need for such a determination prior to the switch approval, it is reasonable to raise this topic in initial meetings with FDA.

• Although the OTC Division will be present for meetings on Rx-to-OTC switches, the principal contact points and reviewers will be in the reviewing division. Issues relating to bridging studies and exclusivity should be raised with the reviewing division rather than the OTC division, which generally has little or no experience with such issues.

• If a product is part of an established monograph, the active ingredients in the product must be properly included for the intended indications in the relevant OTC drug monograph, if final, and be the subject of a relevant USP monograph. If the relevant OTC monograph is not final, the ingredients must be included tentatively as category I (safe and effective) or III (inadequate data to determine safety and efficacy) ingredients.

• To the extent that the OTC active ingredients have not been included in a final monograph and it is necessary to submit data to confirm the GRAS/E status of the substances (either to the tentative monograph or as a monograph amendment), it is useful to discuss with the relevant OTC monograph division officials the scope of data necessary and how that data compares to the safety data existing for previously-approved products.

• Because test methods for OTC drugs have become more sophisticated, it is important to confirm with FDA the appropriateness of the test methodology intended to be used to demonstrate GRAS/E status.

• OTC drug product manufacturers are beginning to use expert panels more frequently to determine whether their products are GRAS/E and, therefore, are appropriate for monograph status. Such expert panels can be useful in persuading OTC division officials that the product is in fact "generally recognized" as safe and effective.

• OTC labeling requirements and format should be considered when proposing OTC status for a product, because such requirements are more standardized than those for prescription drug labeling and these will significantly affect trade dress strategies.

• If your OTC active ingredient has only been marketed abroad, compliance with the FDA's proposed rule on consideration of such products should be closely followed (i.e., collection of adverse experience data, evidence of five years' worth of marketing abroad, etc.) as a basis for requesting review of such products.

Bogdan Dziurzynski

MedImmune, Inc.

CHAPTER 2

How to Get Your Biologic Product Approved

I. Introduction

Utilization of complex technologies is characteristic of the biologic therapeutic research and development process. These complex technologies present challenges to both the regulators and the regulated. I strongly recommend that the skill set of the regulatory team correspond to the technical and management challenges that will be confronted.

The goal of biologic research and development is to provide safe, effective, and innovative products that offer health-enhancing options for both physicians and patients. The effectiveness of the regulatory guidance and management provided will have a profound impact on the identification and development of approvable candidate products. For those candidate products that have demonstrated safety, effectiveness, and an acceptable risk-benefit profile, the timeliness and likelihood of approval will be determined by the quality and professionalism of the regulatory leadership exercised.

The information and recommendations provided in this chapter are offered under the assumption that one of your goals is to expedite the development and approval of a biologic product candidate that proves safe and effective.

II. Planning and Management

A regulatory and development strategy should be developed for every candidate. The initial regulatory strategy should include: product development expectations and available guidelines; test and monitoring criteria; underlying assumptions; anticipated clinical requirements; potential manufacturing limitations; forecasted market opportunities; and targeted indication(s) and desired labeling. The regulatory strategy should evolve with new experience and knowledge.

The regulatory project manager should keep abreast of new developments in the field as they relate to technological advances, clinical applications, regulatory expectations, quality standards, good manufacturing practices (GMPs), and validation requirements. Many regulatory staff members excel in their ability to identify problems; a creative regulatory professional should also recommend possible solutions to those problems, describe alternative courses of action, and recognize opportunities. In other words, the regulatory manager should not just tell the development team what it cannot do, instead the regulatory manager must understand what the objectives are and help to delineate a process that moves the project closer to the goal. Throughout all phases of the project, operational constraints must be identified and resources managed to attain objectives.

III. Phases of Development and Clinical Study

A. Preclinical Development

Well-planned and well-executed preclinical studies can assist the development team in projecting the potential human clinical experience. The preclinical development phase should provide preliminary evidence of pharmacology (product activity) and toxicology (safety) to support the rational design of human clinical trials. Product candidates should be examined using *in vitro* and *in vivo* methodologies to understand mechanisms of action, viable routes of administration, projected pharmacokinetics, feasible frequencies of administration, potential dosage limitations, and potential toxicities.

Because many preclinical studies typically are performed very early in the development scheme, the investigational product intended for human clinical trials should be compared to the material used in preclinical tests. Modifications to either the active form or the final formulation should be assessed, and it should be prospectively determined whether any of the original preclinical tests should be repeated or if additional tests should be performed. In general, first ask yourself and the development team what are the questions that you are trying to answer by the pre-clinical studies.

Establishing an early dialogue with Food and Drug Administration (FDA) preclinical regulatory scientists is recommended to reduce uncertainty regarding the necessity and design of preclinical good laboratory practice (GLP) studies. The potential for using *in vitro* and *in vivo* biological model surrogates should be discussed. Provide a contextual framework for preclinical GLP studies by reviewing possible indications for the product candidate and whether the goal is to develop it for acute or chronic use.

Discuss relevant species, numbers and gender, duration of studies, and preclinical dosage schema based upon the projected maximum human dose, the appropriateness of single or repeat dosing, the desirability of alternative routes of administration, intended monitoring processes (including assessments of antigenicity, reactogenicity and tumorigenicity), and methods of final evaluation (including necropsy). Obtaining preclinical safety and pharmacokinetic data on doses at least two to ten times greater than the maximum anticipated human dose may prevent delays during later-stage human trials. Become familiar, and provide FDA, with the literature that is pertinent to the scientific field and medical application.

B. Early Product and Assay Development — Pre-Phase 1

Prior to initiation of Phase 1 studies, you should have data regarding preclinical pharmacokinetics and safety. Begin to establish the characterization of product structure; document the history and construct of any cell lines used to produce the product candidate. Initiate tests for adventitious agents, and perform a preliminary assessment of viral clearance capabilities for the proposed manufacturing processes. Establish master and working cell banks, and document the sources of any materials of animal origin. Begin to develop and document methods for purity and potency assays, and for in-process release tests. Assess which analytical methods might be of value as stability-indicating assays. Examining product characteristics under conditions of accelerated degradation may help identify stability-indicating assays.

C. Pre-Investigational New Drug Meeting With FDA

The sponsor should determine whether a pre-investigational new drug (IND) meeting is necessary. A meeting probably is not necessary if the sponsor has no questions about: the clinical study design; the inclusion and exclusion criteria; the informed consent process; the selection of endpoints; the study's execution; the statistical analysis; or the manufacture, formulation, and testing of the product. Make good use of FDA's time. It is a valuable commodity and should not be wasted. A reasonable alternative to a pre-IND meeting may be to request a pre-IND teleconference with key FDA reviewers in cases where only a few points of clarification may be needed.

A sponsor should ask, and answer, several questions as to whether a pre-IND meeting or teleconference with FDA is warranted. Do the preclinical data support approval of the IND? Is the initial phase 1 study proposal reasonable as to the number of patients to be enrolled; the intended dosing strategy (including dose escalation, route and duration of administration, and volume to be administered); the safety monitoring plan (including the type and duration of follow-up after the last administration); the target population to be studied; and anticipated risks for volunteers enrolling in the study? Does the sponsor have a rationale for the formulation, the manufacturing process, and the analytical assessment of the product candidate?

Pre-IND meetings and discussions with FDA are important to sponsors seeking to optimize the development of new products. These meetings also can be especially important to young companies with few or no products in the marketplace because the company's valuation may rely heavily on products under clinical investigation.

Any meeting with FDA requires planning, preparation, and practice. The pre-IND meeting provides the company with a forum to introduce, often for the first time, a product candidate to FDA. A well-planned and organized meeting has the potential to create a positive impression at FDA about the product candidate and the company.

Planning for a pre-IND meeting with FDA should begin with a clear understanding and agreement of the objective of the meeting. The overall goal of the pre-IND meeting is to take the regulatory and clinical environment into account in advance of IND submission in order to eliminate delays in both obtaining IND approval and further developing the product candidate. The plan should include preparation of a meeting request and development of a pre-IND briefing document.

The meeting request should present: the objective of the meeting; an agenda; a list of people that will represent the company at the meeting; a list of company-requested FDA participants; a briefing document that describes product manufacture, formulation, and testing; a preclinical summary that supports the clinical plan, the clinical design, and strategy for development of the product; and several dates that are convenient for all company-planned participants. Specific questions should be asked clearly in the meeting request so that FDA may prepare responses in advance of the meeting. The request for a meeting should be submitted well in advance so that FDA has a reasonable opportunity to allow staff to add the meeting to their schedule.

Preparations for the meeting should include an outline of all planned presentations, presenters, and time allocations for each topic. There should be sufficient time for questions and discussions with FDA. A general rule to follow is to schedule half the time allocated by FDA for the meeting for presentations and the remaining half for questions and discussions. Provisions should be made for several rehearsals or practice sessions to refine presentations. Consider including medical, scientific, and technical experts as participants in practice sessions to provide constructive suggestions and to make the presentation succinct.

To demonstrate an appreciation for FDA's time, avoid presenting in more than just a summary fashion information that already is included in the briefing document. One of the biggest weaknesses of sponsors is failing to discuss at meetings topics that may be problematic or difficult for the sponsor. On occasion, sponsors have left a meeting erroneously concluding that, because FDA did not independently surface the problematic or difficult topic, the agency would not find fault with sponsor's perspective of the issue. In truth, FDA could raise future questions or objections that could have financial ramifications and could result in developmental delays.

Companies should present to FDA their plan to address problematic or difficult issues, to elicit FDA's view and to obtain comments, suggestions, and, in some cases, agency requirements, so as not to delay product development. Occasionally, these problems may have little or no impact on the initial IND or on the Phase 1 study. Sponsors then proceed with a product development plan and timeline that assumes a faulty regulatory strategy. Prudent counsel dictates that if a sponsor really wants to know if an intended strategy or approach to an issue would be problematic for FDA, the sponsor should engage the agency in a discussion of that issue.

D. Phase 1

Typically, the first human clinical exposure to an investigational product takes place in Phase 1 studies. This early clinical experience will begin to provide evidence of human tolerance to the product candidate. Comprehensive monitoring of the safety experience is the primary objective of a Phase 1 study, and FDA reviewers will be alert to the safety profile established in these early studies.

Companies should assess whether a blinded Phase 1 study could assist in establishing the true safety profile of the product. Phase 1 experience will directly influence future clinical strategy, so attempts should be made to include male and female volunteers and assessments should be made as to the benefits and liabilities of studying healthy volunteers or patients in that phase.

Reflecting on preclinical experience and using the clinical setting as a contextual framework, companies should carefully outline the strategy for doses selected. In normal volunteers, finding the maximum tolerated dose may be desirable, while in some patient volunteer cohorts, finding the minimum effective dose may be a more appropriate strategy. Determine if immune responses to the product are anticipated, and collect volunteer sera to assess the presence of these responses in volunteers. Expectations of antibody responses such as Human Anti Mouse Antibody (HAMA) would likely negate the use of normal volunteers.

During Phase 1 and prior to initiation of Phase 2 studies:

- begin to establish acceptance criteria for components;

- begin to validate stability assays and estimate stability based on biologic activity and/or product degradation under accelerated conditions;

- monitor stability based on biologic activity and purity;

- establish and qualify a product reference standard to anchor test results during product development;

- begin to validate in-process release tests;

- begin to validate purity and potency assays;

- develop initial written production and test procedures;

- complete the qualification of cell lines;

- generate a detailed description of product structure; and

- validate the processes that demonstrate viral load reduction (to avoid overestimating viral reduction capabilities of the manufacturing process, count steps with similar inactivation and removal characteristics only once).

E. Phase 2

Phase 2 studies are intended to evaluate the safety and effectiveness of a product candidate for its intended use in target populations. Final product formulation and presentation should be defined during Phase 2 studies.

During Phase 2 and prior to initiation of Phase 3 studies:

- begin to finalize written production and test procedures;

- begin to establish production yields;

- complete the validation of purity and potency assays;

- complete the validation of in-process and release tests;

- complete the validation of stability assays;

- finalize and document acceptance criteria for components;

- estimate product expiration dating based on stability data;

- develop production and test standard operating procedures (SOPs);

- begin to develop acceptance criteria for assessment of product comparability;

- begin to validate production processes and establish acceptable ranges for process performance;

- finalize product formulation and product presentation (e.g., vial or syringe size, concentration, liquid or lyophilized, single-use or multi-dose, convenience of use, packaging configuration, shipping, and storage requirements); and

- begin to obtain market projections to match manufacturing capability with market need.

F. Pre-Pivotal Study Meetings with FDA

Pre-pivotal study meetings are generally requested by sponsors to present the outcomes of Phase 1 and Phase 2 studies and to propose and finalize the study design and endpoints for a pivotal Phase 3 trial(s). Planning and preparation for this meeting should begin prior to the completion of Phase 2 studies. The pre-pivotal study meeting may be the most important clinical development meeting between a sponsor and FDA.

You should meet with FDA before pivotal trials to obtain agreement regarding the proposed trial design, endpoints to support the proposed labeling of the product, and the analysis plan. To assess the approvability of a product in anticipation of completing a "successful" pivotal trial, you should present the criteria that will be used to conclude that significant pivotal trial results have been obtained and how data will be analyzed and interpreted. Disagreement with FDA regarding study size, study design, selection of endpoints, data analysis, or interpretation of results offers a significant threat to product approval.

An appropriate briefing document (see section on pre-IND meetings) should be submitted well in advance of the meeting, and sponsor preparations for the meeting should be thorough. An important note: At this point the sponsor already should be assessing if, and when an advisory committee may review the product, and which committee may receive that assignment.

G. Phase 3

Phase 3 trials will determine the safety and effectiveness of a product. A well-designed and well-executed trial should lead to product approval. Sponsors must, however, recognize that the product label generally will reflect the clinical design, endpoints, and results of a pivotal trial. The wording of the indication will determine the ease with which third-party reimbursement is obtained as well as the marketability of the product. Therefore, draft the intended indication prior to initiation of the trial, to ensure that the completed trial will support the desired indication.

During phase 3 and prior to biologic license application (BLA) submission:

- complete the validation of production facility utilities;

- complete the validation of production equipment;

- complete the validation of production processes;

- place multiple lots on stability using validated assays; refine product specifications;

- define yields;

- finish development and approval of SOPs;

- define product expiration dating;

- define acceptance criteria for assessment of product comparability;

- refine market projections to match manufacturing capability with market need; and

- evaluate scale-up of processes.

IV. The Biologic Application Process

A. Pre-BLA Meetings with FDA

It is recommended that sponsors meet with FDA prior to preparation and submission of a BLA. The purpose of this meeting is to introduce FDA reviewers to the outcome and results of the pivotal study. This meeting may serve to clarify any remaining manufacturing issues so that delays are avoided in BLA review and approval. An appropriate briefing document (see pre-IND meetings) should be submitted well in advance of the meeting, and sponsor preparations for the meeting should be thorough.

B. Biologic License Application

The preparation of the BLA should be a well-orchestrated event. All components of the BLA should be reviewed several times prior to submission. Follow the International Committee on Harmonization guidelines for the appropriate sections. Provide sufficient detail in the Chemistry, Manufacturing and Control sections to allow FDA reviewers to understand how the product is manufactured.

The BLA should provide:

- clear descriptions of process parameters;

- manufacturing flow charts and facility floor plans;

- complete description of cell line and banking procedures;

- in-process and final product specifications and analytical methods;

- lists of raw materials, components and equipment;

- clear descriptions of relevant molecular biology;

- complete characterization of the product;

- viral clearance validation data;

- acceptable ranges for each process step; and

- intermediate product hold times and stability.

V. Other Significant Issues on Points in the Process

A. Pre-Approval Inspection

Perform multiple simulated inspections of facilities and documentation. Some of the best consultants in this area are former FDA investigators and reviewers. Sponsor companies should conduct thorough inspections of all operations to detect all areas of weakness or deficiency. FDA will focus on validations of computers, utilities, equipment, and processes; intermediate process-hold times; air, water, and surface monitoring; filling and packaging; and bulk and final product storage and shipping. FDA will review systems for change control; in-process and release testing of raw materials, components, and product; out-of-specification and failed test results; and adverse event and complaint processing. A seasoned quality assurance and regulatory affairs team is essential to successful inspection.

B. Advisory Committee Meetings

Companies should begin to prepare for presentation to an advisory committee as soon as it is apparent that Phase 3 results are satisfactory. The advisory committee process frequently is fraught with problems for sponsors. Ambiguity, grand-standing, misunderstanding, theoretical concerns, and incompetence all have been observed at meetings. Companies may avoid these mishaps through review of videotapes of previous committee meetings and work with clinical-medical experts and consultants to prepare for the meeting.

C. Advertising and Promotion

Preparation of advertising and promotional pieces for launch should begin as soon as Phase 3 results are known.

D. Post-Approval Commitments

Companies must follow through on all of their post-approval commitments made to FDA. Do not be misled into believing that commitments made as a contingency of approval can be negotiated away at a later date. Only in truly extraordinary circumstances will FDA waive sponsor company commitments after the fact.

C
H
A
P
T
E
R

3

Eugene I. Lambert
Jeannie Perron

Covington & Burling

How to Get Your Animal Drug Product Approved

I. Introduction — How Animal Drug Regulation Differs From Human Drug Regulation

The regulation of animal drugs is at once strikingly similar to — and markedly different from — the regulation of human drugs. While animal drugs, like human drugs, are approved for specific indications, drugs for use in animals are distinctive in that they may be approved for use in one or more species. Also peculiar to animal drugs is the fact that they fall into two distinct categories. Animal drugs may be approved for the prevention and/or treatment of disease, like their human drug counterparts, but they also may be approved to enhance the production efficiency of food animals.

New animal drugs fall under the jurisdiction of the Food and Drug Administration's (FDA's) Center for Veterinary Medicine (CVM). The approval process for drugs intended for use in nonfood-producing animals, such as pets and exotic animals, is very similar to the approval process for human drugs. The new animal drug application (NADA) applicant must demonstrate that the drug is safe and effective for the particular species and indication, at the dose range for which approval is sought.

Additional complications are inherent in the approval process for drugs intended for use in animals that may or will enter the human food chain. For drugs intended to treat or prevent disease in food animals, the NADA must also address the issue of how to minimize to safe or undetectable levels residues of the drug in the animal's tissue at the time the tissue enters the food chain (e.g., when dairy cows are milked or beef cattle are slaughtered).[1] Hence, there is a human food safety aspect to the approval of drugs intended to prevent or treat disease in food-producing animals.

---

[1] Generally, CVM ensures that levels of drugs in animal tissues entering the human food chain will be at acceptably low levels by requiring the establishment of a "withdrawal period" for the drug. The withdrawal period is the time prior to slaughter or milking by which the drug must be discontinued so that the residues will reach acceptably low levels when the treated animal's tissues enter the food chain. Many drugs are so benign or produce such low levels in the tissues that they have a "zero" withdrawal period, and can be used right up to slaughter.

Production drugs comprise a unique class of drugs. These are drugs that do not prevent or treat disease, but that enhance food animal production. (Some production drugs may also prevent or treat disease at the same or higher dose levels than the levels at which they are used for their production-enhancing effects.) For example, production drugs may improve the weight gain of the animal or the efficiency of its utilization of feed. NADAs for production drugs must also address the issue of whether unacceptable levels of drug residues will be present in the animal's tissues when those tissues enter the human food chain. Hence, human food safety is also a consideration for this category of drugs.

Both treatment/prevention drugs and production drugs come in varying dosage forms. Where the drug is produced in an injectable or solid dosage form, it may be marketed immediately upon approval. Where the drug is intended to be mixed into feed, there is the additional consideration of determining whether only licensed feed mills can mix the drug initially. In addition, special rules apply where the feed contains more than one drug, perhaps from different drug companies.

II. Contents of the NADA

A. Parts of the Application

There are six major parts of an NADA: safety, efficacy, residue chemistry, manufacturing chemistry, labeling, and environmental considerations. An applicant may make a unified submission of a total NADA, or choose the "phased submission" process.

1. Safety
a. Target Animal Safety — The NADA must contain information related to safety in the target animal. Of concern is not just acute toxicity, but the range of adverse events and the compound's margin of safety. FDA commonly looks for studies performed at three times and ten times the level at which no adverse effects are demonstrated, (i.e., no observed adverse effects level (NOAEL)).

b. Human Food Safety — NADAs for drugs intended for use in food-producing animals must also contain evidence of human food safety. This process is similar in approach to that for a food additive approval. An acceptable daily intake level must be established through laboratory animal studies, and that level is compared to the estimated daily intake of the drug when used as directed in food-producing animals, taking into account estimated levels of use of the food produced by the target animal — meat, milk, or eggs — in the human diet.

As in the case of food additives, the Delaney Clause bars the approval of cancer-causing animal drugs. Animal drugs, however, have an escape hatch from the effect of the Delaney Clause, called the DES Proviso, which permits approval of a new animal drug *if* no residues are found in the food-producing animal's tissues at a level of detection that is equivalent to a one-in-a-million-human-lifetimes risk of getting cancer.

2. Efficacy
The efficacy standard for animal drugs is the "substantial evidence" standard. This standard, while facially similar to the standard applied in the approval of human drugs,

includes a potentially wider array of "adequate and well controlled studies" that can form the basis for an animal drug approval.

3. Residue chemistry

NADAs for drugs intended for use in food-producing animals must include information regarding the appropriate method of detecting residues of the drug in animal tissues. The development of analytical detection methods can be one of the most prolonged and difficult parts of the approval process. While studies can determine the safe level of drug residues, that level must be "translated" into a practical method of detection based on the edible tissue in which there is the slowest depletion, and upon the presence of the "marker compound" (i.e., the drug or one of its metabolic by-products that is used to track the depletion process). There is increasing pressure for the development of "quick tests" (i.e., tests that can be used in U.S. Department of Agriculture (USDA)-inspected establishments to test meat, poultry, and eggs during the inspection process for the potential for violative residues). The "regulatory method" (i.e., the residue detection method accepted by FDA for the particular residues) must be able to confirm or refute the presence of such residues.

4. Manufacturing Chemistry

For dosage form drugs, the issues of manufacturing chemistry that must be addressed by an NADA are essentially similar to those for dosage form human drugs, and involve the application of pharmaceutical current good manufacturing practices (cGMPs). Complexities are added, however, when the drug is intended to be used in animal feed, because the drug is typically sold in an initial dilution of feed ingredients and fillers (formally called a "Type A Medicated Article," and informally a "premix") that facilitate its subsequent dilution — perhaps once or twice more — to actual feeding levels. Both in its initial form and in subsequent dilutions performed at feed mills or on farm, drug present in the feed must be detected and its amount quantified to ensure proper distribution. This can be a difficult process when initial levels may be at hundreds of grams per 100 pound-bag, and feeding levels may be at grams per ton.

A separate but related problem arises from the use of "biomass" fermentation products in feed drugs. Antibiotics are derived from an initial fermentation mass, or "biomass." Particularly in the case of antibiotics used in animal feed, rather than isolating the active antibiotic, as done with dosage form products, the entire biomass would be added to the feed. Analytical procedures must be able to measure the active drug in the biomass to ensure proper dosing. Additional safety considerations also apply in evaluating the content of the biomass.

5. Labeling

The NADA must contain samples of the intended labeling. A much higher proportion of animal drugs is available over the counter than is the case with human drugs. This is particularly true with respect to food-producing animals, where professional producers of such animals have the expertise to evaluate the needs of their animals and administer both feed form and dosage form drugs. Thus, labeling for over-the-counter (OTC) drugs for use in food-producing animals must convey in "expert" lay terms the indications for the drug, the manner of its use, any withdrawal time requirements, and any side effects or contraindications that must be considered. Drugs for companion and exotic animals are much more likely to be limited to use on the order of a veterinarian, so that labeling parallels the format for human prescription drugs.

6. Environmental Considerations

For drugs used in food-producing animals, FDA is required to evaluate the environmental issues that may arise from the use of the drug, including the excretion of the drug or its metabolic by-products into soil and water. Drugs used in aquaculture pose issues of direct addition to water. The applicant's environmental assessment must be submitted in the NADA. The best outcome is that FDA will find no significant environmental impact (FONSI) for the drug.

B. Standards of Proof

The standard of proof for safety of animal drugs required by section 512(d)(1)(A) of the Federal Food, Drug, and Cosmetic Act (FDCA) is based on the submission of adequate tests "by all methods reasonably applicable to show whether or not such drug is safe under the conditions prescribed, recommended or suggested in the proposed labeling . . . ." Animal drugs also must meet the same standard as must be met by food additives under the Delaney Clause. Specifically, section 512(d)(2) of the FDCA requires that CVM consider the effect of the probable consumption of such drug and of any substance formed in or on food because of the use of such drug; the cumulative effect on man or animal of such drug, taking into account any chemically- or pharmacologically-related substance; safety factors that in the opinion of experts are appropriate for the use of animal experimentation data; and whether the conditions of use prescribed, recommended, or suggested in the proposed labeling are reasonably certain to be followed in practice.

The standard of proof for efficacy of animal drugs changed with the passage of the Animal Drug Availability Act of 1996 (ADAA). Before passage of the ADAA, CVM was required to refuse approval of an NADA unless the sponsor submitted "substantial evidence" that the drug would have the effect it purported or was represented to have under the conditions of use prescribed, recommended, or suggested in the labeling. The term "substantial evidence" was defined in section 512(d)(3) of the FDCA as comprising:

> adequate and well-controlled investigations, ... including any field investigation[,] ... by experts qualified by scientific training and experience to evaluate the effectiveness of the drug involved, on the basis of which it could fairly and reasonably be concluded by such experts that the drug will have the effect it purports or is represented to have under the conditions of use prescribed, recommended, or suggested in the labeling or proposed labeling thereof.

For production drugs, FDA imposed an additional requirement that the field trials be conducted in at least three geographic locations in order to provide an adequate statistical base for evaluating the drug's effects. This requirement was based on 1975 guidelines promulgated by CVM.

The ADAA was designed to simplify and expedite the animal drug approval process. Its stated purpose was to enhance the flexibility of the approval process for NADAs, without compromising FDA's ability to ensure that the approved products are safe for animals as well as for humans who consume animal-derived food products. The ADAA provided this flexibility by amending the definition of "substantial evidence." Under the amended definition, substantial evidence may consist of *one or more* adequate and well-controlled investigations, such as studies in the target species or laboratory animals, field investigations, or bioequivalence or *in vitro* studies. Thus, the ADAA potentially reduced the minimum testing required for a particular new animal drug so that, as few as one adequate and well-controlled investigation may be sufficient to support approval.

In 1999, FDA published final regulations in which 21 C.F.R. section 514.4 defined "substantial evidence" under the ADAA as:

> [E]vidence consisting of one or more adequate and well-controlled studies, such as a study in a target species, study in laboratory animals, field study, bioequivalence study, or an in vitro study, on the basis of which it could fairly and reasonably be concluded by experts qualified by scientific training and experience to evaluate the effectiveness of the new animal drug involved that the new animal drug will have the effect it purports or is represented to have under the conditions of use prescribed, recommended, or suggested in the labeling or proposed labeling thereof.

With respect to the number of studies required, the regulation states that "substantial evidence" shall consist of a "sufficient number of current adequate and well-controlled studies of sufficient quality and persuasiveness" to allow experts to determine that the tests and test results reliably reflect the effectiveness of the drug, are repeatable, allow valid inferences to be drawn to the target animal species and determine efficacy. Because the evaluation of production drugs is primarily statistical, CVM has continued to require that trials be conducted in multiple locations.

FDA is also considering new requirements to evaluate the potential for antibiotic resistance from the intended use of antibiotic drugs in food animals. FDA drafted a proposed framework for modeling pre-approval studies and post-approval surveillance of all antimicrobial drugs for use in food animals to determine the potential for the transfer of food-borne strains of antibiotic-resistant pathogens to humans. CVM proposed to classify antibacterial drugs used in food-producing animals depending on factors such as the drug's importance in treating human disease, the severity of any disease treated by the drug, and the availability of acceptable alternatives. The proposed level and type of pre- and post-approval monitoring required depends on the categorization of a particular drug. CVM is also studying the use of risk assessments in evaluating the effect of particular antibiotics in food animal species.

The ADAA also promoted approvals of new combinations of animal drugs that previously had been approved separately for the same uses or conditions of use as intended for the combination. If one or more drugs included in the combination is intended only for the same use as another drug in the combination, the sponsor must show that each drug contributes to the effectiveness of the combination. If one drug has a different use than the others in the combination, the sponsor need only demonstrate that the combination therapy is appropriate for the target population. If CVM has reason to believe the drugs may be incompatible, the sponsor must submit evidence that the drugs are physically compatible. These special combination rules do not apply to dosage form drugs that contain nontopical antibacterials.

C. Tips for Success

1. Presubmission Conferences

The ADAA provided for a binding presubmission conference between FDA and the NADA applicant so that agreement could be reached regarding required submissions. This mechanism (obtaining a binding agreement from FDA on what testing will be required before that testing is conducted) can save applicants considerable time and expense. Because the time between planning a study and its eventual submission to FDA may be lengthy, the presubmission conference also assures the drug sponsor that there will not be a "drift" in approval requirements without a clear institutional evaluation of the need for new data. Advantage should be taken of this procedure whenever possible.

2. Phased Review

Another difference between the human and animal drug approval processes is CVM's encouragement of the use of "phased review." Under this procedure, as each research segment of the NADA is completed, it is submitted for review under the *investigational* file that has been opened for the drug. CVM essentially commits to reviewing each segment under a 180-day clock as if it were part of an NADA submission.

Particularly in the case of submissions for drugs to be used in food-producing animals, the phased review permits, for example, the human food safety evaluation to be completed while work is continuing on residue chemistry, as that work will be driven in large measure by the conclusions reached with respect to the target organ for residue studies, the marker compound, and the "safe" residue level that must be measured. Similarly, target animal safety (TAS) can affect the range of doses that will be studied in efficacy trials, so the completion and CVM evaluation of TAS studies can facilitate efficacy trials. Once the research segments have been completed and approved, an "administrative NADA" is submitted that references the prior CVM evaluations, and includes labeling, draft Freedom of Information Act (FOIA) summary, and environmental submissions (although the latter also may have been submitted earlier for a CVM FONSI).

CVM has committed to a sixty-day review of the administrative NADA. Thus, rather than waiting until all the research segments are finished and a "complete" NADA is filed (and hoping that CVM will have the resources to review all the segments within the same time frame), the "phased review" permits applicants to submit segments, and have review of those segments completed, while continuing other research. Both industry and CVM have found that this procedure facilitates the overall approval process.

3. Timing of Approval Regulation for Drugs Used in Animal Feed

The approval of drugs for use in animal feeds is subject to a different mechanism and timing than approvals for dosage form new animal drugs. Like drugs for humans, dosage form new animal drugs can be marketed as soon as they receive FDA approval. Each approved drug will become the subject of a regulation, but the manufacturer need not wait for publication of the regulation to market the drug.

Manufacturers of drugs for use in animal feeds, however, must wait for publication of the regulation reflecting the approval of the drug before it can be mixed into feeds. The reason for the different procedure in the case of drugs for use in animal feed is that these drugs are mixed into feed by feed mills or on-farm users, rather than by the drug manufacturers. CVM historically has taken the position that the regulation must be published in order to advise these mixers how to use the drug and to regulate such use.

Normally, regulations reflecting the approval of a new animal drug for use in feed will be published within a few weeks of the manufacturer receiving notice of approval of the NADA. The manufacturer should be aware, therefore, that the time lag inherent in publication of the regulation will delay the ability to market the drug for use in animal feed. Despite the repeal of the system of individual feed licenses and its replacement by a system of feed mill licensing, the required approval regulation still forms the legal basis for shipping feed premixes for subsequent mixing into animal feed.

4. Classes of Veterinary Drugs

There are both "prescription" and OTC veterinary drugs. Prescription veterinary drugs are those defined in the FDCA as "not safe for animal use except under the professional supervision of a licensed veterinarian" or those that are limited by their approvals to such use. As explained above, the range of OTC drugs available for use in animals is generally broader than those for use in humans because the expertise of ranchers, farmers, and other animal husbandry professionals permits drugs to be used safely in the care of animals in ways not permitted for human OTC drugs.

In comparison to human drugs, an additional class of veterinary drugs exists as well. These drugs are referred to as veterinary feed directive (VFD) drugs. The law defines a VFD drug as one for use in animal feed for which an approved application requires that the use be under the supervision of a licensed veterinarian. Under a VFD, while drug premixes may be shipped to feed mills, and intermediate dilutions may be made, no animal feed containing the drug may be shipped to the end user except pursuant to a VFD issued by a veterinarian, which in turn requires the existence of a valid veterinary-client-patient relationship and the maintenance of copies of the VFD by the veterinarian, the end user, and the mixing mill. The VFD, like a veterinary order under FDCA section 503(f), must specify the conditions of use of the drug, but unlike a veterinary order for a dosage form animal drug, it may not vary the conditions of use from those permitted in the authorizing animal drug regulation.

III. The Generic Animal Drug and Patent Term Restoration Act and Abbreviated New Animal Drug Applications

New animal drugs were left out of the Drug Price Competition and Patent Term Restoration Act of 1984. Patent and generic drug issues for animal drugs were codified four years later in the Generic Animal Drug and Patent Term Restoration Act of 1988. Under the provisions of that Act, the patent holder has the option of choosing to base its patent term extension on an initial companion animal approval or on a subsequent food animal approval. By contrast, holders of patents claiming drugs approved for human use were required to base their extension on the first approval for the use of the drug.

The rationale of affording to the animal drug patent holder the option to choose the approval on which to base the patent term extension derives from the fact that the food animal approval for a particular drug may take longer to obtain than the approval in companion animals because of the human food safety issues inherent in the food animal approval. The option allows the animal drug patent holder to exploit for longer periods the potentially more lucrative food animal market, even though the patent may expire earlier for the companion animal uses of the drug.

Sponsors may seek approval of generic animal drugs through abbreviated new animal drug applications (ANADAs). The principal burden on an ANADA applicant is to show that the generic drug is bioequivalent to the pioneer product. If an appropriate showing of bioequivalence is made, CVM will apply the proofs submitted in support of safety and efficacy for the pioneer product to the generic drug.

CVM also has the option to require data in addition to bioequivalence, such as bioequivalence in every potential target species, tissue residue studies in target species, and other data it considers to be appropriate. Safety data for generic antibacterial drugs used in animal feed commonly must include information in addition to data for the purified drug itself. Because antibacterials used in animal feed are unpurified fermentation products, the generic manufacturer is required to submit the results of toxicological evaluations of the uncharacterized portion of the fermentation product proposed for marketing. Generic sponsors can seek approval of alternative forms or combinations of the pioneer drug through the submission of a suitability petition, in the same manner as such a petition may be submitted for human generic drugs.

IV. Post-Approval Issues

A. Records and Reports

While FDA has regulations governing records and reports for all approved veterinary drugs, these currently differ from the counterpart human regulations. FDA has underway a project to revise the NADA regulations, including regulations relating to ANADAs, so that the animal drug regulations more closely parallel the human drug requirements.

1. Standard Conditions

The principal purpose of recordkeeping and reporting requirements is to maintain FDA oversight of the safety of the drug under actual conditions of use. Despite widespread pre-approval testing of a drug under conditions similar to those under actual commercial use, only such use (either by veterinarians engaged in day-to-day practice or through over-the-counter sales) can uncover low-level safety issues. For the first year of approval, drug experience reports (DERs) of all adverse events, even if covered in approved labeling, must be submitted to CVM every six months. Subsequent reports must be submitted on an annual basis. In addition, any "unexpected" DER, meaning an adverse event which by kind or frequency is not covered in approved labeling, must be reported promptly to CVM, and the drug sponsor must consider amending the approved labeling on an expedited basis to cover the new information.

2. Special Surveillance

In addition to the general regulations governing reports and records, the statute authorizes FDA to establish individual reporting requirements. In a few instances, special reporting requirements have been established for a class of drugs, and in some cases, they have been established on an individual basis. These individualized requirements are called "Phase IV" reports of post-approval studies, and can include organized oversight of actual use conditions.

B. Supplemental Applications

The Act requires an approved supplemental application for any changes in manufacture, composition, or labeling beyond the variations specified in the initial application. In practice, FDA increasingly permits notifications of changes, either when they occur or as part of annual reports, rather than requiring prior approval of the changes.

Additional conditions of use, altered dosage forms, and similar major changes still require pre-approval.

C. Promotional Oversight

Product promotion is under constant surveillance by CVM. Increasingly, CVM is cooperating with regulators of human drugs in developing guidance on promotional practices. These guidance documents, available on the FDA website (www.fda.gov), should be reviewed for insight into the kinds of activity or promotion of approved claims that can create regulatory problems.

1. Promotional Labeling

Under the general reporting regulations, CVM requires that all promotional labeling be submitted at the time of first use. In its regulations, FDA distinguishes labeling from advertising. Labeling must be consistent with approved uses; must reflect all warnings, contraindications, and precautions; and, in the case of drugs subject to a veterinarian's order, must include full package labeling.

2. Veterinary Prescription Drug Advertising

The FDCA sets certain requirements for prescription drug advertising and gives FDA exclusive jurisdiction over such advertising, thereby effectively excluding Federal Trade Commission jurisdiction. Since the initial adoption of rules governing prescription drug advertising, FDA has taken the position that veterinarian order drugs are prescription drugs within the meaning of FDCA section 502(n). While industry has regularly objected to that position on the basis that the prescription drug provision of the FDCA had been amended in 1950 in a manner that deliberately excluded veterinarian order drugs, the issue has never been resolved in the courts. Industry therefore generally complies with these regulations in the advertising of veterinarian order drugs, despite its stated position to the contrary. While the statutory provision requires only that the advertising contain "information in brief summary relating to side effects, contraindications, and effectiveness," FDA's regulations are more expansive, particularly in that they require there to be a "fair balance" between information on effectiveness and information on side effects, warnings, precautions, and contraindications. As CVM seeks to place more new animal drugs under section 503(f) controls, the FDA regulations on prescription drug advertising play an increasingly important role in the development and deployment of advertising. It should be noted that FDA has taken the position that drug company (or drug product) home pages on the Internet are labeling rather than advertising, and thus are subject to FDA's even broader controls over labeling of both prescription and nonprescription drugs.

Dvorah A. Richman

King & Spalding

How to Get Your Medical Device Product Approved

A little neglect may breed mischief, ... for want of a nail,
the shoe was lost; for want of a shoe the horse was lost;
and for want of a horse the rider was lost.
Diligence is the Mother of good luck.
— Poor Richard's Almanac

If Ben Franklin were here today, he would show great skill in getting product applications through the Food and Drug Administration (FDA). While his technologically-advanced mind certainly would be an asset, Franklin's common sense approach to preparation, hard work, acquisition of knowledge, and other such virtues would be the real keys to his success.

With Franklin's maxims as the starting point, this section uses premarket notifications (510(k)s) and premarket approval applications (PMAs) as examples to illustrate how use of these time-worn principles can be the keys to success.

Failure to prepare is preparing to fail. It sounds simple. Companies, however, regularly fail to engage in the most basic planning and analysis prior to embarking on, or submitting to FDA, a 510(k) or PMA. These basics include discussions of: whether there are other, similar products on the market; what indication(s)/intended use will "fly" with the agency; whether there is a market for the product; any potential off-label uses and, if they exist, what kind of issues this might raise; what, if any, clinical or other data will be required; how much time will be needed to assemble the necessary data; and whether the regulatory pathway will likely be straightforward or complex. Preparation of a 510(k) or PMA is not a static process, so a company should continue to reassess at least some of these issues throughout the application process.

An investment in knowledge always pays the best interest. Once a company has addressed the most basic issues, and has decided to move forward with a device application, it is time to gather as much information as possible. Obtaining relevant FDA guidance documents and industry testing standards is essential. Guidance documents include those that are product-specific, as well as those that pertain generally to product application issues (e.g., the *New 510(k) Paradigm*, *PMA Refuse to File Procedures*, and *Suggestions for Submitting a PMA Application*). Draft guidances can also be helpful, because they provide insights into the agency's thinking and often reflect current policies. Many of these documents are accessible via FDA's Web page <www.fda.gov>. More than one guidance document may be applicable to a particular type of device (e.g., an application for a software-controlled device should adhere to relevant device-specific guidance documents, as well as software-related guidance documents). Panel transcripts may also provide insights into FDA's thinking about and/or treatment of certain types of devices.

Even if it seems that the proposed product application is a straightforward, simple one that is very similar to others that have been submitted, the company should check with FDA to ensure there are no new requirements or some other circumstance that should be addressed. This is true even if a recent device-specific guidance document exists.

To clarify any of these issues, call the appropriate branch at the FDA's Office of Device Evaluation and speak with a reviewer who handles these kinds of applications. FDA's Program Operations Staff can be helpful in identifying the appropriate review division or the person with the most expertise in a certain area. Communication between reviewers and industry currently is encouraged, so this contact should be positive. Such conversations should take place early in the process, when FDA input will be most helpful in assessing the feasibility of the product application, time needed, and a regulatory strategy.

Additional contacts with FDA can, and should, be made when necessary to obtain further information or clarification. Depending on the sensitivities, if any, surrounding a particular application or question, such calls can be placed by an outside party who will not be identified with a particular company, but who can ask all the right questions. When the application is complex or company personnel are inexperienced, it may be helpful to get outside help to draft the submission or to provide insights on strategy, FDA preferences, and so on.

If a product is novel, or there are significant questions about such aspects as data requirements, clinical study design, or the 510(k)/PMA status of the device, it is both appropriate and advisable to ask for a meeting with FDA. Companies can benefit from such meetings only if they understand the "rules of the game" and come well prepared.

Who is wise? He that learns from everyone. Before putting together a 510(k) or PMA, it is generally helpful to build from — or at least be aware of — what others have done in the past. For 510(k)s, this includes: finding valid predicate devices; obtaining the 510(k)s (if possible) or the 510(k) summaries for these devices; reviewing competitors' websites and disease-specific websites; obtaining operator's manuals and promotional materials for potential predicate devices; and conducting a literature review for relevant publications. A company preparing a PMA should obtain the publicly-available *PMA Summary of Safety and Effectiveness* for any competitive devices, as well as other materials that could demonstrate the device's safety and effectiveness.

He that lives upon hope will die fasting. Companies often approach a meeting with FDA with the hope that the agency will provide answers — translated as the "right answers" — to all the company's questions. Using this approach, a company is more likely to receive answers it does not like, a reputation for being unsophisticated, and criticism for wasting FDA's time. Instead of simply hoping for the best, companies must carefully prepare for the meeting and have a well-thought-out strategy and proposal for what is to be done. The proposal must include sound justifications and should explain how the company's plan meets FDA's requirements.

Current FDA law/policy provides for both formal and informal meetings with FDA regarding certain product applications. Companies should evaluate the benefits and drawbacks of the different types of meetings, and determine which would be most beneficial. Before any such meeting, a letter should be submitted to FDA fully explaining the product and the issues that need to be addressed. The letter must be submitted in sufficient time for the attendees to read and absorb the material. It is important to plan who will attend the meeting on the company's behalf; regulatory and clinical staff, engineers, statisticians, software designers, and outside FDA counsel or other advisors are appropriate candidates. Depending on the circumstances, it also may be helpful to bring one or more well-respected physicians or other medical experts knowledgeable about the product, its principles of operation, the clinical study design, etc. Although they may want to attend, representatives from marketing, the investment community, or company board members are typically out of place at these meetings.

Assuming the device is portable, it is often a good idea to bring a product sample because seeing is believing. The same holds true for graphical representations of bench, animal, or any clinical data, which are often very effective.

Contrary to Woody Allen's observation that "90% of success is just showing up," companies must carefully plan and coordinate what will be said at the meeting, and who will say it. It is necessary to determine what difficult questions, might be asked, who will field these questions and what answers will be given. Although it might sound like overkill, it is very helpful to have a practice meeting to coordinate all aspects of the event. Even something as basic as how everyone will get to the meeting — and on time — is important, because getting there is the first step to success.

Someone should be designated to take detailed notes during the meeting with FDA. The company should submit a letter after the meeting, summarizing its understanding of what, if anything, was agreed to and noting any necessary clarifications. If the meeting with FDA is a formal meeting prescribed by law, the company must make certain that all requirements/guidance associated with such a meeting are understood and observed.

Where sense is wanting, everything is wanting. Companies should designate an individual or team to work on and be responsible for the application. (A team typically includes representatives from Regulatory Affairs, Clinical Affairs, Development, Marketing, Quality, and Manufacturing divisions; statisticians and technical writers may also be on board.) The team is responsible for defining the product, creating product specifications, ensuring that design input equals design output, conducting design reviews, developing labeling, and so forth. In addition to addressing all the substantive issues associated with a product application, the individual/team leader must assign responsibilities and establish a realistic timetable for accomplishing the many tasks associated with the project. Unfortunately, company dynamics are often such that the timetable is abandoned in the face of pressure to quickly submit an application to FDA.

Such pressure may be inevitable and difficult — or sometimes impossible — to overcome. Nevertheless, wherever possible, Regulatory Affairs personnel must provide reality-based advice and guidance (i.e., some "common sense") about the amount of work that needs to be done and when the submission can realistically be submitted. That message should include the fact that the better course of action is to "do it right the first time" — that achieving a short-range goal (e.g., telling shareholders that an application has been filed) is less important than the long-term goals of getting product clearance/approval in a reasonable period of time and maintaining a positive relationship with the agency.

Some companies — even those who have gotten good input from their Regulatory Affairs Department and who understand that an application is not ready for submission — generally adhere to the philosophy that the first order of business is to get the application in the FDA queue. With this approach, companies submit data to the agency on a piecemeal basis — as it becomes available or when and if FDA asks for it. Unless special circumstances exist, this is generally a bad idea because it usually takes longer to get the application cleared/approved (assuming it gets through at all), is more frustrating, and can give the company a bad reputation. In addition, that approach may cause FDA to assume that the company is withholding relevant safety and/or effectiveness data. Once such a conclusion has been made it is hard to overcome.

The sleeping fox catches no poultry. As a result of recent legislation, as well as reengineering and other efforts by FDA, there are new policies and procedures that relate generally to product applications. Many of these (e.g., *Modular PMA, "Real Time" Review of PMA supplements, Expedited Review, Special 510(k)s, Use of Published Literature, PMA Interactive Procedures*) are available for use but may not be very familiar to many reviewers. FDA generally will not suggest the use of particular policies/procedures, so companies need to be aware of these new policies and procedures — as well as older ones that are not used frequently — to understand how they can be applied appropriately. It may even be necessary for a company to educate the reviewer about the FDA policy/procedure, including an explanation of how and why it is being applied to the product under review. Particularly when a company tries to do something a little different or unusual, educating the reviewer is well worth doing if it means that the company may gain some advantage.

There are no gains without pains. There is no getting around it — it takes a long time to prepare a good application, and the more complex or novel the application, the longer it will take. For any application, one of the cardinal rules is to make it something the reviewer will want to read. First and foremost, it must be well-organized, well-written, and understandable. An application should be revised and rewritten until it can be followed easily even by someone unfamiliar with the product.

A company should never assume that the FDA reviewer understands how its device works, or why the device should receive a favorable review. Instead, it pays to assume that the opposite is true; companies should provide the reviewer with very clear and comprehensive explanations at each step.

Include a cover letter with the application that provides a "roadmap" to the application. Alternatively, this "roadmap" can be included at the beginning of the application in an Executive Summary. For a 510(k), describe the product; its indication(s)/intended use(s); how it is similar to other products; what, if anything, is new and different about it; and why this distinction does not impact the safety and effectiveness of the device. For a PMA, describe the product; its indication(s); intended use(s); other existing practices and procedures; marketing history; risks; potential benefits; safety issues; and both nonclinical and clinical data demonstrating the product's safety and effectiveness.

Make the body of the application logical and easy to read. To make the document flow, it is generally best to put most of the technical information -- including charts, test reports, and risk analyses — in appendices. The body of the application should, however, at the appropriate reference points, include brief summaries of what is in each appendix, rather than relying on the FDA reviewer to flip back and forth to different parts of the application. Thus, the reviewer's task is made easier and the company has an opportunity to briefly explain the appendices in a way that will help the reviewer understand what they contain, how they relate to the rest of the application, and how the documented evidence supports the product's clearance/approval.

Be an advocate. Do not let the reviewer come to his/her own conclusion as to why a product should be approved/cleared. For example, in a 510(k), the substantial equivalence section is perhaps the most important portion of the document. In addition to a table of comparisons, the submission should include a clear textual explanation of how the new product is similar to, or different from, existing legally-marketed products; why any differences in the product under review do not raise new questions of safety and effectiveness (referring, when possible, to data supporting this claim); and why the product should be deemed substantially equivalent. Conclusory statements not supported by data or other valid argument are not persuasive.

The application itself should be aesthetically pleasing. (Sometimes you can tell a book by its cover!) There should be sufficient *white space*, consistent formatting, continuous pagination, a means of setting off one section from another (e.g., tabs and colored pages between sections) and other hallmarks of a carefully prepared application. FDA requirements and recommendations for product applications — including administrative details such as margin size, and number of copies — also must be observed.

Want of care does us more damage than want of knowledge. The application must be internally consistent and without errors. It is not unusual to see typographical errors, nonsensical sentences, pagination problems, and internal inconsistencies in applications submitted to FDA. Such errors or omissions may give the reviewer a sense that the application is intrinsically faulty; they can also lead to more questions and an overall perception that the company is careless.

An empty bag cannot stand upright. A pretty face is not enough. In order to succeed, any FDA application must, of course, have the substance that FDA is looking for. First, all regulatory requirements must be met. If there are one or more guidance documents relevant to a device, they must be followed religiously once the company has confirmed that there have been no changes to the guidance. Alternatively, if something in a guidance document is not relevant to the company's product or, for example, a different approach to testing is desired, this should be discussed with FDA ahead of time or, at least, be explained in the application. Pieces of the application should never simply be left out on the grounds that the information is not available, the requirement is unclear, or it appears to be inapplicable to the device at issue. It is unlikely that the omission will simply be overlooked by the agency. Instead, the application may be rejected or the company will be questioned about the information in a deficiency letter. If the company cannot submit the information in the allotted time, FDA may, at that point, withdraw the application.

Proclaim not all thou knowest, all thou owest, all thou hast, nor all thou canst. There are many things that must or should be included in a product application. However, companies often put in too much information — some of which is merely irrelevant and some actually damaging. Sometimes this is done to provide extra background information to the reviewer. Another theory seems to be that if the reviewer sees a lot of bulk to the application, he or she will not notice that some of the required elements are missing. As noted above, it is unlikely that this ploy will work. While companies must be careful not to make any significant omission in an application, it is equally important to take care in determining how much information should be provided, how it should be presented, and what legitimately can be omitted. Too much information can raise many new questions, which in turn have the potential to slow down or derail an application altogether.

Think of three things: Whence you came, Where you are going, And to whom you must account. Companies must recognize that, in the end, they are accountable to the agency. Because the agency is made up of people, companies should, whenever possible, develop a give-and-take working relationship with the reviewer or others in the relevant agency division. One way to do this is to ask well thought-out questions prior to submitting an application.

Be a straight-shooter. While companies must be careful about what is said, and how it is said, it is never acceptable to mislead or appear to mislead a reviewer or other FDA staff. Aside from legal issues associated with failure to tell the truth to a government agency, there is no quicker way to destroy trust or have the reviewer question the company's integrity. Reviewers who have had less-than-satisfactory experiences with a company's written work product or who have had ongoing negative interactions with company representatives may not forget this when a new application lands on their desk. As Ben Franklin astutely observed, "Glass, china and reputation are easily cracked and never well mended."

A company may disagree with a reviewer's request, or take issue with a decision that has been made, if it does so respectfully and with substance to back up the difference of opinion. Depending on the circumstances, it may be beneficial to work with someone outside the company who can interact well with the agency, understands the problems associated with the application, and can help the company rectify those problems. If the disagreement is significant to the company, and cannot be resolved at the reviewer level, it can be taken up one or more levels within FDA. There is FDA guidance regarding avenues for dispute resolution. In any case, the reviewer should be given a "heads up" each step of the way.

He that best understands the world least likes it. There are times that an FDA request or decision does not seem fair, is unreasonable, or is even contrary to law, regulation, or written FDA policy. Under these circumstances, it may be worthwhile to contest an FDA action, if both short-term and long-term benefits and drawbacks have been evaluated carefully. At other times, even though the agency's decision may not be a good one, the company's best choice may be to cut its losses and accept the request or decision. Nothing says a company needs to be happy about it, but sometimes acceding to the agency's decision is the most expedient approach.

Careful planning, knowledgeable and thoughtful analysis, good writing, and adequate time and attention are the hallmarks of success when it comes to getting device applications through FDA. There are times, however, when even the best efforts fail to bear fruit — or to bear fruit quickly — due to the complexity of the device, its poor performance in studies, certain policy concerns at FDA, or myriad other factors. Under these circumstances, a company may decide to substantially revise its current application, modify the device, proceed down a different regulatory path, or pursue administrative remedies. If all else fails, however, it may be best to remember Ben Franklin's infamous words, "Nothing in this world is certain but death and taxes."

Richard S. Silverman

Hogan & Hartson, L.L.P.

CHAPTER 5

How to Get Your Food Additive Product Approved

I. Introduction

The Food and Drug Administration's (FDA's) premarket clearance process for food additives can be long and frustrating for companies anxious to bring new additives to market. A recent study commissioned by FDA and conducted by the Research Triangle Institute of Center for Economics Research concludes that, under current review procedures and based on the amount of information and material required for review, FDA is incapable of meeting its 180-day statutory deadline for all but the simplest of food additive petitions.

The impact of FDA's statutory mission on the time it takes the agency to review the various types of applications for premarket approval of food additives cannot be overstated. FDA has, in essence, but one statutory mission — to protect the public health. Not surprisingly, this goal is completely compatible with the goal of food suppliers, ingredient suppliers, food processors, and food packaging manufacturers in supplying the market with only wholesome, unadulterated products. To this extent, the missions of the corporate sector and the government are the same.

In one important area, however, the interests of FDA and industry diverge. FDA, unlike a company, is not "in business" to make a profit. The agency's sole charge is to protect the public health. FDA, therefore, is in no rush to clear a food additive so that production timetables can be met or a marketer's dream can be fulfilled. Rather, thorough scrutiny is the rule.

This approach often seems needlessly detailed and slow in the eyes of the businessperson. Thus, it is vitally important that food additive manufacturers first choose the least burdensome regulatory pathway to market, and then provide FDA with complete information to ensure that the company's entry to market is not delayed unnecessarily.

II. The Regulatory Pathway

Depending on the dietary exposure to a given food additive, whether its use raises any special toxicological concerns, and the type of customer assurances demanded by the marketplace, a manufacturer may have more than one choice as to how best to introduce a new ingredient. Most often, the appropriate regulatory pathway is governed initially by whether the food ingredient is for direct food use, secondary direct use, or for indirect uses.

A. Direct Food Ingredients

There are two potential regulatory pathways for introducing a new direct food ingredient into commerce: the food additive petition process or the generally recognized as safe (GRAS) notification procedure (the latter is currently a proposed rule under which the Center for Food Safety and Applied Nutrition (CFSAN) is accepting submissions). In addition, a company may, under the Federal Food, Drug, and Cosmetic Act (FDCA), determine for itself that a direct food ingredient is GRAS under the intended conditions of use. There may be customers, however, who require greater assurance than a self-determined GRAS position. In essence, this would require a company to submit a GRAS notification to obtain official agency recognition that a product is GRAS under the intended conditions of use.

If an argument exists that use of a direct food ingredient under the intended conditions is GRAS, there are several advantages to submitting a GRAS notification instead of a food additive petition:

- the agency has proposed to respond by letter within ninety days of the date of receipt of the notification, whereas FDA can take as long as two or more years to act on a food additive petition that is not fast-tracked; and

- although a full discussion of all toxicological data, some of which must be published, and a summary of dietary exposure estimates must be included, the company does not need to provide FDA with the raw safety and exposure data for review.

There are several advantages to submitting a food additive petition in place of a GRAS notification:

- FDA does not require publication of the critical toxicology data supporting the safety of the additive;

- because part of a GRAS determination involves common knowledge that the use of a substance is safe, the common or usual name of the substance, its intended use, and the basis for the GRAS determination are publicly available upon receipt of the notification by the agency; some of this information may be kept confidential if submitted as part of a food additive petition;

- favorable agency action on a food additive petition results in a regulation published in the *Code of Federal Regulations*, which provides the highest level of customer assurance;

- if the petition qualifies for CFSAN's special projects team, time to a final regulation may be as little as nine to twelve months; and

- a food additive regulation is generally revoked via notice-and-comment rulemaking, whereas FDA reserves the right to revoke an accepted-for-filing GRAS notification at a later date.

If the GRAS notification option is available, business concerns will dictate which approach is the most appropriate.

B. Secondary Direct Food Ingredient

Like direct food ingredients, secondary direct ingredients may be marketed under a cleared food additive petition or, when applicable, an accepted-for-filing GRAS notification or the company's self-determination that a substance is GRAS. However, secondary direct ingredients also may qualify for FDA's threshold of regulation exemption. This regulation (21 C.F.R. sections 170.39, 174.6) applies specifically to food contact materials and food processing equipment. FDA has granted exemptions to secondary direct additives from regulation as food additives under the threshold of regulation, provided the secondary direct additive met all the other criteria. A substance may be eligible for the threshold of regulation review if its proposed use would result in a dietary exposure of less then 0.5 parts per billion or if the substance is currently regulated as a direct food additive, its proposed use would be at or below one percent of the acceptable daily intake.

In deciding among the three options, the same analysis applies as for direct ingredients when determining whether to submit a food additive petition or a GRAS notification for a secondary direct use. With regard to the threshold of regulation route, there are three major practical advantages to submitting a threshold of regulation request over formally petitioning the agency:

- It is generally sufficient simply to identify the substance of interest and provide data on its potential level in the diet.

- Companies are not required to conduct any toxicology testing on the additive or its impurities, but rather must merely provide FDA with an analysis of existing toxicological information on the additive and its impurities to show that the additive is not a suspected carcinogen (and in the case of impurities, that the substances are either not suspected carcinogens or have a TD_{50} greater than 6.25 mg/kg-bw/day).

- FDA usually can complete its review of a threshold of regulation request within six to twelve months, as compared to the two or more years it often may take the agency to act on a food additive petition.

As with GRAS notifications, companies filing threshold of regulation requests must anticipate that FDA will make the following information publicly available: 1) the identity of the substance that is the subject of the request; 2) the level at which the substance may be used in the given application; and 3) all applicable use limitations, such as time and temperature limitations. Some companies may consider such details about a product's use to be highly confidential, commercial, business, or trade secret information. In this instance, despite its other advantages, a threshold of regulation request would not be advisable.

C. Indirect Food Ingredients

In addition to the four options available for placing secondary direct food ingredients in commerce, a company may market a new indirect food ingredient:

- based on a memorandum to file or a third-party opinion letter stating that, based on either migration studies or worst-case dietary exposure calculations, the indirect food additive is not a food additive within the meaning of the FDCA (i.e., the substance is not reasonably expected to become a component of food under the intended conditions of use) and, based on other safety data, that the substance does not otherwise adulterate food; or

- via a premarket notification for food contact materials, assuming that Congress continues to fund the premarket notification program or user fees are instituted.

When deciding among the four options that are available for both secondary direct ingredients and indirect ingredients, the same analysis applies to both kinds of ingredients. There are several advantages to consider, however, if a company can establish that a food-contact material or a piece of food processing equipment is not a food additive within the meaning of section 201(s) of the FDCA:

- because the substance falls outside the scope of FDA's premarket clearance authority pursuant to section 409 of the FDCA, a company may market the substance without any prior authorization from, or consultation with, FDA; and

- the company is not required to share any information upon which its determination is based; however, to adequately assure customers regarding the suitable FDA status of the substance, the company may need to share some information with customers (in this instance the company will have complete discretion over which information to reveal).

Unlike an indirect ingredient that is marketed pursuant to a food additive regulation or threshold of regulation exemption, FDA can challenge the company's decision to market the ingredient at a later date.

There are several advantages to filing a notification over filing a food additive petition, GRAS notification, or threshold of regulation request:

- FDA is required to act on the notification within 120 days of receipt of the notification; and

- favorable agency action on a notification will not result in a generic regulation upon which any other manufacturer may rely, but rather an effective notification will grant the company submitting the notification a proprietary right to market the food contact substance pursuant to the notification.

Because FDA has just initiated the notification program the complete list of advantages and disadvantages associated with filing a premarket notification cannot be known.

III. Compiling a Complete Submission

Once a food ingredient manufacturer decides the appropriate regulatory pathway for bringing a new food ingredient to market, it is imperative to provide FDA with a complete submission to avoid unnecessary delays and to build FDA's confidence in the company's competence. In this regard, some helpful hints for ensuring a complete submission are provided below.

A. Food Additive Petitions

- Before submitting a food additive petition, verify that use of the substance under the intended conditions is not already covered by an applicable food additive regulation.

- Consult the regulation (21 C.F.R. part 171) to ensure that all required information is included.

- Always estimate dietary exposure to the substance based on the specific intended conditions of use outlined in the food additive petition. Because the amount of dietary exposure will dictate the amount of toxicology data needed to support the safe use of the additive, do not leave this important job to FDA. For help with determining dietary exposure: 1) to a direct additive, consult with FDA's guidance document, *Estimating Exposure to Direct Food Additives and Chemical Contaminants in the Diet;* and 2) to an indirect additive, consult with FDA's guidance document, *Recommendations for Chemistry Data for Indirect Food Additive Petitions.* Both of these documents are available on FDA's homepage (www.fda.gov).

- Always consult with the agency before undertaking any toxicology testing to demonstrate that the substance is safe for the intended use. Because toxicology testing often is the most expensive testing performed in conjunction with a food additive petition, and given that review by the toxicology group is usually the most time consuming part of the food additive petitioning process, it is helpful to have FDA's concurrence that the battery and design of tests proposed by the company is appropriate. When considering which toxicology tests are needed to demonstrate the safety of an additive, consult FDA's guidelines, *Toxicological Testing of Food Additives,* which also is available on FDA's homepage.

- Submit meeting minutes regarding any discussions of the appropriate toxicology testing scheme, and ask FDA to review the minutes to ensure that a true "meeting of the minds" has occurred.

- Always design toxicology protocols in accordance with FDA guidelines and not the Organization for Economic Cooperation and Development (OECD) guidelines, because FDA's guidelines are broader in scope and more detailed in their requirements. Therefore, testing under FDA requirements will generally satisfy both OECD and FDA requirements. Moreover, FDA often will refuse to calculate a "no-observable-effect level" (NOEL) based on toxicity data collected pursuant to an OECD protocol.

- If the food additive petition involves an antimicrobial, refer to FDA's guidance document, *Antimicrobial Food Additives – Guidance*, to ensure that FDA, not EPA, has jurisdiction over the substance. Also, if appropriate, be sure to request expedited review of the petition.

- If the food additive petition involves an enzyme preparation, consult with FDA's guidance document, *Enzyme Preparations: Chemistry Recommendations for Food Additive and GRAS Affirmation Petitions*, to ensure that all specific information that relates directly to enzyme preparations is included in the petition. This guidance document also is available on FDA's homepage.

- Check to see if the company can include an abbreviated environmental assessment or if the product qualifies for a categorical from the environmental assessment.

- In addition to three copies of the petition, provide FDA with a fourth copy from which all information that the company considers confidential and trade secret has been redacted. Although FDA may disagree with the company, the agency may decide it is easier to use the company's redacted version to respond to Freedom of Information Act (FOIA) requests rather than to create its own redacted version of the petition.

B. GRAS Notifications

- Consult the proposed regulation (62 Fed. Reg. at 18,938) to ensure that the company includes all information requested as part of the GRAS notification proposal.

- Always calculate dietary exposure in the same manner you would calculate dietary exposure for a food additive petition.

- Confirm that at least some of the critical toxicity data supporting the safe use of the additive is published. The published data may be supported by unpublished data.

- Be sure to have complete files containing the toxicity data that is summarized in the notification, in case FDA requests the information as part of its review. Responding immediately to FDA will build agency confidence.

- If the subject of the notification is an enzyme preparation, consult with the guidance document noted above to ensure a complete submission.

C. Threshold of Regulation Requests

- Using the list provided at FDA's homepage, confirm that the additive under the intended conditions of use is not already the subject of an exemption. If it is, the company may market the additive pursuant to the exemption.

- Consult the regulation (21 C.F.R. section 170.39) to ensure that all information required by the regulation is included.

- Calculate dietary exposure based on the specific intended conditions of use to determine whether dietary exposure is less than 0.5 parts per billion (ppb). For example, if the additive is intended for use in polyethylene packaging that contacts only fatty foods, use both the consumption factor for polyethylene and the food type distribution factor for fatty foods. Failing to apply the latter factor would result in an overestimation of dietary exposure.

- When dealing with a physical mixture of additives, the dietary exposure to each component of the mixture must be below 0.5 ppb; the dietary exposure to the mixture as a whole may be above 0.5 ppb.

- If the toxicology search on the additive does not reveal any studies, state this fact and inform FDA regarding which databases you used to search for the information.

- Attach complete test reports from any migration testing done in support of the request.

- Provide FDA with a redacted version of the threshold of regulation request for the agency's use in responding to FOIA requests.

D. Premarket Notifications for Food Contact Substances

- Continue to watch for FDA to publish proposed regulations implementing the premarket notification program for food contact substances.

- Notifications are likely to require the same quantity and quality of information that is currently required in food additive petitions.

- Provide FDA with a redacted version of the notification for its use in responding to FOIA requests.

IV. Conclusion

Determining the least burdensome regulatory pathway is the first, and perhaps most important, step in bringing a new food ingredient to market. For example, careful consideration of the intended conditions of use of a new food processing aid may allow a company to calculate a dietary exposure that falls within FDA's threshold of regulation exemption, thus obviating the need for the company to submit a lengthy food additive petition. Likewise, a literature search on a Concern Level II direct food ingredient may yield a published article detailing the results of subchronic rodent and nonrodent feeding studies, thereby creating the possibility that the substance may be marketed pursuant to a GRAS notification.

Once a food additive manufacturer determines the proper regulatory pathway, the company must focus its complete attention on providing the agency a comprehensive submission to avoid needless delays during the review period. Providing FDA with an incomplete submission at an earlier date, rather than a more complete submission at a later date, will always cost time in the long run.

Moreover, providing FDA with a complete submission can create a high level of confidence in the company's abilities, and perhaps lead to reviewers extending some benefit of the doubt when reviewing the company's dietary exposure calculations and safety data. Although following this common sense advice may not allow a company to market a new food additive as quickly as the company would like, adherence to these basic precepts should ultimately help speed along the process.

C
H
A
P
T
E
R

6

Daniel A. Kracov
Jennifer J. Spokes

Patton Boggs LLP

How to Get Your Dietary Supplement Product Approved

I. Introduction

The Food and Drug Administration (FDA) does not officially "approve" dietary supplement products or ingredients for marketing in the United States. Dietary supplements, however, are subject to several notification and review procedures related to composition, safety, and labeling. Several of the procedures, such as those for filing health claim petitions and authoritative statement health claim notifications, also are applicable to conventional foods. This chapter will focus on the two notification procedures mandated by the Dietary Supplement Health and Education Act of 1994 (DSHEA) that are unique to dietary supplements.

The first notification process requires that a manufacturer, packer, or distributor of a dietary supplement product submit a notification to FDA if its product bears a particular type of product claim, called a statement of nutritional support. The second process requires a manufacturer or distributor of a dietary supplement product to submit a notification to FDA if its product contains a new dietary ingredient. Both notification procedures alert FDA of the marketing of the dietary supplement and its claims or new ingredients, and enable the agency to evaluate the submitted materials, notify the submitter of any problems or issues, and take actions to help ensure that the product complies with the laws and regulations applicable to dietary supplements.

II. Statements of Nutritional Support

A. Claim and Notification Requirements

If a dietary supplement product bears a statement of nutritional support on a dietary supplement label, the manufacturer, packer, or distributor must submit a notification to FDA. A statement of nutritional support is one that:

- claims a benefit related to a classical nutrient deficiency disease, and discloses the prevalence of the disease in the United States;

- describes the role of a nutrient or dietary ingredient intended to affect the structure or function in humans;

- characterizes the documented mechanism by which a nutrient or dietary ingredient acts to maintain such structure or function; or

- describes general well-being from consumption of a nutrient or dietary ingredient.

For such claims — which must be accompanied by a mandatory disclaimer — the manufacturer, packer, or distributor must notify FDA that the product's labeling bears a statement of nutritional support. The notification must be filed no later than thirty days *after* the first marketing of the dietary supplement. The notification must include:

- name and address of the manufacturer, packer, or distributor;

- text of the statement;

- name of the dietary ingredient bearing the claim, if applicable;

- name of the dietary supplement (including brand name); and

- signature of a person certifying the accuracy and completeness of the information in the notice, and certifying that the notifying firm has substantiation that the statement of nutritional support is truthful and not misleading.

Upon evaluating the notification, FDA ordinarily will notify the firm via a "courtesy" letter if the claim may be subject to regulatory enforcement action. FDA, however, is under no obligation to issue such a letter prior to initiating an enforcement action.

B. Formulating a Claim

Extensive thought and research should go into formulating an appropriate claim for a dietary supplement product. The following steps should be taken prior to formulating a claim:

Consult FDA's final rule on structure/function claims. On January 6, 2000, FDA published a final rule that attempts to distinguish between acceptable dietary supplement claims relating to the structure or function of the body ("structure/function claims") and claims that could render products unapproved new drugs. The final rule contains several examples of acceptable dietary supplement claims. For example, FDA considers "helps promote digestion," "supports the immune system," and "helps support cartilage and joint function," to be acceptable structure/function claims. In addition, "relieves stress and frustration," and "improves absentmindedness," are acceptable according to FDA. In the final rule, FDA permits some structure/function claims that FDA previously deemed unacceptable, such as claims related to natural processes like menstruation, pregnancy, and aging. FDA also acknowledged that some OTC drug monographs contain structure/function claims that can be used with dietary supplements, such as the antacid, sleep aid, and weight control monographs. Thus, when formulating structure/function claims for dietary supplement products, you should consult FDA's final rule for model claims.

Do not implicitly or explicitly claim that the product is intended to diagnose, cure, mitigate, treat, or prevent a disease. Often, there is a fine line between an acceptable structure/function claim and a disease claim that renders the product an unapproved new drug. Although FDA has limited resources to enforce against unacceptable claims, the final rule indicates that the agency takes a broad view on what constitutes a disease claim.

For example, FDA considers claims that a product "decreases the effects of alcohol intoxication," "provides support for the cold and flu season," or "reduces joint pain," to be disease claims. FDA also considers claims to be disease claims if they state that the product affects a characteristic set of signs or symptoms of a disease or disease class, affects an uncommon or harmful abnormal condition associated with a natural state or process, is a substitute for a disease therapy, augments a drug therapy or action, or treats or prevents diseases associated with drug therapy. For example, FDA does not permit the claim, "helps maintain normal intestinal flora when using antibiotics." Once again, it is advisable to thoroughly research the status of a claim before presenting it to FDA.

Ensure that you have adequate substantiation for the claim. To make a claim on a dietary supplement label, you must have substantiation that the statement is truthful and not misleading. The Federal Trade Commission (FTC) has issued guidance on advertising claims for dietary supplement products that, although not directly applicable to product labeling, can provide assistance in determining whether substantiation is adequate. For example, the guidance advises that a claim should directly reflect study results. Furthermore, certain types of studies, such as human, controlled, double-blind studies, are the most effective substantiation. Importantly, a representative of the company must certify to FDA that the information contained in the notification is not false and misleading, and that the claims are substantiated (although you need not submit the claim substantiation).

Survey "courtesy" letters issued by FDA. It is helpful to survey the courtesy letters issued by FDA to other firms and companies doing business in this area, to determine if any have been issued for claims similar to the claim that you are proposing. If FDA has issued such courtesy letters, you should consider revising your claim to a lower-risk claim. Keep in mind that some courtesy letters issued before the final rule might not accurately reflect the current regulation.

Survey warning letters issued by FDA. Warning letters are issued by FDA when the agency determines that a product and/or company (or individual) may be subject to regulatory action. Thus, Warning Letters also provide insight into certain claims that FDA deems unacceptable for dietary supplement products.

Conduct consumer research. Often, consumer surveys can help determine which potential claims are most effective at relaying your intended message to consumers. For example, consumer research may indicate whether consumers better understand a claim that a product "maintains" a body function or "supports" a body function. Keep in mind that if your consumer survey shows that consumers interpret your proposed claim as indicating an intended effect on disease, then the survey shows that the claim may not be an appropriate structure/function claim for a dietary supplement.

Conduct market research. Market research on potential claims can provide information as to claims currently being used. For example, structure/function claims about supporting mental function and mood enhancement, have received few courtesy letters and are among the most common claims on the market. Claims referring to energy, vitality, and stamina also have not received many courtesy letters and are common. Although the presence of a particular claim does not guarantee that FDA will not object to the claim, and thus will not initiate an enforcement action against the product, market research may provide a perspective as to FDA's enforcement priorities and the amount of regulatory risk involved with certain claims.

Submit all the claims that will appear on labels and labeling. Although you need not submit your advertising claims, you must submit claims appearing in all labels and labeling, including package inserts. In addition, FDA currently considers Internet information accompanying the sale of a product to be labeling. Thus, if you do not submit your Internet claims, FDA may request them or may conduct its own research on your Internet claims.

Do not claim that the product's mode of action is anything other than by ingestion. Dietary supplements, by definition, are ingested. FDA has informed manufacturers that their products are not dietary supplements, and thus cannot make certain claims, because the products were not intended for ingestion. For example, do not state that the product is a lozenge intended to soothe the throat by dissolving in the mouth. Also, do not claim that the product should be taken sublingually for faster absorption.

Do not represent the product as a conventional food. By definition, a dietary supplement is not represented for use as a conventional food or as a sole item of a meal or the diet. For example, FDA objected to the marketing of a product as a dietary supplement because its label bore pictures of the product being used in the same manner as butter. FDA has also objected to a yogurt drink marketed as a dietary supplement with claims that the product serves as a "breakfast drink," and "part of a balanced breakfast," as well as a dietary supplement characterized as a "soup" with identity statements commonly associated with soups such as "chunky tomato." FDA asserts that these products are conventional foods and may not be marketed as dietary supplements.

Do not submit your proposed labeling or your substantiation for the claims. FDA does not require the submission of these materials. If you submit them with your notification, you invite additional FDA review and criticism.

III. New Dietary Ingredients

A. Determining Whether to File a New Dietary Ingredient Notification

A dietary supplement that contains a new dietary ingredient is adulterated unless 1) the dietary supplement contains only dietary ingredients that have been present in the food supply in a form in which the food has not been chemically altered, or 2) there is a history of use or other evidence of safety establishing that the dietary ingredient, when used under the conditions recommended or suggested in the labeling of the dietary supplement, will reasonably be expected to be safe. If the second condition forms the basis for safety, the manufacturer must provide FDA with information supporting that finding, at least seventy-five days *before* introducing or delivering the product for introduction into interstate commerce. FDA keeps the filing confidential for ninety days after its receipt, at which time the filing is placed on public display (except for trade secrets or confidential, commercial information).

During the seventy-five days, FDA reviews the notification and may notify the manufacturer if the agency determines that the ingredient will not "reasonably be expected to be safe" for marketing. If the manufacturer does not receive such a notice within seventy-five days, the manufacturer can market the product with some assurance that FDA did not object to the product on safety grounds. FDA's failure to respond, however, does not constitute an official finding by FDA that the new dietary ingredient is safe.

Before filing a new dietary ingredient notification, you should ascertain whether the ingredient in question qualifies as a "dietary ingredient." A dietary ingredient is a vitamin, mineral, herb or other botanical, amino acid, or a dietary substance for use by man to supplement the diet by increasing the total dietary intake (or a concentrate, metabolite, constituent, extract, or combination of these ingredients). FDA will object to a new dietary ingredient notification if the ingredient does not constitute a dietary ingredient. For example, FDA concluded that an ingredient consisting of a variety of pathogenic microorganisms was not a dietary ingredient because pathogens are not substances that are food or that are used for food.

Once you have determined that the ingredient is a dietary ingredient, you must determine whether the ingredient is a "new dietary ingredient." A "new dietary ingredient" is an ingredient that was not marketed in the United States before October 15, 1994. Thus, you do not need to file a notification if the dietary ingredient appeared in foods or dietary supplements in the United States prior to October 15, 1994. As mentioned above, you also do not need to file a notification if the ingredient has been present in the food supply in a form in which the food has not been chemically altered. The legislative history for DSHEA clarifies that "chemically altered" does not include the following physical modifications: minor loss of volatile components, dehydration, lyophilization, milling, tincture or solution in water, slurry, powder, or solid in suspension. Thus, before filing a new dietary ingredient notification or marketing a dietary supplement, you should research the history of use of the ingredients present in the dietary supplement to ascertain whether any ingredients are new dietary ingredients and thus require the submission of a notification.

B. Filing the Notification

A notification for the marketing of a new dietary ingredient must include:

- name and complete address of the manufacturer or distributor;

- name of the new dietary ingredient, including the Latin binomial name and the author of any herb or other botanical;

- description of the dietary supplement or dietary supplements that contain the new dietary ingredient including:

  - level of the new dietary ingredient in the dietary supplement; and

  - conditions of use recommended or suggested in the labeling of the dietary supplement, or, if none, the ordinary conditions of use of the supplement;

- history of use or other evidence of safety establishing that the dietary ingredient, when used under the conditions recommended or suggested in the labeling, will reasonably be expected to be safe. This should include citations to published articles or other evidence that forms the basis for the conclusion that the ingredient is safe. References to published literature should be accompanied by reprints or copies of the references and should be in English; and

- signature of a designated person.

When compiling the notification, you should keep the following helpful hints in mind:

Include evidence from scientific studies, especially human studies. The FTC's standards on evaluating substantiation for claims can also prove helpful in determining which scientific studies best demonstrate the ingredient's safety. For example, while many different types of studies can be listed, including animal studies and epidemiological studies, large, long-term, double-blind human clinical studies are the most highly regarded for assessing safety. Because FDA has rejected notifications that did not provide sufficient evidence related to long-term use, chronic toxicity testing of at least six months is advisable, as is reproductive toxicity testing. Furthermore, FDA will examine whether the human studies reflect conditions of use similar to those recommended on the product label. (Note: It is advisable to use higher dosages in animal studies than is recommended in the human product's labeling.) Remember that studies cited in the notification should focus on safety; effectiveness studies are not required. It also may be helpful to include a literature search with the notification.

Include information on the history of use. FDA likely will assess the totality of the safety evidence from information provided in the notification on history of use, existing literature, and original studies. Therefore, although you obviously cannot make up for a complete lack of scientific studies, the history of use information can be used to complement and round out the other safety evidence provided in the notification.

Provide as much evidence as possible on the current use of the ingredient and the ingredient's effects on the body. A significant amount of evidence about the ingredient being used in various ways can provide further support for a conclusion that the ingredient is safe. Evidence of use is most helpful if the ingredient is in comparable forms and levels as the supplement; however, any information may be helpful. In addition, although use in the United States is usually preferable, foreign uses also can support your position. It also may be beneficial to provide background information on how the ingredient is taken into the body and its mode of action.

Do not include drug uses or disease claims in the notification. Because you must indicate the recommended conditions of use for the product, do not indicate an intended drug use for the product. For example, FDA deemed a product to be an unapproved new drug because the new dietary ingredient notification contained claims that the product helped the immune system fight disease and treated respiratory disease. It is better to establish the labeling claims for the dietary supplement product before filing the new dietary ingredient notification, and to include these acceptable dietary supplement claims in the new dietary ingredient notification.

Review FDA's response letters indicating that certain new dietary ingredients are not safe. Ninety days after submission, FDA places new dietary ingredient notifications on public display, including FDA's response to the notification. Therefore, you can consult the public docket, as well as the trade press, to determine why FDA rejected certain notifications. For example, it may be helpful to know if FDA has objected to new dietary ingredients because only animal studies were provided in their notifications. Many of FDA's objections do focus on the nature or quality of the scientific research data provided, and FDA's past objections have led many to claim that FDA essentially requires safety evidence akin to that for a food additive petition.

Indicate in the notification which materials are confidential. FDA will not place information on public display if it is trade secret or otherwise confidential commercial information. Designation of confidential information must be in writing. Therefore, you should indicate in your notification any information that you deem confidential. If you accidentally omit certain designations, FDA may permit you to designate additional materials confidential within a reasonable period of time after the filing date. Be aware, however, that FDA could disagree with any such designations and could attempt to make the information publicly available. If you are uncertain as to whether FDA might make the information public, you should consult FDA before submitting the notification to avoid unexpected disclosure of important information.

Remember that you cannot market the product until seventy-five days after you file the notification. In preparing for product development and marketing, take into account that marketing of the product will be delayed seventy-five days while FDA examines the new dietary ingredient notification. In addition, if FDA has objections or requests additional information, the time period before marketing could increase. Although FDA will notify you if the agency objects to the safety of the ingredient, FDA will not notify you if it does not object to the new dietary ingredient. Therefore, if the seventy-five days pass and you have not heard from FDA, you can begin marketing the product.

File a complete notification — do not plan to supplement it later. If FDA does not object to your new dietary ingredient notification, you can market the product seventy-five days after the filing date. If you must, however, supplement the notification with additional information, FDA will assess whether the additional information is substantive. If it is substantive, FDA will notify the company and will "restart" the seventy-five-day time period. Thus, if you submit your notification before gathering all the necessary information, you may not be able to market the product until well after the initial seventy-five days have passed.

Although not required, manufacturing information provides additional support for the product's safety. By providing FDA with information on how the ingredient and/or product is produced (including quality assurance information), you offer FDA further assurance that the ingredient is safe as used in your dietary supplement product.

During the seventy-five days after a notification filing, advertise with caution. Although there is no legal prohibition on advertising during FDA's seventy-five-day review that your product is "coming soon," you should consider the possible consequences of such advertising. For instance, FDA may request more information or object to the notification, creating substantial delays in the time it takes to get your product to market. In addition, if FDA has any problems with the notification, you may not want to inadvertently put pressure on FDA, through product advertising, to accept the notification. A major advertising campaign could alert FDA as to the potential proliferation of the product and may cause the agency to exert closer scrutiny or to raise additional concerns. Advertising language based on claims regarding the safety or effectiveness of the new dietary ingredient should be minimized during this seventy-five-day period.

IV. Conclusion

Notifications to FDA for dietary supplements should be carefully reviewed and analyzed prior to submission. For statements of nutritional support notifications, it is important to invest a significant effort to formulate an appropriate claim before submitting the notification. For new dietary ingredient notifications, include all relevant information on the ingredient's safety, including scientific studies. Also remember to allow your company, and your attorneys or consultants, ample time to prepare the notifications.

FDA's Office of Nutritional Products, Labeling, and Dietary Supplements, the office responsible for regulating dietary supplements, has limited time, resources, and personnel. Companies should work with FDA, as appropriate, but should seek to resolve their own problems in submissions rather than test sampling new concepts with the agency. If FDA requests additional information, make sure that you fully understand the request so that you provide the correct information and do not create additional delays. If you invest sufficient time and effort in developing products and product claims in compliance with FDA's requirements, the regulatory clearance process for dietary supplements can be efficient and effective.

Andrea E. Chamblee

Regulatory Consultant

7

CHAPTER

Obtaining Information From FDA

I. Introduction

The extraordinary number and diversity of products and regulatory standards under the purview of the Food and Drug Administration (FDA) can make retrieving information like searching for the proverbial needle in a haystack. It can be difficult to know how to narrow a particular search to retrieve the specific information you desire. Requests under the Freedom of Information Act (FOIA) can be lengthy and expensive, and Web searches can result in hundreds of unrelated "hits." If you try to circumvent the morass by calling FDA staffers directly, you are likely to be sent back to "square one:" to the Web, or to the FDA's Freedom of Information (FOI) Office. There are, however, some lesser-known ways to speed your search.

II. FDA Contacts

After determining that the information you seek is not easily accessible in your files or on the Internet, you may try a quick telephone call or e-mail directly to an FDA staffer. Unless you are extraordinarily lucky, you will probably be referred to the FOI office, as dictated by FDA procedure. FOI offices have the equipment and the budget to catalog requests, search records, purge confidential information, keep frequently-requested documents accessible, and mail out responses.

FDA staff members are not *forbidden* from responding directly to individual requests, although in the grand scheme of things, it is best for the reviewer and the public if these functions remain separate. Even though you may not agree with that at the time you are hoping for a quick turn-around to your own request, you would not want to learn that your product approval was delayed even by a day because your reviewer was tending to tasks that should have been performed by another office. The FOI office also needs to track requests, and the funds that go into fulfilling requests, for staff, equipment, and budget planning. Others will be incensed when they find they went through channels, paid for, and waited for a document while their competitor received instant answers by phone, at no charge. These are the considerations that give pause to many FDA employees outside of FOI who are uneasy about handling such requests.

Still, there is a fairly good argument for the direct route of communication if the FOI office will have to ask that office to produce the documents to respond to your request in any event. If there are no contentious issues about information to be purged before release, or if you are willing to let the employee perform the purge while erring on the side of caution, the FDA office may be willing to send it to you directly. In this case, a direct request may actually save FDA a few steps. If the employee still hesitates, you may be able to prod them gently with a reminder that an e-mail to inform the FOI office, perhaps with a copy of the documents released, will satisfy most FOI staff concerns about tracking and budgeting.

Another instance when a contact may not object to a direct request is when the office has the document at the tip of its collective fingers (*e.g.*, a regulations writing office may have a document on display for *Federal Register* publication, or the Office of Policy may have a policy statement handy). While you should assume that agency personnel are busy, if they owe you a favor or welcome a break from some other task, you may consider throwing yourself on the mercy of your contact, or try to catch them at a good time to get that quick response.

Chances that the direct approach will be successful are inversely proportional to the resource-intensiveness of responding to your request. Factors that go into that determination include the sheer volume of documents sought, and whether the documents you seek are difficult to distinguish from others or are difficult to locate.

One good example of a simple, yet time-consuming, request involves one of my current assignments. A client asked for a registration number of an old biological establishment. I called some colleagues who I had hoped might remember its notable closing about seven years before. They did not seem to mind the interruption, but they did not remember the precise circumstances, and certainly not the registration number. Although the actual piece of information is small, registration numbers of establishments closed that long ago (before most information was in files on desktop computers) are buried in boxes off-site. It is not information readily called up from computer disks.

Even if the original documents are in the hands of a Center or field office, if they will be difficult to purge for release then the direct approach to ask for them will not work. FDA staff not trained in FOI procedures will be hesitant to tackle a contentious or difficult editing job, and the entity that provided the information, or is mentioned in it, will surely make its objection known.

In sum, a call to a responsible party may provide a rapid turn-around, if the document or a Web link to it is easily at hand. As the response becomes more resource-intensive, you may be better off saving any favors owed and calling them in on another day.

III. FDA Website

FDA's website continues to evolve, in a valiant agency attempt to keep pace with the World Wide Web. Some general tips for using the site will stand the test of time.

Unfortunately, the agency's Centers haven't "piggy-backed" on site names for such common addresses as site maps, FOI, indices, or "what's new." Once you get beyond www.fda.gov/ [Center abbreviation], the addresses are cumbersome and not universal; clicking through seems faster than typing lengthy names of forgetful acronyms. Perhaps the next redesign will result in common site names, so that comparing biological policy on feed for food-producing animals with biological medical devices, for example, requires knowing only parallel addresses such as fda.gov/cber/biopolicy, cdrh/biopolicy, and cvm/biopolicy.

A. Use What's New

Each FDA Center has is own web page, so you can limit your browsing to the appropriate Center. FDA's search page also allows you to restrict your search to one Center. Nevertheless, you still can end up with search results that fill pages and require hours to eliminate irrelevant hits. Moreover, when you click through the links listed on the search results, your web pages are addressed from a temporary "search bin" instead of the permanent document address. When this bin expires in several minutes, return visits to the site are very complicated.

One way to avoid the maze is to have FDA send you e-mail with summaries and direct links to the events of the week. The Center for Drug Evaluation and Research (CDER) and the Center for Devices and Radiological Health (CDRH) have this service; limited resources may prevent the Center for Biologics Evaluation and Research (CBER), the Center for Food Safety and Applied Nutrition (CFSAN), and the Center for Veterinary Medicine (CVM) from having the same. For "What's New at CDER," sign up at: <www.fda.gov/cder/cdernew/listserv.htm>. For devices, go to <www.accessdata.fda.gov/scripts/cdrh/cfdocs/cfCDRHNew/listman.cfm>.

All the Centers post new entries on their sites through a button on each Center's homepage. Go to the appropriate Center's main page, select "What's New" (currently in a box on the left margin) or go to <www.fda.gov/opacom/newonweb.htm>.

B. Use Other Web Search Engines

If you are not looking for something new, you will have to search, but the FDA search page may not be the best place to start. Consider other search engines that let you impose more limits on your search. For example, you may limit by date, so you can forego extraneous records discussing your topic of interest long before it became a rule. If you type in enough keywords, you should pull up the FDA page in the top list of your results, and perhaps get a bonus in the form of related hits from sister agencies or trade groups, which can add dimensions to your research that you would not want to have missed. To further limit searches on "off-site" search engines, you may be able to contain the search to FDA's website if the engine allows you to type in the domain name <fda.gov> (or <.gov>). HOTBOT, SNAP, and MAMMA are engines that search across several smaller search engines, and allow you to limit your search by date and site in this manner. These engines also allow you to add complete phrases and to exclude words without bothering with the grammar rules of composing a search; the connecting words (e.g., AND, BUT, and NOT) are already placed for you.

C. Use FDA's Dockets Page

The FDA dockets page is an invaluable source, and recently has been redesigned. It serves as a default starting point for a search, with links to most documents added to the FDA public record in the past few years. The dockets page also allows for comments to be submitted electronically. FDA dockets can be found at <www.fda.gov/ohrms/dockets>.

D. Hidden Indexes

Another way to search on the FDA web pages is to scour through the indexes. By omitting the <html> tag on many office's web addresses, you can bring up their indexes and get another perspective on the mysteries locked in there. For example, by typing <www.fda.gov/opacom/> on November 29, 1999, you would get a much better idea of what is organized there by the Office of Press Affairs then you would with a straight search. You can see the site documents are divided by year and by how the information was issued (e.g., *Talk Papers*, which are cleared through the Commissioner's Office, versus press releases, which also must be approved by the Department of Health and Human Services (DHHS) and therefore may not be cleared as quickly). There are also directories for Fact Sheets and the *Enforcement Report*. You can also see the date that the information was posted by FDA (although that is not necessarily the document date). If you know a little about how the information you seek was originally released, you may be able to browse those directories more quickly than reviewing the results of a search. As another example, on <www.fda.gov/opacom/morechoices> you can find a potpourri of policy issues.

At <www.fda.gov/bbs/topics>, FDA's Bulletin Board System Topics Directory, which was instituted before the agency had a web page, you can find categories for:

- *Enforcement Reports*

- Press Releases (see also "Talk Papers") [1998] [1997] [1996] [1995] [1994] [1993] [1992]

- Public Calendar

- Speeches

- Talk Papers

At <www.fda.gov/ohrms/dockets/dockets> the documents in the index are listed by docket number. In a related directory, <www.fda.gov/ohrms/dockets/ac>, you will find a list of advisory committee transcripts and, where available, committee meeting summaries.

IV. Use Small Manufacturers Assistance Offices

CDRH's Division of Small Manufacturers Assistance is a role model for offices that interact with small manufacturers; hopefully it will be a model for the other FDA Centers soon. FDA has posted an overall agency-Web guide, with many links helpful to businesses of all sizes, at <www.fda.gov/opacom/morechoices/smallbusiness/toc.html>.

CDER has a new small business office at 301-827-1494, Ron Wilson is the Office Director, and John Friel is the Division Director.

FDA also has Small Business Representatives (SBRs) who help businesses whose products are regulated by FDA. These SBRs are located in six regions around the country. The SBRs can respond to inquiries, conduct or participate in workshops and conferences, or visit plants, at your request, to offer assistance. SBRs are listed at <www.fda.gov/opacom/morechoices/smallbusiness/smbusrep.html>.

V. Freedom of Information Act Requests

FOIA, codified at 5 U.S.C. section 551, was revised in 1996. The Act as revised endorses FOI responses to be customized not only between agencies but within agencies as well. FDA and other agencies are still looking to the Department of Justice (DOJ) for guidance on the myriad of permissible interpretations. FDA's FOI pages may be found at <www.fda.gov/foi/foia2.htm>.

In sum, the new FOI law allows for what it calls multitrack processing. The DOJ allows different tracks based on the nature of the request and the office that serves as the repository of the records. If you want to position your request to be in the faster track, you need to know how the requests currently are prioritized. The law also addresses other issues, including one that has caused some confusion, namely the point at which agencies must post information on the Internet or otherwise make it available.

A. Nature of the Request

1. Expedited Review
Certain requests are entitled to the fastest process, called expedited review. Few will qualify for this fastest track. Under this provision, requests from persons *primarily in the business of disseminating information* should qualify for this review, apparently on the theory that releasing the information for further dissemination gets a better "bang for the buck," and perhaps in deference to media deadlines. *Not only the press, however, may qualify for this fastest track.* If the information you seek is of importance not only to you but to an educational organization, it would be worthwhile to join forces so the request can be associated with that organization and its purpose. Then, seek expedited review on the basis that the organization as an educational one is primarily in the business of disseminating information.

Requests regarding an imminent threat to the life or physical safety of an individual also are expedited. These requests must be accompanied by certification that they are truthful. According to Les Weinstein, a regulatory counsel on FDA's FOI staff, there must be an "urgent need to inform the public about an actual or alleged federal government activity; a mere deadline is not enough."

FDA has ten days to grant a review as expedited (*not* ten days to respond to the information request). A denial can be appealed through the DHHS. Assuming that the request is not moot by then, an aggrieved party can seek judicial review.

2. Multitrack Processing

If FDA staff can respond to a request on-the-spot, they also have discretion to put aside those requests that are voluminous and labor-intensive to answer later. Requests need not be prioritized solely on a first-in-first-out basis. Under the Electronic FOIA Amendments of 1996 (E-FOIA), FDA can establish different tracks based on the complexity, voluminousness, and labor-intensity required to respond. Within those tracks FDA assumably should respond on a first-in-first-out basis. FDA is not limited to two tracks of faster and slower, but can have several middle tracks as well. The statute does not dictate how FDA will prioritize between the longest and shortest tracks, or how it will prioritize among several "middle" tracks. The Department of Justice (DOJ) answers questions and issues guidance periodically, which can be viewed at <www.usdoj.gov/oip/foi-act.htm>.

Les Weinstein provided an example of a voluminous request — one that sounds suspiciously as if he has seen it before — for "any and all information FDA has on 'fen-phen'" (Fenfluramine (Pondimin) and Dexfenfluramine (Redux)). "What they really want," he suggested, "is [adverse drug reactions] ADRs, or ADRs from a particular timeframe." Or perhaps the requestors are seeking only ADRs mentioning cardiac valvular dysfunction or other heart ailments from 1996 to 1997.

If you really do need all that information, you may not want to send your request as one large "white elephant," but if appropriate, as multiple requests divided to reduce the documents that must be combed through or copied, and to avoid the slowest track.

B. The Office Responsible for the Request

FDA need not set up one office with one tracking system. Under the E-FOIA Amendments, the requests can be tracked differently by different offices. FDA has decided to have different tracks for each Center and for field/regional offices.

It is likely that a request that goes to one busy or ill-equipped Center or field office can expect a different priority and timeframe for response then a similar request routed elsewhere. You may want to tailor your search to go to an office with a shorter backlog. Because the system is new, it is hard to predict which office or route will be considered the fastest, or whether that accolade will be passed to other offices over time.

Many factors will affect turn-around time, including the extensiveness of the search, the volume of the documents involved, the size and sophistication of the particular staff, its ability to compete for the time of staffers within the agency who have the source documents, the office budget, and the sophistication of the equipment. You may want to submit the request to more than one office, if feasible, and cancel one when you get a response from another. The potential disadvantage is, if you do not cancel the second search before it starts, you may be billed twice for the results.

According to E-FOIA, regardless whether the priority is selected because of the nature of the request or the tracking system of the responsible office, the procedure for prioritizing requests *must include a provision to allow the requester an opportunity to limit the scope of the request to qualify for faster processing.* Therefore, be sure to provide an address where you can be located early in the submission process, to ensure that your request is on the fastest, most appropriate track.

C. Will FOI Requests Be Obsolete? The "Rule of Threes"

One of the more interesting and perhaps least understood provisions is that regarding documents that must be indexed or posted on the Internet. With proper document selection, sufficient resources, and ever-increasing public access to the World Wide Web, FOI requests increasingly will be replaced by the sound of "mice" clicking. As with many new initiatives, however, there is no new funding to cover start-up costs, in this case to get the documents loaded and agency staff updated on the new requirements. This continues to be true, even though it would seem that increasing access to documents on the web may save costs in the long run. It also should be noted that costs for documents produced via FDA's website cannot readily be passed on to the requester.

At a recent trade association annual meeting, one FDA staffer explained that without at least three separate requests for production of a document, the Center would not devote scarce resources to posting that document on the Internet. When the moderator of the session asked, "How do we know what to request?" there was an uncomfortable silence.

This "rule of threes" does not quite reflect the actual statutory requirement. Three actual requests are not necessary; the statute reads that for documents "that have become *or are likely to become* the subject of subsequent requests for substantially the same records . . . *because of the nature of their subject matter*," the documents should be available in electronic format and indexed for easy (electronic) retrieval. In effect, such materials should be available on the World Wide Web, fax-on-demand, or some other accessible format. Although you should not have to explain this statutory information to FOI staff, you may need to serve as an instructor for other FDA staff less familiar with all the passages of E-FOIA.

D. Form and Format

The new E-FOIA also requires agencies to provide the record in any "readily reproducible form and format" requested. Therefore, if you can use the information faster in the form of CD or disk, or even e-mail, it would be worthwhile to request it that way even if you have to wait another day for it to be placed in that format. On the other hand, if FDA has not yet reproduced the particular record in the format you requested, you may want to give FDA a chance to send it to you in the form it already takes, rather than wait for administrative staff to scan it.

VI. FAX-on-Demand and Other Electronic Document Retrieval

FDA keeps a list of Frequently Requested Numbers on the World Wide Web that includes the Fax-on-Demand for the Centers that maintain this service, as well as other important numbers. The list of documents is updated too frequently to try to reproduce here; it is available at <www.fda.gov/opacom/morechoices/smallbusiness/freqcall.htm>. The Fax-on-Demand numbers and some other important numbers are printed in Table A of the Appendix to this chapter, for easy reference.

VII. Other Sources of Related Information

Clearly, there are too many sources of FDA-related information to list them all; health-related sites on the web are springing up faster than the borderline industries offer to link to them. Nevertheless, many are worth special mention. Some information sources, like the "Pink Sheet," the "Gray Sheet," and their multicolored relatives of the traditional trade print media, and like drkoop.com on the Web, are well-known. Table B in the Appendix to this chapter lists some of the lesser-known health-related websites that stand out.

VIII. Conclusion

The universal rule for obtaining information, whether it is a Web search, a FOIA request, or a call to an FDA staffer, is to make sure your request is as narrow as you can make it and still receive the information you need. Ask for the more expedited tracking and leave complete contact information so that you can get help to ensure your request is narrow enough to qualify. Note that you are willing to discuss alternative kinds of requests if they will provide you with what you need in better time.

Appendix

Table A
Fax-on-Demand and Related Addresses and Telephone Numbers

Center for Biologics Evaluation and Research	
Fax-on-Demand	Local (301) 827-3844 or toll free at 888-223-7329

Center for Devices and Radiological Health	
Facts-on-Demand Index at	toll free at (800) 899-0381 http://www.fda.gov/cdrh/dsma/fod.html#contents
Electronic Docket (Documents via computer (modem))	(800) 252-1366

Center for Drug Evaluation and Research	
Office of Training and Communication	(301) 827-4573 or fax (301) 827-4577
Fax-on-Demand	local (301) 827-0577 or toll-free at (800) 342-2722

Related Important Addresses and Telephone Numbers

Office of the Commissioner	
Office of External Affairs, Industry and Small Business Liaison Team:	(301) 827-3430

National Institutes of Health	
Small Business Institutes Program (For information about grants involving FDA regulated products)	(301) 435-0715

Small Business Administration	
409 3rd Street S.W. Washington, DC 20416	
Small Business Answer Desk or Wash. D.C. area	(800) 827-5722 (202) 606-4000

Superintendent of Documents	
Mail to: New Orders Superintendent of Documents P.O. Box 371954 Pittsburgh, PA 15250-7954	(202) 512-1806
For on-line subscriptions	(202) 512-1530

Table B
Health- and Business-Related Information Sources

About.com	
	About.com has "guides" with a wealth of information on many subjects, and you can get newsletters on various subjects you choose delivered to your electronic mailbox. About.com sites include:
http://home.about.com/health	Health, including medicine, alternative medicine, disease, global issues, women's health, and fitness
http://home.about.com/business	Business, including industries, and professions
http://usgovinfo.about.com/culture/usgovinfo/	Government, including laws, industries, international and local issues, and agencies
http://globalbusiness.about.com	Global issues, including global business information.
	One of my favorite sites here addresses small business help with exporting and importing <http://globalbusiness.about.com/business/business/globalbusiness/library/weekly/aa062899.htm>
HealthWeb	
	Medical librarians throughout the MidWest collaborated to create HealthWeb.org
HealthHippo	
	Health Hippo is a collection of policy and regulatory materials related to health care, provided by FindLaw. <http://hippo.findlaw.com>.
HealthFinder	
	Healthfinder® is a free gateway to consumer health and human services information developed by the Department of Health and Human Services. It contains links to selected online publications, clearinghouses, databases, websites, and support and self-help groups, as well as the government agencies and not-for-profit organizations that produce reliable information for the public. <http://www.healthfinder.gov>.

Table C
Important sites

All sites begin with http://www.fda.gov/ unless otherwise noted

	CBER	CDER	CDRH	CFSAN	CVM
Site map	cber/sitemap.htm	cder/site/sitemap.htm	Only for Mammography, at cdrh/mammography/site_map.html	http://vm.cfsan.fda.gov/list.html	cvm/sitemap.html
Index	cber/cberac.htm	cder/directories/qi.htm	http://www.accessdata.fda.gov/scripts/cdrh/cfdocs/cfTopic/topicindex/topindx.cfm	vm.cfsan.fda.gov/sitelist.html	cvm/fda/mappgs/specificsubj.html
FOI	cber/eFOI.htm	cder/FOI/index.htm	cdrh/FOIcdrh.html	http://vm.cfsan.fda.gov/~dms/FOIa.html	cvm/fda/mappgs/eFOI.htm
Frequently requested numbers	cber/pubinquire.htm	not listed	not available	http://vm.cfsan.fda.gov/~lrd/emaillist.html	not available
Manufacturer's assistance	available by e-mail at matt@cber.fda.gov	Small manufacturer's assistance office may be under consideration at CDER	cdrh/dsma/dsmamain.html, or Device Advice - http://www.fda.gov/cdrh/devadvice	http://vm.cfsan.fda.gov/~dms/industry.html	not available

C
H
A
P
T
E
R

8

Wayne L. Pines

APCO Associates

How to Win With an FDA Advisory Committee

I. Introduction

You cannot spend too much time preparing for an appearance before a Food and Drug Administration (FDA) advisory committee. You can, however, go about the process inefficiently; you can assign too few, too many, or the wrong people to the project; and you can make the worst mistake by failing to listen carefully to the agency or to interpret properly the positioning of FDA.

Managing the process of presenting before an FDA advisory committee is important from many perspectives. A scientifically-sound, professional presentation can impress the committee and FDA, and can create a higher level of confidence in the company's professionalism and basic competence. This confidence provides the basis for gaining the benefit of any doubt about the product or about the data supporting its safety and effectiveness. The advisory committee's views also influence how FDA manages the labeling negotiations that will take place if the product is ready for approval.

The media and Wall Street frequently attend advisory committee meetings. How well a new drug or device is positioned with the health care community and the public will depend, to a large extent, on the media reports emanating from a committee meeting. Very often, the meeting provides the first opportunity for major public exposure for a new drug or device. Wall Street's view of the potential for the product and of the company's value, especially for smaller companies, is influenced by how professionally that company's representatives appear in public before an advisory committee.

Preparation for an advisory committee meeting should begin in earnest about three months before the committee meeting. At the time an application is filed, the company can learn from FDA which committee will review the product, and when that committee will meet over the next year. Depending on the product's review time, it is possible to "guesstimate" when the presentation will be.

II. The Initial Steps

There are a few initial steps that should be taken to prepare for a meeting:

(1) Profile the committee so there is a good understanding of its members and how it functions. There are many sources available for such a profile. Videotapes of previous meetings can be obtained from commercial sources and can provide a flavor for how the committee asks questions and debates issues. Some committees have strong chairmen who keep tight reins on the committee. Other committees are less focused. Key points to look for are the extent to which FDA staff seeks to influence the committees during the meeting and the extent to which there is debate among FDA staff members themselves.

You also can get the resumés of the committee members from many sources, including Internet sites for the institution with whom the committee member is affiliated. A call to the committee member's office is a very direct way of obtaining the resume. The resume provides an indication as to the committee member's clinical experience and focus, as well as his or her research interests and potential conflict of interests.

A third way to obtain information and insights into advisory committee members' views is to interview people who have watched them at advisory committees or who have discussed with them their clinical interests. Within large drug companies in particular there usually are physicians, researchers, or others who are familiar with at least some members of a committee. Smaller drug/biotechnology companies and medical device companies may need to call on outside resources to obtain these insights.

(2) Establish a master timetable for all events so they can be planned and scheduled. The master timetable should list all tasks and major meetings, such as major rehearsals and mock advisory committee meetings, that are to take place. These meetings should be planned and scheduled as far in advance as possible, especially those meetings that require attendance from outside advisers or that require significant time commitments from outside presenters. Outside adviser-experts usually have very busy schedules, especially when they are practicing medicine or teaching. It is essential to schedule their time early in the process.

The key sessions that involve outside participants are rehearsals and mock advisory committee meetings. Also needing to be scheduled are the rehearsals that immediately precede the actual committee meeting.

(3) Assign sufficient staff to do the job. Many large drug and device companies assign too many people to prepare for an advisory committee meeting, and very often the people assigned have other responsibilities. I have found that a small dedicated team of people, most of whom are relieved of other responsibilities, usually works best. This approach enables the team to focus its attention on the presentation and related is-

sues, to get the work done quickly, to respond promptly to FDA requests, and to keep to schedules. It also allows for consistency in the preparation process, because once a decision is made, it will not constantly be second-guessed except by that same group. The team should include people who are familiar with the disease or condition; who understand the history of the application and the relationship with FDA; and, most importantly, who know the data, its strengths, and its vulnerabilities.

(4) Be sure it is clear who is in charge. Very often, when senior managers from different departments are assigned to coordinate an activity, it is not clear who is in charge. In preparing for an advisory committee meeting, when basic decisions need to be made every day and there is no "right" or "wrong," it is essential to have a single person who can make the decision and have it stand unchallenged. The leader can be from any one of a number of different departments: research and development, regulatory affairs, medical affairs, or senior management. Who will serve best depends on the leadership skills of the individuals, but the point is that someone must be recognized as "in charge."

(5) Hire the right consultants. Decide early in the process who the best people are to help with the preparation. Inevitably, some of the investigators should be involved. Experts in the disease or condition being treated or diagnosed often are useful. Others who are almost always needed are experts in statistics, slide production, and FDA strategy. The earlier the consultants are hired, the more useful their contributions will be.

III. The Early Decisions

At the initial organizational meetings, certain decisions should be made:

What data will be presented? This often is a complicated decision. An application consists of vast volumes of data from the various phases of product development. All the relevant data will be in the briefing book prepared by the company for the advisory committee, but in developing an hour-long presentation, not all the data can or should be presented. The pivotal studies generally will be presented in some detail, as will major safety information. Any data that FDA regards as particularly significant also should be presented. The data selection process should be discussed extensively.

Which points will be emphasized? There is a difference between information (facts) and messages. Messages are those thoughts that you want the listener to remember. In addition to presenting information, a presentation also should deliver messages. There needs to be discussion of what the basic messages are for each segment of the presentation. The initial presentation should be an overview and should summarize the main points that will be made by later presenters. FDA knows the product and committee members have read the briefing book, or at least glanced at it, so the presentation need not cover every point about the product. Instead, the presentation should provide the most persuasive case for why the product should be approved.

Who will speak? The best presenters must combine knowledge of the data, an ability to communicate with an audience, an ability to respond to questions, and inherent credibility. Presenters often are selected solely on the basis of what they know, but if they are not persuasive or they cannot respond in a focused way to questions, then perhaps they should not stand at the podium on your behalf. You have to consider many factors in deciding who will present.

Who will be the liaison with each speaker? The company should assign someone to act as liaison with each outside speaker. The outside speakers should receive regular information from the company as to how the presentation is progressing and what questions FDA is posing. Speakers cannot just show up at the rehearsals and on the day of the advisory committee meeting. They must be an integral part of the development process.

Who will answer questions? The hardest part of the advisory committee meeting to coordinate is the Q&A. The best strategy is to have a single person field the questions and then answer them or call on an expert to answer them. The people designated to respond to questions must know in advance what is expected of them. What are the company's answers to the tough questions? How long should an answer be? What back-up slides will be needed to answer the questions? When should the back-up slides be used, and when is it better not to use them?

What is the best way to prepare the slides? Most companies now use PowerPoint to prepare the slides, and use the same system to present to the advisory committee. PowerPoint is less expensive than producing slides.

Who will manage the slide process? This can be done either inside the company or outside. But someone must be assigned to manage the slide process. This person should know how to produce Power Point slides that are readable and can be changed quickly, since many of the changes are made during meetings. It also is a challenge to produce slides with tables and graphs that are easy to read.

How will the Q&A be compiled? The best way is for everyone involved in the presentation development process to write and send to a central source all the likely questions that the committee will ask; this may be hundreds of questions. Then this person should categorize the questions according to topic: safety, efficacy, etc. The people designated to respond to committee questions in that area should review the questions and determine who is best at responding, and which back up slides, if any, will be used.

How will external audiences – e.g., media and Wall Street – be managed? Usually someone in the public relations or IR department of the company, working with the presentation team, will take responsibility for working with external audiences before, during, and after the committee meeting. The important thing to achieve at the planning meeting is to decide who will be responsible for this function. It is important for this individual to have intimate knowledge of the progress of the presentation and the people presenting, as well as having a relationship with FDA, so he or she can communicate appropriate information to the external audiences. It is common for a "war room" to be set up at the advisory committee meeting to handle external audiences. The extent of the "war room" and its capabilities can be determined based on the interest likely to be expressed in the product being reviewed. The "war room" should have all necessary communications technologies, such as computers, modems, and faxes – all of which should be compatible with any other technologies that the company will bring in, such as laptop computers.

Will there be presenters at the open public session? The open public session that starts each advisory committee meeting is an opportunity for noncompany representatives to speak. They may be physicians, patients, patient advocates, or any member of the public. The company can invite speakers to attend the open public session and provide a perspective on the product to be presented to the committee. If a company invites such speakers, they should be prepared to present for five minutes or less. They should make clear their affiliation or financial relationship with the company. Speakers will seldom receive any questions.

Who will be the liaison with FDA? The company should designate who will be the liaison with FDA regarding advisory committee matters. Usually this is a person in the regulatory affairs department. This person has a special responsibility to listen carefully to FDA's staff as they complete the review of the product; to set up meetings if needed; to learn from FDA the logistics of the meeting (where, when, etc.); and to provide FDA with the company's briefing book and, if requested, slides. This is an important liaison function that should be managed by a senior person who has experience in dealing with FDA.

Agree with FDA on the process. The kinds of issues that must be discussed with FDA early in the process include:

- When is the briefing book due? Usually FDA wants copies of the briefing book three to four weeks before the committee will meet.

- When will we see FDA's own internal product review? FDA traditionally has provided this to the company, though litigation has made it more difficult of late for FDA to do this. If provided, it must be read and re-read carefully and objectively, to ascertain FDA's main concerns and fine-tune presentations accordingly.

- When will we see FDA's questions for the committee? FDA always prepares questions for the committee to answer at the conclusion of the meeting. Companies can obtain the questions in advance of the actual meeting. Obviously, the further in advance the questions can be obtained, the easier it is to focus the presentation on the questions.

- Does FDA want to see our slides? Sometimes FDA staff has the time and willingness to review the company's slides, if submitted far enough in advance. This review generally is a good idea, as FDA feedback can help fine-tune the presentation.

How will the briefing book be prepared? At the same time that the presentations and slides are being prepared, a briefing book also must be written. This book is sent to committee members before the meeting. It represents the best case that the company can make for its product. The briefing book must be well-organized, well-written, and powerfully persuasive. It should contain only data that FDA has seen, and its outline should track the oral presentation to be made before the committee. The tables must be consistent, if not identical, with those in the oral presentation. The person assigned to draft the briefing book must be an active member of the committee preparation team, but must have the time to focus on the book until it is provided to FDA three to four weeks before the committee meets.

IV. A Few No-No's

There are a few things that should be avoided during the advisory committee preparation process. It is inappropriate to communicate with committee members, for instance. To do so invites concerns about tampering. A company also should not take anything for granted. No product presentation goes perfectly, and no advisory committee should be regarded as a "slam dunk," no matter what FDA says.

V. Organize Rehearsals Efficiently

You can get a lot out of a rehearsal, or it can be a waste of time and money. In my experience, rehearsals lose their value when they are scheduled before the company is ready to make a coherent presentation; it is better to spend the day working on the presentation. They also lose value if the key presenters are not available.

The first rehearsal should be at a time when the company is ready to make a presentation along the lines of what it expects its final presentation to be. By the time of this first rehearsal, basic decisions should have been made about the order of the presentation, the messages to be communicated in each part of the presentation, and the likely speakers. A first draft of the slides and of the oral presentation should be available.

At the first rehearsal, which generally should be without the "mock" advisers, hardcopy handouts should be made available to everyone in attendance so they can make comments on the presentation or the slides. Handwritten comments that can be turned in at the conclusion of the day make it easier for the presenters to amend their presentations and slides. It usually is a waste of time to review every slide with the entire group present, when the comments on the slides can be delivered in writing. It is a good use of time to discuss major messages, whether those messages are being communicated, what can be eliminated, and what should be added to the presentations. Invariably the first rehearsal produces a presentation that is much too long.

The first rehearsal is not a good time to work with speakers on their presentation skills. The order of business should be to improve the presentations. There is time at later rehearsals to work on presentation skills. At the second rehearsal, which should take place when the presentations are further along in planning, there should be discussion of major messages and also how to improve each slide.

The third rehearsal, and a fourth if needed, might include a "mock" advisory committee meeting consisting of former members of the committee to which the presentation will be made. The mock advisory committee rehearsals must be run tightly if the company is to gain any insights and knowledge. The "mock" committee members should receive advance copies of the briefing book and they should be asked to listen and ask questions as if they were attending a real committee meeting. In particular, they should be instructed to be as tough as they can be; mock advisers often feel they should be gentle and vote for approval of the product, even if they identify deficiencies.

Final rehearsals take place in the days immediately preceding the actual committee meeting. The company may commandeer a hotel in the Maryland suburbs and spend all waking hours practicing and refining the presentation and how questions will be answered. This is a time when every presenter and every potential answerer of questions should be involved actively in the rehearsals. The only way that the team can work together at the public meeting is to rehearse together. In particular, attention should be paid to how the company will respond to questions, how quickly the back-up slides can be called up, and the presentation skills of the presenters. This is also the time when the press and investment community strategies can be unveiled; I have found that there is not much value in discussing press or investment strategies with the presenters until this time, as they should be focused on matters that are more central to the presentation itself.

VI. At the Meeting Itself

A. Etiquette

Companies usually bring large contingents of employees to witness the meeting. These employees should be given very precise instructions on what to do. They should be cautioned not to speak with the media or investors unless they are designated spokespeople. They should not discuss with each other the progress of the meeting, lest they be overheard. Meetings are usually attended by swarms of competitors, and must be approached with this knowledge in mind.

Company presenters should introduce themselves to the committee chairman and greet other members of the committee as appropriate, especially if they have met before. It is not appropriate to discuss substantive issues with the committee members in private.

B. Answering Questions

If the preparation has been done correctly, the biggest challenge at the actual meeting is responding well to the committee's questions. The company should have in place a system for how questions are to be answered – who will field the questions, who will answer questions, and how back-up slides can be accessed. The company should prepare for any question that might arise, and also prepare to answer "off-the-wall" questions that might be asked. Questions about pricing, labeling, and Phase IV study commitments usually can be deflected because they either are inappropriate (e.g., pricing) or are subject to discussion with FDA staff (e.g., specific labeling and Phase IV). Of course, if labeling issues or follow-up studies are an issue or are central to FDA's own questions to the committee, the company should be prepared to respond.

C. Managing the Unexpected

There are many things that can wrong during an advisory committee meeting. For example, during the public session, there could be unexpected presentations by individuals or groups who oppose approval of the product or who make other adverse statements. One of the company's own speakers may fall ill and not be able to present. FDA could make unexpected statements. The committee may be unsatisfied with some of the answers or could react differently than expected. During the committee debate, members could make misstatements about the product or the data supporting it, leading other members of the committee to a negative vote.

Preparing for the unexpected has some inherent contradictions. The best way to prepare is to decide who among the company speakers is best equipped to handle unexpected events, and then delegate to that person the right to make decisions on the spot if needed. For example, if an outside speaker during the open session makes an inflammatory remark that could prove damaging, the company may seek to rebut it; or if FDA makes an unexpected remark, it may be necessary to respond. The decision must be made quickly and efficiently, and a system should be put into place to handle the unexpected.

D. Working With the Media/External Audiences

Only the designated spokespeople should have any contact with the media, investors, or other external audiences. During the meeting, it usually is unwise to make any statements, as it is always difficult to predict the outcome based on remarks heard during the meeting itself. During the meeting, the target external audiences should be identified so that information can be provided to them immediately afterward. Statements projecting all possible outcomes should be prepared in advance so that the company can move quickly to announce the results and put its own spin on them.

VII. Conclusion

Preparing for an advisory committee meeting is a long, intense, and focused effort. If the product is successful before the committee, all the work is worthwhile. If the outcome is negative, then second-guessing begins and an evaluation needs to be made of what went wrong. In my experience, companies that have negative outcomes usually can look back and not only see their errors but also reinterpret the signals from FDA or other sources that were ignored or not effectively addressed.

At the end, what carries the day at an advisory committee is good data; a product that is safe, effective, and needed; and a positive recommendation by FDA staff. How a company presents itself at the committee meeting provides underpinning for a positive outcome.

Kate C. Beardsley

Buc & Beardsley

How to Appeal an Adverse Product Approval Decision

I. Introduction

If you are lucky, you will never have to think about appealing an adverse decision made by someone at the Food and Drug Administration (FDA). But most people who deal with FDA find themselves or their management considering an appeal at one time or another. When a company must decide whether and how to appeal, either because FDA declines to approve a product based on the information available or will not act at all, there are a range of available choices. Every situation is different, and the right choice will vary depending on the circumstance. Nevertheless, in thinking about an appeal, a few principles are worth keeping in mind. This article comments on how to think about framing an appeal, where to take an appeal, and how to handle an appeal.

II. Framing an Appeal

As a rule, the place to begin an appeal is not at FDA, but rather in-house by taking a clear-eyed look at the situation, what you have told FDA, and what FDA has told you. Even though you may be reporting to an outraged management and/or board of directors, try not to approach your review defensively. The existence of a dispute does not mean that either the company or FDA is wrong, stupid, or venal. Product approval decisions are complicated, and there is plenty of room for good faith differences of opinion. The trick is to find ways to narrow those differences, and that is what your review should be about. Sometimes one person can do such a review intuitively, moving the pieces around in his or her head; at other times the process needs to be collegial. Often, it is useful to add one or more outsiders to the process (e.g., medical experts, consultants, or lawyers) who can bring additional perspective and experience. However you approach the job, it is worth taking the time to do it well; a cogent, consistent position is the key to successful appeals. Some of the most important issues to consider are discussed below.

A. Can You Define the Points of Disagreement?

It is not always easy to find out where the points of disagreement are. Are you facing a scientific or technical conflict, a regulatory conflict, a policy conflict, a difference related to a change in approach, or just miscommunication? One place to start is with FDA's correspondence. But FDA's correspondence is often conclusory; it will tell you what FDA wants to see, but not always why it wants it. The "whys" may be important, because they define the real points of disagreement. Can you call one or more people at FDA to get more information? If so, that should be done quickly to help you frame the issues.

B. Is the Science on Your Side?

Presumably, the company would not have submitted an application in the first place if it did not believe that the product was safe and effective (or, in the case of an investigational product, that it was worth investigating). But take another look. Has FDA identified a real flaw in the logic or a real gap in the data? If so, you may decide not to appeal, but fill in the gap.

C. What Are Your Strongest and Weakest Points?

Almost all products have strong points and weak points. Prevailing in an appeal means keeping the emphasis on the reasons your product should be approved. If you are in a situation that potentially involves an appeal, the chances are that FDA is focusing on weak points in your submission. You need to avoid losing sight of, or taking for granted, the strong points in your case.

You also need to know how to handle weak points. Sometimes, you can compensate for weaknesses with labeling changes; for example, a narrower indication or an extra warning. In an appeal, you will need either to explain persuasively why the weak points are not important or be able to provide FDA some comfort that the weaknesses can be handled.

D. Have You Met the Regulatory Requirements?

Meeting the requirements for approval is not always the same thing as proving that a product is safe and effective, although the two usually are linked. For example, FDA cannot clear a 510(k) submission for a device unless the 510(k) submission includes a summary of safety and effectiveness or a statement that the company will make such a summary available. When you get a letter saying that FDA wants material that may seem peripheral, it may be that the regulatory requirements have not been met. To approve a product, FDA needs a complete file, and it is unlikely to render a favorable decision unless it has one.

E. Have You Made Your Points Effectively?

Many FDA reviewers will tell you that the number one cause of disputes is failure to present information about the product clearly and completely. Often, the company just knows too much, but has not done all it could, or should, to help reviewers understand the submission — in general and down to the smallest specific. Maybe each section of the application was written by a different person or group, and no one has pulled it all together and made sure it has a theme and is coherent. Sometimes, communication problems stem from the way a submission is formatted, making it hard for reviewers to find particular information in the many volumes that make up a submission. Sometimes, a company has left out information that seems obvious, but provides context for FDA; a reviewer may not start with the same assumptions or level of knowledge about a health condition that a company does. Sometimes, there is just so much information that it does not add up to anything; it is too hard to distinguish the important from the unimportant. If communication seems to be the problem, your appeal may not work any better than the original submission. Perhaps a clarified and strengthened resubmission will work better than an appeal.

F. Is FDA Facing Other Pressures Regarding Your Application?

In reviewing applications, FDA faces both inside and outside pressures. For example, FDA is under constant pressure to treat competitors equally or at least similarly. Therefore, precedent may be important, and the agency will not want to give your company a better deal than the company that came before it. Also, as a federal agency, FDA sometimes has little choice but to pay attention to its parent, the Department of Health and Human Services, as well as the White House, Congress, the medical establishment, and the press. This is not necessarily a bad thing; it is a fact of democratic government. In recent years, xenotransplantation has been a good example of this phenomenon. In allowing xenotransplantation clinical trials to proceed, FDA has had to cope not only with the real benefits that xenotransplants could offer, but also the equally real public and scientific fears that animal viruses could cause unknown diseases in humans. The more you know about the kinds of pressure FDA is facing, the better the decisions that can be made about your appeal.

G. Is There Common Ground?

Appeals work best when someone has thought through ways to solve everyone's problem. A company cannot expect FDA to do that; chances are that your product is just one among many that FDA reviewers are trying to handle. For that reason, it is up to the company to find a way to give everyone most of what they want, and there may be more than one way to do that. The more choices you can put on the table, the better the odds of finding one that FDA can live with.

III. Where to Appeal

While you are ensuring that your own position is clear and well-reasoned, and that you have identified your strongest arguments and made the best of your weakest ones, you also will be deciding where to appeal.

In rare situations, there may be statutorily-defined routes to appeal. If, for example, a premarket approval (PMA) application is denied, the law provides for submission of a petition for review and a specific process to manage such petitions. It is rare, however, that product approvals reach this stage. More commonly, an appeal is related to a less definitive action from FDA; for example, a request for more or different data. In these circumstances, companies have a range of choices, from re-raising the issues with the initial reviewers to filing a formal appeal.

The most common kinds of appeals can be grouped into four categories, each of which is briefly described below.

A. Appeals to the Division Director

You can be reasonably sure that, if a dispute concerns a matter of importance or has a history, the director of the division reviewing the application is aware of it. If he or she has not heard about it from you and your colleagues, however, he or she may not have heard the best presentation of the company's viewpoint. Generally, it is worth trying to discuss the issue directly with the director. FDA regulations provide that any interested person may obtain review of an agency decision by raising the matter with the supervisor of the employee who made the decision. While the regulation contemplates a review of the administrative record rather than direct contact with the applicant, it is rare that a division director will refuse to discuss a problem application.

The best way to start an appeal is to tell the reviewer that you want to discuss the matter with the division director. Very often, the reviewer or branch chief will want to arrange a meeting; if not, you can call the division director directly. Generally, you will be asked to submit preparatory materials, which provide an opportunity to state your case in writing prior to the meeting. In recent years, FDA's procedures for requesting and scheduling meetings have gotten more cumbersome, so it is worth starting the process as early as possible.

B. Appeals to the Ombudsman

Most of FDA's Centers have an ombudsman, one of whose functions is to help resolve disputes. The term "ombudsman" means, literally, "administrative man," and that is a fair description. The ombudsmen have no power to overrule the decision of a division or a reviewer, but they have the power of persuasion and the advantage of working for the Center Director. At a minimum, they can facilitate communication and make the process work better. At best they can be effective mediators, bringing a fresh and reasonably independent viewpoint to a problem situation. One other advantage of consulting the ombudsman is that the consultation can be confidential; the ombudsman is about the only place for a guaranteed-confidential FDA insider perspective. Although one can, in theory, involve the ombudsman at any point in the approval process, it generally is best to take the matter at least to the division level before turning to the ombudsman.

There are several ways to take advantage of the ombudsman's help to resolve a dispute. Sometimes, it is helpful just to get an FDA perspective on the problem, and get some advice on the choices available to you. While the ombudsman cannot be expected to give detailed advice on the basis of a single phone call, he or she often can provide informal reactions very quickly. The ombudsman may be particularly helpful if your concerns raise sensitive issues (e.g., personality conflicts, unfair or unequal treatment, or violations of the law). The ombudsman can help you sort through whether the treatment bothering you is unusual or just routine FDA practice; whether your concern is likely to be taken seriously; and where to pursue it within the agency. It is in this advisory context that the confidentiality offered by the ombudsman can be most useful.

Another choice is to ask the ombudsman to play an active role in mediating the dispute. Whether that makes sense depends both on the ombudsman and on the dispute. It is probably fair to say that, as a general rule, the more procedural and less scientific the controversy, the more likely it is that the ombudsman can help. For example, if phone calls are not returned, meetings not scheduled, or responses not received in a timely manner, the ombudsman may well be able to help.

If the Center ombudsman cannot help, or if the problem seems so intractable or so important that the company would prefer that it be addressed at a higher level, FDA also has an agency-wide ombudsman, who reports directly to the Commissioner. The agency ombudsman will give advice on process, for example, on which agency offices to contact on a specific issue or possible paths to resolve a problem; and can also investigate complaints and mediate disputes within one of the Centers.

C. Appeals to Center and/or Agency Management

If a dispute cannot be resolved at the division level, another choice is to take it to Center management, starting with the Office Director and moving to a Center Deputy Director or Director, if necessary. FDA's regulations provide for an appeal as far as the Commissioner. Generally, however, the informal version of this kind of appeal takes the form of a request for a meeting with specific individuals in Center management. If the dispute is scientific or medical, FDA's drug regulations provide that FDA will try to grant requests for meetings involving important issues, and that requests should be made through the division director. An applicant may suggest that FDA seek the advice of outside experts, and that FDA may then invite one or more members of an advisory committee or other consultants. The Center for Biologics Evaluation and Research also has adopted this policy. While the Center for Devices and Radiological Health has not laid out quite so formal a pathway, its leadership will schedule meetings in appropriate circumstances.

Making an appeal at the Office or Center level requires a good deal of thought. This kind of meeting is often scheduled to take sixty-to-ninety minutes, which means that the company must be able to state its position cogently and persuasively in no more than thirty minutes. Taking the right experts and having available the right information can make important differences in the result. It is almost always worth testing a presentation with experts before the meeting, preferably people who are not intimately involved with the product. It may be worth practicing more than once.

FDA's guidance applicable to drugs and biologics also suggests a more formal variant of this process, to which the guidance refers as Formal Dispute Resolution. To start the formal process, a sponsor submits a request to a Dispute Resolution Project Manager, along with supporting information. It is then referred to the appropriate official who will provide a response, usually written. For products under the Prescription Drug User Fee Act, the guidance establishes a strict timetable. Formal dispute resolution is designed more as a review of the administrative record than as an interactive exchange of ideas. It may be appropriate in a situation where positions are completely polarized or where there appears to have been an important procedural or regulatory flaw in the review process. It is likely to be less well-suited to working through complicated scientific or data-related issue.

FDA's regulations also provide other methods for resolving disputes, primarily petitions of various kinds, the most common of which are citizen petitions. Petitions, which can be filed at any time, are usually not good vehicles for resolving application-specific disputes. For one thing, they are public, as is the agency's response. Also, except in unusual circumstances, FDA rarely acts on petitions very quickly, and petitions sometimes languish for years without any response.

D. Appeals to Dispute Resolution Panels

In recent years, the most often discussed form of dispute resolution is the process established in the Food and Drug Administration Modernization Act of 1997 (FDAMA), which provides for a sponsor to request a review of scientific controversies by an FDA advisory panel.

FDA has promulgated a brief regulation implementing the law, but the two draft guidances, one covering drugs and biologics and the other covering medical devices, provide greater insight into how the process actually would work. At the outset, it is important to note that the law does not provide a right to advisory committee review, but rather a right to request a review. Both guidances make an effort to explain the kinds of situations in which review is not appropriate; the medical device guidance also gives some examples of situations in which review might be appropriate. Both speak to the internal process for making a decision about whether a request would be granted. The Centers for Drugs and Biologics contemplate using their regular advisory committees as dispute resolution panels. The decision of an advisory committee is not binding, and need not be followed by the Center Directors, who act on the advisory committee's recommendations.

Even a cursory reading of the draft guidances suggests a major drawback in seeking this kind of review — the extensive time needed to request the review, for FDA to decide whether to grant the request to schedule the meeting, and for the agency to decide how to handle a recommendation. It seems clear that advisory committee review will be appropriate only for disputes that do not require timely resolution.

IV. Handling an Appeal

There are no hard and fast rules for deciding how to handle an appeal. There are, however, a few general principles to bear in mind.

Informal appeals usually have the best chance of success. Although, at the behest of industry, FDAMA focused on the more formal kinds of appeals, these usually are best reserved for "last-ditch" efforts. An appeal that is quiet, that is undertaken before positions have hardened, that aims for consensus rather than argument, and that stands the least chance of embarrassing FDA or the applicant is most likely to succeed. One can imagine a dispute that is appropriate for advisory committee review — perhaps a highly public affair in which industry and the medical establishment were ranged against FDA's position. But that kind of dispute is rare; most often, the issues are neither that universal nor that clear-cut.

Identify potential allies within FDA. Appeals involve people as well as process. FDA is not monolithic; there are likely to be as many views inside FDA as outside. In deciding how to appeal, consider who will be involved, and how to involve the people or organizational units who are most likely to be helpful.

Try to offer a solution. Appeals should be designed not to force a decision maker to reconcile irreconcilable differences, but to offer the opportunity to find common ground. Some background is always required, but dwelling on past failures by FDA reviewers is more likely to divide than to unite. While you want to be careful not to negotiate against yourself, offering a solution that gives both parties some of what they want often provides the best hope of success.

Almost all appeals add time to the review process. Almost all applicants seek both speed and certainty in the review process. Appeals beyond the division almost always are messy and slow. FDA does not operate on business timetables. Anyone who has tried to schedule a meeting at FDA knows that just to get the meeting scheduled is a major undertaking. And there is no guarantee that one meeting will resolve the issues. More often, one is looking at two or three such meetings. Appeals, then, should be reserved for issues that are central to getting a product approved.

Maintain procedural good faith in any appeal. You may not be able to pursue an appeal without sacrificing some esprit in your relationship with FDA reviewers, but you stand the best chance if you are forthright about your intentions and you respect FDA's hierarchy. As a rule, if you intend to appeal, you owe the person whose decision is being appealed an explanation and an opportunity to participate.

Expect repercussions from an appeal. Anyone in FDA's management will encourage you to exercise your right to appeal if you believe an appeal is warranted, and will tell you that retaliation against appellants is strictly prohibited. At a seminar on dispute resolution last year, one Device Center official made the point well with a slide that said "From the clash of differing opinions comes the spark of truth." Our experience is that most FDA employees believe that statement and do their best to live it. At the same time, disputes can change perceptions, and cause those who disagree to view each other with less openness and more suspicion. That can have consequences for future dealings. You want to be seen as a person or organization who will stand up for themselves in an appropriate situation, but not as one who causes trouble for no good reason. That can be a fine line to walk.

Avoid threats of litigation or bankruptcy. FDA is in the business of protecting the public health, and any appeal should be based on respect for that mission. Whether your company goes out of business or sues FDA is, for the most part, irrelevant to the protection of public health. Besides, your allegations are likely to be discounted; FDA has heard too many empty threats of this kind, and generally will not be able to distinguish between a genuine intention and an expression of frustration.

V. Conclusion

At the end of the day, disputes are likely to be resolved on the strength of the science, and the product's potential impact on the public health. But different people, both inside and outside FDA, will evaluate science and public health differently. Dispute resolution processes are ways to get viewpoints aired before a new audience with a different, sometimes broader, perspective. Handled properly, that can make a big difference.

10

Marlene K. Tandy

Health Industry
Manufacturers Association

How to Hold a Meeting With FDA

Having a successful meeting with FDA is a crucial aspect of developing and marketing an FDA-regulated product. Here are tips on how to set up, prepare for, and conduct a successful meeting.

I. Ten Tips on How to Set Up a Meeting

(1) *Request the meeting in a written submission to FDA.* The format can be a letter, a memo, a response to the FDA Form 483 (Notice of Inspectional Observations), a response to a warning letter or untitled letter, or any other suitable written vehicle. A written request provides a record of the request, outlines the issue(s) and reason(s) for the meeting, and gives the agency something tangible that will require a response.

(2) If the subject of the meeting relates to business that your company has conducted with a specific FDA staff person, or relates to a matter that you expect will be referred after the meeting to a specific person that you have worked with in the past, then *you may choose to call that person in advance of sending the written meeting request.* This will give him or her a "heads-up" that your meeting request will be appearing in the near future.

(3) *In the written request, include the following items*:

- an introductory paragraph summarizing the basic issue(s) to be discussed and a statement to the effect that "we would like to meet with the agency to discuss this subject";

- a section that discusses the background of the issue(s). If there is a significant amount of background material that needs to be provided, consider putting it into a separate volume that can either accompany the meeting request letter or be sent at a separate time. If you send background material at a separate time, the request letter should indicate this. Also, plan to send separate background material either by an overnight mail service or by messenger, to arrive at FDA at least two weeks before the scheduled meeting date;

- a section that provides more detail on the issue(s) to be discussed and lists any specific questions or decision items that you will present to FDA at the meeting;

- a suggested timeframe for the meeting. One hour is standard, however, in some special cases (e.g., complicated product issues or extensive enforcement matters), more than one hour may be necessary. If you think this is the case, be sure to explain why you are requesting a lengthy time period for the meeting;

- identify any person(s) from FDA whom you would like to have attend the meeting. For example, if you have been working with a particular reviewer, it may be wise to request this person's attendance at the meeting. Or, if the issue to be considered includes any special scientific discipline (e.g., biostatistics or toxicology), it may be wise to note this and request attendance by an FDA scientist with expertise in that area;

- identify any audiovisual aids that will be necessary (e.g., slide projector, overhead projector, set-up for projection from laptop computer, phone for conference call). It is also a good practice to mention your audiovisual requests to the FDA contact person on the phone; and

- conclude with statement(s) similar to, "Thank you very much for your attention to these issues. We will contact your office in the near future to arrange a meeting date." Plan to call the person to whom the meeting request was sent approximately three to four days after the letter was faxed or sent by messenger (or a week after the letter is sent by regular mail).

(4) A situation may call for *sending copies of the meeting request letter to several people* within the agency that you would expect to attend the meeting, in addition to the person to whom the meeting request is directed. *If you cannot identify any of these people*, then it is always appropriate to *send extra copies of the meeting request letter* to the person to whom the meeting request is directed, *for their use internally at FDA.* This is especially true if you are submitting extensive background material.

(5) In general, *the date for the meeting will be driven by the FDA attendees' calendars,* so it is sensible to wait to obtain the available date(s) from FDA before asking about the schedules of expected attendees from the company. Company officials seem to be able to adjust their calendars rather quickly once informed about the only date(s) that FDA has available for a meeting. One exception to this is when a specific company person with a difficult calendar or travel situation (e.g., the CEO or a research scientist from outside the United States) is involved in the meeting. In that case, it helps to have available date(s) from that company person in advance of the phone call to FDA, in order to convey those dates to the person at FDA who is scheduling the meeting.

(6) When you call the FDA person who is scheduling the meeting, *remember to be polite and gracious*, particularly if it takes several calls to schedule the meeting. Resist the temptation to call this person every day. Try to allow a few days between calls, or

ask the person about the best date/time to call back. Be sensitive to how difficult it is for that person to mesh many FDA staff calendars to arrive at an available meeting date.

(7) When you are working on the phone with the FDA person who is scheduling the meeting, *you may have an opportunity to select among days of the week and times of day for the meeting.* If so, you should consider the following suggestions. Generally, Mondays and Fridays are the worst days for a meeting due to travel difficulties. Early in the morning is generally not preferable, because that may not allow time for a pre-meeting and it leaves little flexibility in case of travel problems. Late in the day is also not preferable; people are a little "burned out" by that time and departing the meeting then will place participants in the Washington, D.C. metropolitan area rush-hour experience. Therefore, meetings on Tuesday, Wednesday, or Thursday, between the hours of 10:00 a.m. and 3:00 p.m., are better days and times to select.

(8) Once the person on the phone gives you the available date(s) and time(s) for the meeting from FDA's perspective, you will need to poll the company attendees to select a definite meeting date. When that is completed, you will need to *call the FDA contact person back and confirm the date and time.* Some people choose to provide a written follow-up confirmation to the FDA contact person concerning the date and time that has been set for the meeting.

(9) When you set the meeting date, *make sure you obtain the exact location for the meeting,* including building name (FDA occupies many different buildings in the D.C. metropolitan area), address, specific conference room, and telephone and fax numbers for the contact person. Inquire about the security procedures necessary to enter the building, because these will have an impact on how early you need to arrive to be on time for the meeting.

(10) Once the meeting date is set, *provide written confirmation to the expected company attendees.* The written confirmation should include date, time, location, and telephone and fax numbers for the FDA contact person. The written confirmation also should include information on how the preparations for the meeting will be conducted (discussed in more detail in the next section).

II. Ten Tips on How to Prepare for a Meeting

(1) *One person in the company should be the administrative contact person* for the meeting. This person should be responsible for obtaining copies of the materials that are to be presented to FDA, for arranging the company pre-meeting(s), and for additional contacts with FDA that may be necessary prior to the meeting.

(2) *At least one pre-meeting should be arranged* to walk through the company presentation(s), to discuss the questions that might come up, and to set the list of decision items that the company wants from FDA as a result of the meeting. There should always be a pre-meeting on the day of or the day before the FDA meeting. This keeps the issues fresh in the minds of attendees. The best pre-meetings are held in person, to simulate the interaction among participants that will occur at the actual meeting with FDA. If necessary to accommodate scheduling constraints, pre-meetings can be held by telephone conference or videoconference.

(3) At the pre-meeting, *roles will need to be assigned to various company personnel attending the meeting.* One person should be designated as the leader of the delegation. This person should be responsible for opening and moderating the company's presentation. This person also should be responsible for conducting the pre-meeting(s). Another person should be designated to take notes at the FDA meeting. In addition, someone should be assigned the task of preparing minutes of the meeting.

(4) At the pre-meeting, *the person(s) who will be presenting information to FDA should practice.* The visual materials (e.g., slides, overheads, or computer presentation) should be used to make sure they are in working order. Constructive comments from pre-meeting attendees should assist in developing concise, logical, and persuasive presentations.

(5) At the pre-meeting, *it is essential to practice questions and answers.* The company should designate someone (either the leader of the delegation or someone else) to develop possible questions. These questions can be generated from many sources, such as: 1) knowledge of the issues to be presented (with emphasis on the weak points in the company's position — and there are always weak points); 2) previous interaction between the company and the agency; and 3) review of previous agency actions or statements on the issue. In addition, the pre-meeting attendees should be encouraged to raise questions based on the presentations. The pre-meeting provides a place for potential answers to be contemplated, debated, and established. The answer should then be assigned to the company person most capable of delivering it at the FDA meeting. A determination of who is "most capable" requires an evaluation of scientific and regulatory expertise as well as meeting presentation skills. Delivering the answers should also be practiced at the pre-meeting.

(6) The leader of *the company delegation, in consultation* with the pre-meeting attendees, *should create an agenda for the meeting with FDA, and assign various topics* to be handled by particular company presenters. Specific questions and/or decision items to be discussed at the meeting may be listed in the agenda. The sequence of company presenters, and transitions among them, should be practiced at the pre-meeting. The leader of the company delegation should call on people by their names to start and transition among presentations, because this will act as a verbal cue for the person during the actual meeting.

(7) The administrative contact person should *fax the agenda and a list of expected company attendees to the FDA contact person* for the meeting. This should be done approximately a week before the meeting. The company contact person should *also request a list of expected attendees from FDA.* This may not arrive from FDA until the day before the meeting.

(8) The administrative contact person should *ensure that copies of all relevant materials will be hand-carried by someone attending the meeting,* including copies of the agenda and any company presentations intended to be left with FDA. Also make sure that someone brings an extra copy of the actual slides or overheads; it is wise not to travel with only a single set of the visual materials to be shown at the meeting. Extra copies should be hand-carried to the meeting of anything the company has provided to FDA in advance of the meeting (e.g., the meeting request letter or background materials). Do not assume that because materials were sent to the agency in advance of the meeting that the FDA attendees will bring these materials to the meeting. It is also a

good idea for one person attending the meeting to bring a copy of the laws and regulations applicable to the issues to be discussed.

(**9**) The administrative contact person should *obtain maps and directions for getting to the meeting location from the hotel and/or airport*. Each company attendee should be given a copy. Each company attendee should know the building at which the meeting will take place, the conference room, the address, and the phone/fax numbers for the FDA contact person. Each company attendee should bring business cards to the meeting.

(**10**) The pre-meeting should *conclude with a discussion and agreement about transportation arrangements*, to make sure that everyone knows how they are traveling and when they are expected.

III. Fifteen Tips on How to Conduct a Meeting With FDA

(**1**) *Plan to arrive at the FDA building* at least *fifteen minutes before the scheduled time*. Each FDA building has security entry procedures that will need to be completed by each visitor. For meetings at the Parklawn Building (5600 Fishers Lane, Rockville, MD), plan to arrive *at least* thirty minutes before the scheduled meeting time, because the security procedures there are more elaborate and more people are waiting to enter this building. The goal is to be in your seat in the meeting room *before* the scheduled meeting time, so that the meeting can start on time. With limited time available for FDA meetings, starting on time is crucial. If you know you will be late, call the FDA contact person to let them know; cell phones and telephones on airplanes have made this communication easy.

(**2**) At the *security check points in most FDA buildings*, you will need to have the name and telephone number of the FDA contact person for the meeting. Also for security purposes at many FDA buildings, an FDA employee will need to escort visitors to the meeting room. Generally, the security guard will call the FDA contact person, who will then be the escort. Try not to complain about the security procedures when you are checking in at the FDA building; most organizations and companies have comparable procedures for visitors entering their premises.

(**3**) *When choosing seats in the meeting room, try to avoid an "us against them" line-up*, with all the company personnel on one side of the table and all the FDA personnel on the other. Such seating can bring a needlessly-confrontational atmosphere to the meeting. Expect that there will be more FDA attendees than were listed by FDA before the meeting. For various internal coordination reasons, the list of attendees that FDA provides is often a vast underestimate of those who will show up in the meeting room. These additional FDA attendees frequently do not sit at the table, but will sit in extra chairs on the side of the meeting room.

(**4**) The leader of the FDA delegation generally will open the meeting by welcoming the attendees. *It is a good practice to introduce everyone in the room.* One person from the company should be assigned to write down the names of the FDA personnel present at the meeting, for the minutes to be prepared by the company.

(5) *Generally, there will be a sign-in sheet that one of the FDA personnel circulates during the meeting.* As the meeting ends, the leader of the company delegation should approach the FDA person who has the sign-in sheet and ask for a copy before they leave the building. It is very handy to have this list immediately after the meeting ends, and most times there is a copy machine near the meeting room.

(6) *One person from the company should be assigned to take notes during the meeting.* It generally works better if this person *is not* the leader of the delegation, because the leader is too busy trying to moderate the meeting to ensure smooth discussion flow and good use of time. The notes will be useful for the company in preparing written minutes of the meeting.

(7) After the introductions of the attendees, the leader of *the company delegation should thank FDA for agreeing to the meeting.* It is very helpful at this point for the leader to note that the company is expecting the meeting to last for the time period that has been assigned, and ask FDA whether this is also their understanding. Sometimes, the timeframe has shrunk (e.g., because the FDA division director needs to attend another meeting that was recently placed on the calendar). It is important for the company to know how much time is truly available for the meeting in order to compress the company presentation to the most crucial points if time is short.

(8) The leader of the company delegation should then *begin the presentation.* There will be situations in which *it may be advantageous for the leader of the company delegation to request that FDA speak first* on the substantive issue(s) to be discussed, particularly if the meeting is in response to an action that FDA has taken (e.g., an enforcement issue or a "not approvable" letter). Requesting that FDA "go first" can be a useful way for the company to hear the reason(s) behind an FDA action or the concerns that FDA still has with a particular situation, before those views are lost in the details of the company presentation.

(9) As the company presentation proceeds, the leader of the company delegation should *be mindful of times when a transition should occur to another portion of the presentation.* When that time is reached, calling on the person by name to start his or her part can provide a verbal cue to begin another portion of the presentation.

(10) *Questions likely will arise* from FDA meeting participants. The most organized way to handle these is for the leader of the company delegation to *direct the response by calling on the person by name* from the company who has been prepared in the pre-meeting to handle the specific question. If the question from FDA is one that has not been anticipated in the pre-meeting, then the leader of the company delegation has a number of options: the leader can answer the question; the leader can direct the question to someone *by name* from the company who the leader believes will be able to answer the question (saying, for example, "That is an excellent question — Bob works in areas that relate to the question you have raised. Perhaps Bob would be able to answer your question."); or the leader can throw the question out to the group and hope for help from the other attendees (saying, for example, "That is an excellent question — who would like to provide an answer?"). Inevitably, it will be difficult to maintain this type of organized response to questions from FDA, particularly in a high-spirited meeting. In those circumstances, the question-and-answer discussion may be free-flowing, which can be a good thing if questions are being adequately addressed. If no one from the company at the meeting can answer the question, it is appropriate for the company representatives to agree to send an answer to FDA as a follow-up item. Ultimately, it is the responsibility of the leader of the company delegation to make sure that questions do not completely side-track the decision items that need to be discussed at the meeting, i.e., to keep the meeting on course.

(**11**) Not only the FDA representatives will have questions to ask. In the pre-meeting, the company should have organized the questions they want or need to ask FDA. And as the meeting goes along, the discussion may be the impetus for more questions from the company representatives to FDA. This may be the company's only opportunity for face-to-face interaction with FDA on a particular issue, so make sure that you *ask all necessary questions before the meeting is over*. Again, it is the responsibility of the leader of the company delegation to manage the use of time during the meeting to make sure that company questions are asked and answered.

(**12**) It is important for the company representatives to *maintain a civil demeanor during meetings with FDA*, particularly when the subject is contentious. It is never appropriate for a meeting with FDA to degenerate into a shouting match. Once someone loses his or her temper, it is difficult to think clearly about the points that are being discussed. If there is a flare-up, the leader of the delegation may suggest taking a short break to calm people down before starting the meeting again.

(**13**) Once the meeting is wrapping up, *there should be a discussion and agreement about the follow-up actions* (if any) *that will be undertaken by FDA and the company*. The leader of the company delegation should ask FDA for the timeframe in which the agency anticipates to complete whatever follow-up actions have been identified. Meetings generally end with the leader of the FDA delegation thanking the attendees for coming, and the company leader expressing the company's gratitude.

(**14**) When the meeting is over, it is tempting to engage in extended informal chat with the FDA attendees. Because visitors to many FDA buildings need to be escorted from meetings by an FDA staff person, situations can arise in which the assigned escort is waiting for an inordinate amount of time for impromptu conversations to end, or may have to escort several groups of visitors at different times. Try to avoid this by *limiting post-meeting conversations to a brief period*.

(**15**) After leaving the meeting, *do not chat about the meeting while you are* anywhere *within FDA grounds*. FDA personnel usually are present in the halls while you are walking out of the FDA building, in elevators on the FDA premises, in cafeterias and snackrooms in the FDA buildings, and in the parking lots. Remember also that FDA personnel travel on planes and trains, so these may not be optimal places to discuss meeting results. Better choices for post-meeting discussion include hotel conference rooms, meeting rooms back at your company, or telephone conference calls.

III. Ten Tips on How to Follow-Up After a Meeting With FDA

(1) *Have a post-meeting conference with company meeting attendees,* and other company representatives as appropriate, *to review the key decision and follow-up items* from the meeting. It is best to hold this meeting shortly (within a week) after the meeting with FDA, to capture impressions while they are still fresh in peoples' minds.

(2) *Ensure that follow-up tasks that the company has committed to are assigned to someone at the company to complete.* It is vitally important that a company establish and maintain a good reputation with FDA by providing the follow-up materials promised to FDA in a timely fashion. If for some reason there is a problem with the follow-up information that has been promised to FDA (e.g., it is not available, it is not the correct information, or it is not relevant information), then prompt contact with FDA (either written or oral) is a good idea to explain the situation.

(3) *The company should always prepare minutes (or a report) of the meeting.* These minutes should include at least the date of the meeting, names of the persons attending the meeting, any decisions reached, and any follow-up actions to be taken. These *minutes should be disseminated as appropriate* within the company.

(4) In some situations, particularly in meetings involving premarket issues, *it can be helpful for the company to agree to share its minutes with FDA.* Because FDA will need to write minutes of the meeting for the agency files, the quicker the company can get its own set of minutes to the writer of the FDA minutes, the more likely that the agency write-up will include decision items and follow-up items. To identify the writer of the FDA minutes, a call to the FDA contact person for the meeting is a good place to start.

(5) It is a wise practice to *request a copy of the minutes that FDA writes for meetings.* These should be available in response to a Freedom of Information request, but a call to the FDA contact person for the meeting is a good starting place for information about obtaining a copy of the FDA minutes.

(6) *Opinions differ on whether to send any written correspondence to FDA immediately after a meeting, in effect a "thank-you letter."* Politeness is a good reason to send such a letter. Another good reason to send this type of letter is to make sure the agency receives something in writing quickly (i.e., before the official company minutes of the meeting are available) that notes the decision items and follow-up items agreed to at the meeting. There may be times when it is a reasonable choice not to send such a letter (e.g., after a contentious meeting in which FDA may have been convinced to reverse a previous position, resulting in a "victory" for the company). Sending a letter to FDA after this type of meeting may not be a wise idea, as it might be viewed as a form of gloating.

(7) Meetings with FDA officials at certain levels within the agency (i.e., the Commissioner or the Center directors) are listed on the FDA Public Calendar, which is available on the FDA website. *Members of the media may contact your company from these listings on the public calendar.* Whether the meeting is listed on the public calendar or not, members of the media (including trade press) may contact your company to ask about a particular issue on which you have met with the agency.

(8) Either during the pre-meeting or post-meeting stage, *company representatives should develop a media strategy* for dealing with these inquiries.

(9) Depending on the subject of the meeting, *a company may want to contact the trade press on its own after the meeting* to spread the word about the issue discussed and/or the results of the meeting. At *other times, the company will be interested in keeping a low profile* with the media after a meeting with FDA.

(10) There might be interest on Capitol Hill in the subject and/or the results of the meeting. Either during the pre-meeting or at the post-meeting stage, *company representatives should consider whether contacts with congressional staff are advisable* after the meeting with FDA.

The opinions expressed in this chapter are those of the author and are not for attribution to HIMA.

Mark E. DuVal

3M Company,
3M Pharmaceuticals Division

CHAPTER 11

Persuading FDA to Your Position

I. Introduction

Anyone who has been in the management of a medical device, drug, or food company knows that a company has, for better or worse, a relationship with the Food and Drug Administration (FDA) that is not unlike a personal relationship with an individual. It consists of ups and downs, positive collaboration, as well as confrontation and frustration. Managers in these industries also know that this relationship is important because of the power FDA has over the company due to FDA's pervasive regulations and jurisdictional reach. This makes it a relationship that must be thought about carefully and attended to.

Companies must begin by acknowledging the importance of FDA to their business and by thinking more strategically about the their relationship with FDA and about how to approach the issues they have before the FDA. FDA has the ability, through its interpretation and application of its rules, to postpone a company's return on investment through a delayed product approval. FDA can impact the amount of such return by something as simple as limiting the content of a product's labeling, which makes the product less differentiable, and thus, a less competitive product in the marketplace. An FDA-regulated company cannot simply think about how it can have its way with FDA in every encounter. Rather, the goal is for a company to think more broadly about its relationship with FDA in deciding which issues to push and how to effectively convince the agency of the company's position.

The regulations are pervasive and the stakes are high. Most non-FDA-regulated businesses do not have to concern themselves with regulations that significantly influence the development, testing, manufacture, and marketing of a product. In FDA-regulated businesses, product development and testing must incorporate FDA's latest thinking on toxicity study requirements, pharmacokinetic guidances, clinical endpoints, and other approval standards. In manufacturing, changes made to improve efficiency, lower manufacturing cost, or substitute raw materials are not simply or inexpensively made. Such changes often require that clinical or bioequivalence studies are conducted to support the change and that FDA approval lead times be factored into timelines. Once approved by FDA, products must be manufactured to meet tough FDA "agreed-upon" specifications under good manufacturing practice (GMP) regulations. Marketing must deal with seeking FDA's pre-approval of product labeling. The initial promotional materials used for product launch also must be pre-approved by FDA to ensure consistency with approved labeling and relevant regulations. Subsequent promotional materials must continue to meet FDA's rigorous standards and expectations.

Not only is FDA regulation pervasive and the interpretation of its regulations not always clear, management knows FDA has enforcement authority to act upon companies that FDA believes are noncompliant. FDA has many statutory and practical tools at its disposal. These include severe measures like product seizures, injunctions on the sale of products, FDA-initiated product recalls, debarment, and the like. Well-known instances of these include the seizure of Procter & Gamble's orange juice due to FDA's concern over the allegedly-misleading labeling of orange juice concentrate as "fresh," the closing of Warner-Lambert's manufacturing plants for failure to meet GMPs, or the fine of $100 million paid by Abbott Laboratories to FDA for alleged GMP violations. But almost more important than its statutory tools are the nonstatutory, practical tools the agency wields. The practical tool used most effectively by FDA is public relations. FDA knows that a company's reputation is key to its relations with shareholders, suppliers, present and future business partners, and customers of all types including distributors, retailers, hospitals, managed care organizations, physicians, and patients.

A company's reputation also means a world of difference to state or federal investigators and prosecutors and public policy makers, whether administrative or legislative. A company's bad reputation can result in product liability exposure as well, not to mention punitive damages. If, for example, FDA sends a notice of violation directed to a company's promotional tactics or claims, the content of that correspondence can be relatively matter-of-fact. If the company has a bad reputation with FDA, the same promotional tactics or claims can result in a warning letter dripping with words critical of the company, which can, in turn, catch the attention of mass tort product liability lawyers trolling for new cases. A good or bad reputation can mean the difference between commencing or not commencing mass tort litigation, a congressional or grand jury investigation, and early settlement discussions.

To be a manager in an industry regulated by FDA is not for the faint of heart because it entails much risk, and opportunities for innocent mistakes and second-guessing abound. FDA-imposed fines, product seizures, plant shutdowns, consent decrees, delayed product approvals, discontinued advertising campaigns, and general frustration are part of the lot in life for an FDA-regulated company.

All of this points to two facts for an FDA-regulated company. First, a relationship with FDA is inescapable. A company must consider what kind of relationship it will cultivate and have with FDA. Second, a good relationship with FDA is important. To conduct business, an FDA-regulated company must often gain the approval of FDA or avoid its critical eye. It also must attempt to influence the content, application, or enforcement of regulations by which its business will be transacted. This means that an FDA-regulated company often must figure out how to influence the FDA to its position, and in that quest its relationship with FDA figures prominently.

II. Addressing Your Issues With FDA

Before a company can address how to persuade FDA to its position, it must understand three fundamental things, among other more subtle considerations:

- The company must recognize that FDA is not a monolithic organization, and different parts of FDA can and do think very differently on issues, so unification of direction comes only from the highest levels at FDA;

- A company must try to understand its relationship with FDA. Is your company known for its integrity, technical expertise, and contributions or for its self-serving positions, delaying tactics, product recalls, or violative promotional campaigns? Do you adopt positions and advance arguments that are specious, disingenuous, and baldly self-serving, or is your company thoughtful, thorough, and fairly balanced?

- How important is the issue to your company, and how assertive or aggressive do you want to be in persuading FDA to your position? A company cannot "cry wolf" on every issue if it wants to be taken seriously on truly critical matters. Do you push the agency hard and unceasingly, or do you reserve such tactics for only the important stuff? What tactics do you want to employ to persuade FDA to your position — e.g., filing citizen petitions or lawsuits, seeking congressional intervention or publicity, or requesting the support of patient or physician groups? A company must contemplate whether it will burn bridges with FDA in employing any of these tactics. A company's relationship with FDA can assist or hinder the company's ability to advance positions or resolve issues with FDA.

III. Understanding FDA

A. Diversity Within and Across Centers

Your company first must recognize what FDA is and is not. Just as your company is not a monolithic organization, neither is FDA. FDA has an Office of the Commissioner that establishes the broadest policy positions and the administrative structure for the agency. The thinking of personnel in the Commissioner's Office is often very different from those *within* the Centers. Personnel within the Commissioner's Office are concerned with the broader policy issues and the impact of those issues upon the public and the agency itself in terms of its relationship with Congress, the Administration, patient and medical associations, industry, public interest groups, the media, the public at large, and other international health authorities.

The Centers are more focused on operational issues. FDA transacts its daily business of product approvals, inspections, compliance, etc. through its Centers. The Centers address very different, yet related, industries — human drugs, animal drugs, medical devices, biologics, etc. Even the attitudes and personnel within a Center can be quite different. The Centers, in turn, transact business through offices and divisions. For example, two offices in the Center for Drug Evaluation and Research (CDER) are the Office of Drug Evaluation (ODE) and the Office of Generic Drugs (OGD). The thinking of personnel can be very directed to the discrete issues upon which they work daily.

A good illustration of how different thinking can co-exist in one Center may be seen in ODE and OGD. Broadly speaking, ODE has very rigorous approval standards before a new chemical entity (NCE) can come to market, and it is a highly physician- and scientific-driven organization. ODE, in a sense, acts as a gatekeeper for society to ensure that only safe and effective new drugs come to market. ODE is continually imposing new and higher standards of proof on the innovator pharmaceutical industry, which adds great expense and additional time for new drug approval. The innovator industry often argues that ODE's standards are higher than necessary to ensure the safety and efficacy of new drugs and that these standards should be more reasonable.

OGD, on the other hand, is statutorily charged with expeditiously, and without unnecessary cost, approving generic drugs that are competitive to innovator products. The generic industry argues that OGD must relax its approval standards to a more reasonable level. The innovator industry often challenges the bioequivalence approval standards that OGD adopts, complaining that OGD allows generic drugs to come too easily to the market without appropriate assurance of bioequivalence. In therapeutic, technical, and medical arenas where decisions of the two offices overlap, OGD and ODE can have significant differences of scientific, legal, and policy opinion. Issues like this often are internally debated by an FDA committee called the Advisory Committee for Pharmaceutical Science.

This tension underscores the point that groups within Centers of FDA can and do have different views because their jobs and the expectations of Congress, the Administration, and the public are different for each of them.

If organizations and individuals *within* FDA's Centers are quite diverse, it goes without saying that personnel *across* Centers make FDA even more diverse. This is driven by the complexity of the issues with which the Centers deal, the sophistication of the industry with which they interact, and the history of regulation to which certain types of products and industries have been subject. Certainly drugs and medial devices historically have been subject to far greater regulation and scrutiny than foods, cosmetics, or animal drugs. Understanding this type of diversity is also key in understanding how to influence FDA to your company's position.

B. Diversity of Functions and Issues Within FDA

In addition to the diversity of personnel within and across FDA, there is a diversity of functions and issues. The type of person with whom one deals also can be quite different within an office, depending upon the role they serve. Anyone who has dealt with individuals in CDER's Office of Compliance will testify how different these personnel are from those in the reviewing divisions that approve drugs, devices, or biologics; that is because their roles are so different. It is like comparing company personnel in clinical affairs to employees who are compliance auditors. They play far different roles within the organization. They see a different part of the world every day. That influences how they view the world and how they interface with others. The company's relationship with the agency can be far different from one function to the next; indeed, a company's relationship with one function may impact the company's relationship with another function.

A classic example is the difference between scientific, technical, and medical personnel within FDA who work on technical issues and those who work in policy or legal positions. Companies are often in the situation of making broad policy or legal arguments to technical FDA personnel focused on very discrete technical rules and issues. Such arguments can fall on deaf ears and can be perceived as obtuse or even irrelevant to the more "practical" issues with which the regulator is faced. Conversely, technical arguments made to policy and legal personnel will be understood to an extent, but these personnel will be more interested in the broader process, procedure, legal and/or policy issues at stake. This organizational diversity requires that companies have an in-depth understanding of the distinct part of FDA with which they are working, in light of a fuller perspective and understanding of FDA as a whole.

Just as FDA's *functions* are diverse, so are the *issues* FDA confronts. FDA is constantly identifying and prioritizing the issues it must address. While your company's issue may be important to you, it may be a speck on FDA's radar screen. At any given time, FDA is dealing with AIDs, tobacco regulation, breast implants, fen/phen, biofoods, international regulatory harmonization, and cloning, to name a few. Even if your issue is deemed important by a group within FDA, such as CDRH's Division of Ophthalmic Devices, it may not be important to, or even known by, the Commissioner's Office, CDRH, or the Office of Device Evaluation (to which the Division of Ophthalmic Devices reports). The key to getting relatively quick, positive FDA action on your issue is knowing how to get large on the radar screen. Your issue must become important to, and immediately actionable, by FDA (i.e., the "squeaky wheel" that gets the agency's "grease").

C. FDA as a Political Entity

FDA as a political entity often appears impervious to political pressure, but it is not. FDA's budget, its direction, and its appointed leadership are chosen by the Executive Administration, but the agency receives funding (and other direction) from Congress. FDA is probably the most insulated and, to an extent, unresponsive agency within the government. Compared to other agencies, like the EPA, whose agendas and enforcement activities are highly scrutinized, FDA often acts as if it is relatively immune from public and political pressure. This derives from the important public charge given to FDA to approve drugs, devices, and other products that are safe and effective.

FDA is a uniquely-situated administrative agency in that it operates in a highly sophisticated field and its decisions touch the life of every American citizen (e.g., in the foods we consume, the medicines we take, and the medical devices we use or that are used on us, etc.). Conferred upon the FDA is an enormous public trust, based on the agency's expertise and dedication to safeguarding the public health. Because the agency is comprised of physicians, pharmacists, biologists, biochemists, and other highly educated and trained individuals, the executive, legislative, and judicial branches of government frequently are reticent to challenge FDA on questions of medicine and science.

As a result, FDA receives much latitude, and even deference, in its decisionmaking. Congress, the Administration, the media, or the public-at-large often do not feel equipped to take on the FDA in its medical and scientific decisionmaking. These groups do, however, feel capable of challenging FDA on policy issues like the speed of product approvals, whether FDA should harmonize its policies with European governments, what enforcement authority it needs to do its job, or whether FDA can restrict commercial-free speech about the off-label uses of drugs. This is important to know because challenging FDA is not an easy undertaking. To influence or persuade FDA often means attempting to persuade the agency in areas where it feels most confident and will not be second-guessed — i.e., on issues of medicine and science.

Knowing when FDA will be granted latitude and deference in its decisionmaking is important for a company deciding to persuade FDA to its position or to challenge FDA. If the issue is purely a scientific or medical issue, you are unlikely to be successful challenging FDA before Congress or in court. A company's efforts are better spent enlisting the support of scientific, medical, or trade associations; other foreign health authorities; or highly respected experts (preferably former FDA consultants). If the issue is a legal or public policy issue, effort should focus on enlisting the support of patient groups, trade associations, the media, Congress, or the Administration.

D. FDA in Its Rulemaking Capacity

Because the arena of rulemaking in which FDA operates is highly technical and dynamic, FDA is justifiably loath to promulgate hard and fast rules. Rules may lock in scientific thinking to a specific point in time; rules, once established, can circumscribe the agency's flexibility. Advances in medicine and science can mean, for instance, that surrogate clinical endpoints used to establish the safety of a medical device, once established and memorialized in a rule, may need to be changed to reflect these advances. For this reason FDA does not want to lock in approval criteria in rulemaking. FDA is very sophisticated and calculated in its attempts to avoid promulgating binding rules.

Regulated industry, however, desires certainty and an understandable regulatory framework. Industry, for example, wants to know what level of medical and scientific proof will be required of it for the approval of products. Industry also wants an opportunity to tell FDA what it expects of FDA. The way industry and FDA temporarily have bridged this gap in expectations is for FDA to issue "guidances" revealing its current thinking on medical and scientific issues. Guidances are not full-blown regulations, but they do offer insight into FDA's current thinking. This regulatory device also gives FDA the opportunity to create a nonbinding document that can be modified as medical and scientific thinking advance.

Many in industry regret acquiescing to FDA's issuance of guidances rather than insisting that regulations be promulgated. FDA considers guidances to be an expression of its current thinking on an issue and not a final, binding policy position. FDA argues that a guidance is not "final agency" action that can be challenged in court. What frustrates industry, however, is that FDA enforces behavior against its guidances. FDA reserves the right to change its mind and depart from its own guidances, without prior notice, within the context of an individual product approval or other specific regulatory decision. The disclaimer FDA issues with every guidance reads:

> This guidance represents the Agency's current thinking on [insert subject]. It does not create or confer any rights for or on any person and does not operate to bind FDA or the public. An alternative approach may be used if such approach satisfies the requirements of the applicable statute.

This regulatory disclaimer is the ultimate regulatory weapon, in that FDA can continually issue its "thinking" on a matter without being bound by or accountable for such. If administered by a despotic bureaucrat, a guidance can be a formula for disaster. If administered with fairness and understanding, it can be useful to both FDA and industry. The key is found in the integrity and fairness of the person administering the rules.

E. Knowing FDA's Authority

While FDA generally is a rules-respecting organization, it can operate aggressively, inconsistently, or even outside of its jurisdiction. For instance, FDA often requests from companies information beyond its statutory or regulatory authority. In fact, FDA's *Investigations Operations Manual* instructs GMP inspectors to do that. Inspectors may ask for information for which a specific statutory exemption exists or they may even ask for nonmanufacturing-related information that is not within the agency's inspectional authority under section 704 of the Federal Food, Drug, and Cosmetic Act (FDCA). In conducting pre-approval inspections, FDA has been known to expand its jurisdiction, playing on company fears that FDA may characterize a company's refusal to provide certain information as a "refusal to inspect." Such a refusal means that FDA may not complete the inspection and that the company's product will not come to market until the inspection has been rescheduled many months later and the company passes.

The agency also is known for sometimes inconsistently applying its policies or scientific views. An illustration of this is when an innovator drug company is required to conduct an expensive, time-consuming clinical study, rather than a simple, inexpensive bioequivalence study, to support a change of manufacturing site, drug delivery device, or inactive ingredients. Later, the agency may approve a generic drug product that has a different manufacturing site, a drug delivery device that differs from the innovative drug product, and new inactive ingredients, among a myriad of other differences, upon the submission of a simple bioequivalence study. The scientific inconsistency in this process is obvious.

All of these examples suggest one important point — FDA wields a tremendous amount of power that, because of the scientific realm in which it operates, inures to its benefit. Regulated industry should be self-aware, should know its rights, and should know when to challenge the agency and when it is more practical to make concessions. While FDA has substantial power, it is not impervious to outside pressure.

IV. Your Company's Relationship With FDA

Depending on your situation, you may not have a "relationship" *per se* with the agency. Your company may be small or it may not be sophisticated in direct dealings with the agency. But for those companies who do or will have dealings with the agency, it is important to cultivate that relationship and address the issues dispassionately. Many companies, even large companies, do not put strategic thought into examining their relationship with FDA. This is especially true of companies who only partially participate in healthcare or have distinct operating companies or divisions selling a variety of drugs, devices, nutritionals, functional foods, and/or animal drugs; each division or operating company might have its own idea of what they want their relationship with FDA to be and how they want to get there.

Some companies' experiences with FDA are benign, or even good experiences. Others may have had severe and intense run-ins with FDA over product seizures, class labeling issues, promotional warning letters, delays in product approvals, and the like. Others have a mixed bag of benign and bad experiences with FDA.

A. The More It Changes, the More It Stays the Same

New FDA administrations can influence the way FDA approaches industry generally. FDA under Commissioner Young, for example, was relatively cooperative with industry, far different than the combative and idealistic FDA under Commissioner Kessler. Commissioner Henney, thus far, appears to be a reasonable and pragmatic leader, but Commissioners come and go. It is the career bureaucrats with whom a company has the most dealings. A company must concentrate its relationship-building on the career employees.

B. A Relationship With FDA Is Not Unlike Other Relationships

A relationship with an organization is not unlike a relationship with another person. Universal to all positive relationships are trust and respect. This may sound too simplistic and like something akin to psychoanalysis, but companies often overlook this simple fact — trust and respect transcend differences and are basic to any personal relationship. This is true for FDA, even though the relationship is among a collection of people, job functions, and divisions within multiple organizations.

A company's job is to ensure that its culture and corporate "personality" are consistently communicated to FDA. This must be done in any encounter with the agency, whether major or minor, long or short, formal or informal. Company representatives should use every interface with FDA to communicate company views on relevant issues. Most organizations want to leave the impression that they are honest, ethical, and concerned about their relationship with the agency. Like it or not, each company has, for better or worse, a "personality" profile or reputation within the agency, and that reputation can be shaped through its interactions with the agency.

Wanting a good working relationship with the agency, however, does not translate into acquiescing to every demand or request or never challenging FDA policy positions. Many companies are under the misperception that to have a good relationship with the FDA, they must accede to every demand or decision FDA makes without question. Other companies believe the agency is the "enemy" so the company must be combative and on the attack at all times. Neither view is a healthy or correct view of the agency.

Any good relationship is built upon good and bad times, harmony and acrimony, agreement and disagreement. Some companies believe they can never publicly criticize FDA, complain to Congress or the Administration about FDA, or even sue the agency. Not only is this not true, it may not even be healthy for a good relationship. An occasional serious difference of opinion allows a company to "air it out" with FDA, and keeps the agency respectful. It keeps balance in the relationship because FDA knows its actions may be contested by the company taking the issue beyond the agency. This can force FDA to re-examine its policies, procedures, and conduct. Just as in personal relationships, it is the honesty and respect extended to the other party throughout the relationship that is important. How companies respond after difficult exchanges or challenges will matter most.

V. How Important Is the Issue to Your Company?

Most companies have a lot of active issues before FDA. Optimally speaking, a company wants a positive, expeditious resolution to *every* issue it has before FDA. If FDA does not decide in a company's favor on any given issue, the company theoretically could appeal every issue it has before FDA, bringing to bear whatever influence it can muster. In a perfect world, this could be done if a company had unlimited time and resources, and there would be no impact on the company's relationship with FDA.

A. Prioritizing Issues

The reality is that companies must prioritize their issues. A company must decide what is truly important. It may seem unfair to a company that it should lose *any* issue with the FDA, but this is unrealistic. The agency does view the world differently than a commercial enterprise. A company will win and lose issues with FDA. It is also an unrealistic view to believe a company can conduct a "full court press" on every issue in which it is engaged with FDA. A company, therefore, must wisely expend its political capital when choosing to challenge the FDA. It also must decide how best to allocate its internal resources and expenditures in pursuit of an issue with FDA. This entails the company having seasoned personnel who know FDA well, and are fully cognizant of both the company's ongoing issues with the agency and the strategic business plan for the company. The company frequently will call upon these individuals to make critical judgment calls and provide advice as to whether and when to push FDA hard on issues, or to relent and wait for another day.

There is a real nexus between the achievement of an FDA-regulated company's strategic business plan and its interface with FDA. Much of FDA's decisionmaking vis-à-vis a company can financially make or break some companies, or significantly change the profitability or potential of others. FDA has significant influence over many issues in the life cycle of a product. FDA's decisions affect the ability of a company to get a return on its investment. This begins with setting the content of clinical studies needed for product approval. This decision dictates the level of investment and the time it will take to obtain approval. Following approval, FDA can disagree with the content of a company's television advertisement and require it to be discontinued, thus affecting the ability of a company to effectively market its product. Once a product's patent is close to expiry, FDA also establishes generic approval standards and interprets their application to the approval of individual generic products competitive to the company's innovator product. From beginning to end, FDA's hand is on the company's affairs and success.

On some issues a company may need to prevail in a dispute with FDA because the stakes are high. Accordingly, marketing and legal departments may advise being very aggressive with the FDA to resolve the issue to the company's satisfaction. This may, in turn, produce some nervousness on the part of executive management and regulatory personnel who intuitively fear "biting the hand that feeds them." Regulatory affairs professionals, in particular, worry that negative encounters with FDA can make their day-to-day jobs more difficult, unpleasant, and stilted.

For instance, imagine a company that is faced with the potential approval of a competitive generic product and it also expects new drug approval (NDA) for a significant new product. Assume the company is on solid ground to challenge the generic product's approval; the company takes serious issue with the Office of Generic Drugs' (OGD's) approval standard and with OGD's application of the standard regarding this particular product. The generic product in this example has the potential to take seventy-five percent of the innovator's ($100 million) market within six months. In prioritizing company issues, you wonder whether, by administratively challenging FDA in an aggressive manner or even suing the agency, you would jeopardize chances of obtaining timely approval from ODE for your new drug product. A delay in approval by six months would mean a loss in revenue from the new drug of approximately $30 million.

B. Does FDA Retaliate?

Those unfamiliar with FDA might jump to the conclusion that by being contentious with any part of FDA, you have infected the whole when it comes to your relationship with the agency. Some companies believe that a challenge will result in FDA retaliation and, therefore, a delay in product approval. There are several problems with this conclusion, however. The first problem is that many companies do not believe FDA truly "retaliates" in the full sense of the word. That is not to say that people within FDA are not affected by a company's perceived attitude toward, and actual dealings with, the agency. On an individual level an FDA employee does have the opportunity to let his or her biases affect their subjective decisionmaking; it may happen, but it is hard to prove.

The better view is that these occurrences are extremely rare and that most decisionmaking is subjected to review by a broader FDA audience, so retaliation is unlikely to occur. If a company's relationship has been honest and respectful, FDA does not fault the company for periodically challenging the agency on good grounds. This implies, however, that if a company consistently games FDA (e.g., with specious challenges, continual threats, or delaying tactics), this may have an impact on FDA's thinking. Many negative company encounters can adversely impact FDA's institutional experience with your company over time, and may result in the company's issues and arguments not being taken as seriously as they should or resolved within desired timeframes.

The second problem in assuming FDA retaliates in the example above is that ODE personnel rarely cross paths with OGD personnel such that a company's dispute with OGD would come to their attention. Companies often presume that FDA has this relatively perfect communications network, in which any bad or good experience is immediately known across FDA and certainly across a Center within FDA. Nothing could be further from the truth. Over time, a company's interface with FDA may result in a general company "reputation" being developed. But specific ongoing events are rarely known by people outside of major FDA working groups. This is true in the agency for the same reasons it is true in companies — people have too much to do in their jobs already and everyone is on information overload.

Assume in the above example that the company went so far as to sue OGD over the approval of a generic drug. To validate the suspicion that FDA would somehow retaliate by delaying approval of that same company's NDA, the following would have to occur. The retaliation theory presumes knowledge of the OGD lawsuit by ODE employees who are working on the NDA. Remember, these are technical employees, generally not interested in legal and policy matters, who typically are preoccupied with their own work. It is a big assumption to assume ODE personnel, in a reviewing decision, would even be aware of the lawsuit, especially given how busy the agency is and the major policy matters with which it is involved. Next, one would have to assume that lawsuits are rare, such that any lawsuit would be newsworthy enough to capture the attention of all relevant FDA personnel. In reality, FDA is sued fairly frequently and it is questionable whether an ODE employee would know or care about the lawsuit.

The retaliation theory also presumes that ODE employees know about, and understand, the nature of the lawsuit. The next assumption is that the FDA personnel have formed an opinion about the merits of the lawsuit — that the company was acting in bad faith or trying to publicly embarrass the FDA, as opposed to simply disagreeing with FDA. Finally, after having had knowledge and understanding of the lawsuit, and having formed an opinion about the company, FDA personnel would have to be motivated to act. Presumably, this motivation would result in an FDA employee doing something with the company's NDA to preclude or delay its approval. All of this would occur, if it did, despite the fact that ODE's work is reviewed and that ODE personnel have yearly product approval targets (as expressed under the Prescription Drug User Fee Act and in FDA management expectations). This suggests that genuine FDA retaliation against companies is highly unlikely.

Although retaliation probably does not occur in the typical scenario set forth above, a bad relationship may nevertheless affect the outcome of some FDA decisionmaking. Certain factors may lead this to happen. The first such factor is when the issue involves a scientific or medical decision that falls within FDA's discretion and judgment. FDA often operates in decisional gray areas where its judgment is difficult, if not impossible, to challenge. A second factor is when FDA is currently working on a company issue and the agency's distaste with that company's conduct is on a related matter in a related work group; the issue is substantively and temporally related and affects the same FDA workgroup. As in the example above, the work of ODE personnel is not going to be affected by a company lawsuit related to OGD's approval of a generic product. ODE personnel reviewing an NDA could be impacted, however, by company behavior that frustrates them on a related matter, such as when the company appeals to senior FDA management about a scientific issue related to product approval. This frustration could later translate into an ODE refusal to agree to certain labeled claims desired by that company for the same product. If ODE decides not to allow the company to use the desired language in the label, the company will be unable to successfully challenge FDA in its medical judgment.

Another factor is the egregiousness of the company's conduct that could affect FDA's outlook on a company and give rise to situations in which FDA could take an opportunity to cut a close issue against the company. This could occur in a situation, for instance, where the Center for Devices and Radiological Health (CDRH) is deciding whether a medical device meets section 510(k) criteria (i.e., whether it is "substantially equivalent to a pre-1976 device"). Devices subject to section 510(k) are subject only to FDA notification before coming to market. CDRH could, in the alternative, determine that the device is a class III medical device, which must be subject to premarket approval by FDA. A medical device company that has a long track record of selling devices that are the subject of many product liability cases, and that has had many compliance issues and a defiant attitude toward FDA regulation, might not get the benefit of a close call with FDA. If the issue could go either way, FDA may decide the issue against the company using a completely supportable rationale.

Once a company is freed from paranoia over perceived retaliation, but recognizes factors that can affect FDA decisions, it can think more productively about its relationship with FDA. In the end, knowing how hard to push FDA is an art, not a science. It is part of prioritizing the importance of individual issues in the context of the overall relationship. As stated earlier, relationships are resilient and are forged out of good and bad times. "Pushing" can garner either respect or contempt, depending on the approach and tactics used. Getting personal with FDA personnel rarely, if ever, helps to successfully conclude a matter, whereas honest and strong differences of opinion usually are tolerated, if not respected.

VI. How to Persuade FDA to Your Position

A pervasive regulatory system is a given in an FDA-regulated industry. The specific content, application, and enforcement of regulations are not a given. It is incumbent upon every FDA-regulated company to see that its commercial interests are maximized in such a regulatory system. The individual agendas of many groups jockey with one another amidst the regulatory system. These agendas belong to individual companies, Congress, the Administration, consumer and medical groups, trade associations, the media, and FDA itself.

A company must figure out for itself how it can make its issue stand out, get attended by FDA, and resolved to its satisfaction. A company often must attempt to persuade FDA to its position on a variety of issues having varying degrees of importance to the company. Merely using the word "persuade" to describe this process can connote something bad, underhanded, or distasteful. In fact, the world is run by persuasion and we all do it to accomplish our jobs and get through life. Lawyers persuade, but so do salesmen, politicians, executives to shareholders, teachers, clergy, parents, and children. As FDA has statutory and practical tools available to it in dealing with noncompliant companies, so does a company have tools in attempting to persuade FDA to its position.

A. Gaining Intelligence

Prior to utilizing other tools available, a company must have information about the agency's position or direction. Information provides insight into what tools it will take to address a particular issue. Hypothetically, assume a company is threatened by FDA with its combination product (a medical device and drug) being pulled from the market for the company's alleged failure to register it as a new drug. The company has been marketing this combination product for years, and it is used throughout the country in hospitals and managed care organizations. Assume also the company has taken the position that the product was lawfully on the market because it met the requirements of a published over-the-counter (OTC) Monograph; the company argues that its product essentially meets the criteria contained in the OTC Monograph, but that it made technological improvements to the product in such a way that it meets the spirit of the monograph without deviating substantially from it. The company's argument is that FDA's monographs should be flexible enough to accommodate slight technological advances that benefit patients. The company is dealing with CDER's Office of Compliance, who has threatened the seizure action. The company executives want to know what it can do.

At the outset of any situation like this, the company is often at an information deficit. While it may have formal written communication from FDA, that is only the beginning, and much must be learned. How did FDA learn of the product in question? Why is it taking this position? What scientific, policy, and legal conclusions has the agency drawn? Has it taken action against anyone else? If not, why not? If so, is this situation distinguishable from theirs? How quickly will FDA act, and what are the options? To answer these questions, a company must understand the scientific, policy, legal, and political issues with which it is confronted.

This litany of questions speaks to the need for quickly gaining intelligence on your situation. To do that, a company must have seasoned regulatory and legal professionals in place and in whom the company has invested time and money. Over the years these people must be allowed to attend meetings with FDA as issues crop up. They also must be allowed to attend relevant seminars to stay substantively on top of issues and FDA structure, procedure, and politics. Participation in trade association working groups enables these professionals to immerse themselves in salient policy and science issues. Speaking at industry/FDA seminars allows them to take their experience and knowledge to the next level by sharing it with others — a learning experience in itself. Company participation in defining and resolving scientific, policy, or legal issues (through scientific, trade associations, and FDA advisory committees) makes the company a "player." Later, in handling company issues with FDA, this involvement and developed expertise gives credibility to the company's arguments with FDA.

All of these activities allow the company's personnel to mix and mingle with FDA personnel and leading professionals within the industry. This accelerates and greatly enhances the institutional savvy of the company and makes the company professionals better able to quickly gather, assimilate, and report information. More importantly, it allows them to provide solid advice to the company. This is critical when an agency action can require an immediate response, under high pressure and exigent circumstances.

Having a network of consultants from a variety of disciplines is also important. FDA lawyers, public relations and public affairs specialists, and scientific and medical experts are necessary to the company. Most frequently, these consultants are former FDA employees or former or present consultants to FDA. While company employees may know seventy-five to ninety percent of what they must know, substantively and politically, on any given issue, consultants bridge the gap for the company. They are hired for their in-depth knowledge of complex scientific, policy, or legal issues. Consultants are often hired because they know how FDA thinks about certain issues; sometimes they enjoy current relationships with key FDA employees and can quickly obtain intelligence about FDA's thinking because they maintain an active network of contacts with FDA personnel, scientific associations, and other FDA advisors. It is important that the company have some continuity among its outside consultants so the consultants understand the company's people, culture, business and regulatory issues that it routinely faces.

The information a company needs can be garnered from a wide variety of sources, such as Freedom of Information Act requests, published regulations and guidances, FDA-sponsored journal articles and symposia, FDA communications with other companies or regulatory agencies, past agency enforcement actions, past and present agency personnel, the FDA's website, etc. Sources of potential information are seemingly endless, but it takes creativity and persistence to dredge out enough appropriate information to help the company make decisions.

B. Dealing With the Right People at FDA

In the example described above, the company is facing a compliance action in which FDA plans to seize its product. The company's position raises an important policy question. The OTC Monograph basically is intended to be a recipe that, if strictly followed, allows similar products to be on the market without FDA approval. The position the company takes is that the OTC Monograph should accommodate moderate technological innovation. Arguably, this policy position enables "me-too" products to come to market with slight improvements that benefit patients. It also allows the company to benefit from reduced regulatory requirements of the OTC Monograph, as opposed to full-blown product approval. Even though the Office of Compliance initiated this matter with a threatened seizure, that office may be the wrong group for the company to deal with at FDA. Because the Office of Compliance serves as both police and prosecutor within FDA, to argue for an expanded view of FDA's OTC Monograph is like going to the police/prosecutor with proposed legislation that takes away their jurisdiction to enforce the matter. They do not have the authority to enact that legislation, and they actually may oppose the change if they feel it hampers or complicates their job.

At times, a company must elevate the matter or shift it to another area within FDA. In this situation, the company is seeking a policy resolution to a prosecutorial matter. FDA personnel in policy positions will ask their compliance people, who are focused on the compliance issue, whether it is in society's best interest to have this product removed from the market. If the product is popular and widely used, for example, seizure of an otherwise safe and efficacious product on a regulatory technicality may look foolish to the outside world. This, in turn, may cause the agency political problems — the public, medical community, media, and Congress may not understand the action and could even call it into question. Policy personnel within FDA may take a broader view and seek compromise, such as requiring a clinical study and giving the company time to complete it. Compromise will allow FDA compliance personnel to save face and will allow FDA policy personnel to derail regulatory action that could draw criticism and embroil the agency in a public relations exercise or congressional oversight. A company must try to ensure, therefore, that its matters are presented to the right personnel within FDA.

C. Tools to Use in Persuading FDA

FDA has *formal* channels and procedures — tools — a company can use to solve matters it has pending before the agency. This includes a dispute resolution guidance that discusses appeals to advisory committees and going up the chain-of-command within FDA. FDA also has an Office of the Chief Mediator and Ombudsman (the Ombudsman) in the Office of the Commissioner, and one in CDER and in the Center for Biologics Evaluation and Research (CBER). CDRH recently has proposed adding an Ombudsman to its organization as well. The Ombudsman acts as a moderator and liaison between the agency and industry. FDA regulations also allow the filing of a citizen petition, which allows a person to put before FDA issues it wants the agency to address. A citizen petition is used by a petitioning party to suggest changes to, or prescribed action on, agency regulations, guidances, enforcement efforts, etc. on issues such as product approvals, product promotion, and GMP enforcement matters — in short, on most anything. The citizen petition process originally was created to open up FDA and allow for more public input.

Problems with FDA's dispute resolution procedures and use of the Ombudsman include the fact that they are cumbersome and time consuming, and they allow the agency to stay in control of managing a company's issue. If your company has an issue that can take time to resolve, then it is acceptable to follow these FDA-preferred routes. Often, however, formal channels are the least effective means of getting things done. Utilizing the Ombudsman, for example, can be a frustrating experience — while wanting to help, the Ombudsman often does not have the internal clout to make things happen, much less to make it happen quickly.

Filing a citizen petition is a company's best bet for getting an issue quickly in front of the agency, and in detail. Once filed, it is public information, which may or may not play well into a company's strategy. The FDA by regulation must furnish a response to a petitioner within 180 days of receipt of the petition. In practice, FDA rarely does so, and has a backlog of petitions that have not been responded to in the designated timeframe. If FDA does not respond to the petition, a company arguably has exhausted its administrative remedies and the issue may be ripe for a lawsuit. FDA has stated that it learns a lot from citizen petitions, and speaks favorably of the process, except in the context of innovator companies who use the process to attempt to delay or prevent the approval of a competitive generic product. To address these cases, FDA has proposed a regulation to eliminate a company's ability to file a citizen petition that could delay or block a generic approval. Overall, however, the citizen petition remains an effective formal tool.

Another formal channel to persuade FDA is to sue the agency. As previously discussed, it may be that a lawsuit every five to ten years actually keeps the agency more respectful of the company's positions. It signals that the company has the conviction and fortitude to take the agency to task if it disagrees strongly enough. The problem with a lawsuit, obviously, is the time and expense to all involved. Additionally, it often is difficult for a company to achieve its objective by suing. Lawsuits are an inefficient tool to use in persuading FDA, but it can be a highly effective one. One need look no further than the *Washington Legal Foundation* (*WLF*) case in which WLF challenged three FDA guidances, the first two of which addressed the dissemination by companies of off-label information contained in medical journal articles and medical textbooks. The third FDA guidance addressed a company's ability to suggest the content of, and speakers for, medical education and symposia.

In the *WLF* case, Judge Lamberth of the U.S. District Court in Washington, D.C., ruled that FDA's guidances were an impermissible infringement on First Amendment free speech. He later went on to rule certain pertinent portions of the Food and Drug Administration Modernization Act (FDAMA) unconstitutional as well. In doing so, he enjoined the agency from enforcing these guidances, and the related parts of FDAMA, against companies. The *WLF* case illustrates the magnitude of the results that can be obtained by resorting to the courts. FDA would never have voluntarily agreed to a result as sweeping as what was constitutionally-imposed on it by Judge Lamberth.

A lawsuit is a powerful tool, but it is actually the *threat* of a lawsuit that may serve a company better. Neither FDA nor a company enjoys the publicity associated with a lawsuit; neither do they like the time consuming effort and tremendous expense. As is true in private disputes between commercial or product liability litigants, both sides often find it to their advantage to seek resolution before a lawsuit is filed or tried. It is important, however, that a company has in its armamentarium the conviction to actually file a lawsuit, if necessary. If a company never has the fortitude to file a lawsuit against the agency, even when the issue is important — whether financially, philosophically, or otherwise — then it becomes a "toothless tiger." This can diminish the effectiveness of company personnel who deal with the agency, because when all else has failed, the company's only recourse may be through an independent arbiter, i.e., the courts. The flip side of the equation is the company who is "trigger happy" and sues the agency fairly frequently. Arguably, such a company loses its negotiating edge because FDA always anticipates a lawsuit. This company can be explained away by the agency as a company that is naturally litigious. Again, it is the *threat* of a lawsuit that is most effective, if it conveys the conviction to follow through with a suit if needed.

Among the *informal* tools available to a company in persuading FDA are: intervention by Congress or the Administration, intervention and/or influence by third parties, using public relations, and contributing to the development of science and public policy. To start, FDA is an agency of the federal government whose very charter is to put flesh on the bones of the FDCA. FDA exists to interpret, implement, and enforce the FDCA through regulations and other administrative interpretive devices like guidances and warning letters.

In its capacity as an agency, it is subject to political pressures. FDA receives budget approval and direction from the White House, and funding and more direction from Congress. Congress often provides FDA clear and formal direction, such as legislation. FDA also can receive "direction" as a product of congressional telephone calls, letters, requested meetings, oversight hearings, and the like. Since FDA fundamentally would rather spend time doing its job, and not dealing with politicians, it does not like congressional intervention. For a company, however, congressional intervention can be very effective. As such, every company must be prepared to invoke congressional intervention when needed. This is a particularly effective tool if the congresspersons involved are on committees having substantive or funding jurisdiction over FDA.

Requesting intervention by the Administration or White House is a much more difficult proposition. When a company goes to the White House to seek assistance on an issue with FDA, there exists both potential opportunity and risk. Every company, constitutionally speaking, has the right to ask any elected official for assistance on any issue it has with an agency, including the President and Vice President. But practically speaking, the level of public interest and media scrutiny will be much higher and more sensitive when a company goes to the highest office in the land. Any approach to the White House must be carefully considered. One mistake companies often make, however, is believing that "going to the White House" means going directly to the Office of the President or Vice President and asking them for a favor. The "White House" is far larger than some realize; it is a large bureaucracy within itself, and there are many secondary offices. Less visible and less risky contact can be made with the Administration through such offices as the Office of Management and Budget, the Office of Science and Technology Policy, or the Council on Environmental Quality. Companies need political experts to assist them in navigating this political minefield, be it in Congress or the Administration.

Another tool available to companies is third-party intervention, which can come in many forms. As a policymaking institution, FDA must take input from a number of constituencies. These include stakeholders, such as patient advocacy groups, medical associations, industry, scientific groups, and public interest groups, to name a few. To advance its issue, it behooves a company to seek broad support. These groups all have their own relationship with FDA and varying degrees of credibility and clout, so their involvement can motivate a company's cause. Their involvement can take the form of position papers, letter writing, petition drives, surveys, press conferences, and joint meetings among the company, the third party, and FDA. In a more serious situation a third party could join the company as a named plaintiff in a lawsuit against the agency. To be effective, a company often must be able to build a coalition of third parties. This entails finding a common denominator among all parties on the issues and advancing them in a manner acceptable to all.

Companies often overlook another tool that it has at its disposal, and that is to participate in the development of scientific and policy issues. A company has a stake in many issues, so it may be helpful to join scientific or trade associations or policy "think-tanks" to influence the content of public discourse and published articles. This requires an ongoing investment, but over time the company's impact can be significant. For example, if a company's expertise and its business is in drug delivery systems, it will have an interest in the science and regulation that encompasses that field. It will want to have its scientists publish articles in scientific journals. It also will want its clinical affairs department to publish relevant medical developments discovered in clinical studies. The company should participate in medical and scientific associations whose agendas include the issuance of scholarly works on topics like "the impact of changes to the physical properties of these devices as they interact with the drug and the patient." The company also will want to find opportunities to provide input to relevant FDA advisory committees or other ports of scientific input into FDA to influence the agency's regulatory thinking.

By doing so, the company will establish itself as a significant voice in scientific and policy matters. And success breeds success. A company initially may fight for a seat at the table in scientific and policy debates. Through long, fruitful participation, the company eventually will be included in all such debates because they will be viewed as having a necessary and important viewpoint.

As a final tool, a company can use public relations as an adjunct to all of the above. Whether the company is boldly holding its own press conference or is able to orchestrate a press conference and media plan through third parties, public relations is an important tool. While FDA is more insulated than most federal agencies, it is impacted by public opinion. A public relations strategy can provide another pressure point on the agency. Public relations can encompass letters to the editor, full-blown press conferences, and lay and scientific articles consistently being placed in the media. The placement of these press pieces is important. At times, newspaper print "within the beltway" of Washington, D.C., in the *Washington Post* and the *Congressional Quarterly*, may be the most effective media placement. At other times, articles targeted for a lay audience in *USA Today* or television news spots are important. This all depends on the importance of the matter, the political palatability of the message, and your ability to package it as newsworthy to the press. Not every issue, or even many of them, will qualify for a public relations plan, but on significant matters it must be considered. Suffice to say, a well-planned public relations plan is an asset when it accompanies the other tools discussed above.

VII. Conclusion

Persuading FDA to your position is an art, not a science. It starts with an understanding of FDA, and your company's relationship with FDA. Once a company has identified what issues it will have before FDA, and prioritizes them, then it can begin planning how to persuade FDA to its position. FDA has many pressure points, and the goal is to apply pressure from as many points as reasonably necessary to affect the outcome in your favor. No one will be mindful of your company's agenda or shepherding your issues except you. It is incumbent on each company to think about how important FDA is to the company — and then to strategize what goes into FDA in order to maximize what comes out of FDA. There are many tools and tactics available to a company in attempting to persuade FDA. A company is limited only by the imagination and creativity of the employees it has assigned to the task.

Richard O. Wood

Bell, Boyd & Lloyd L.L.C.

CHAPTER 12

Petitioning the FDA

I. Introduction

The right of citizens to petition government is ensured by the U.S. Constitution. The Food and Drug Administration (FDA) fulfills its constitutional obligation by giving anyone the right to file petitions requesting the agency to take or refrain from taking certain actions. A petition submitted under this authority is known as a "Citizen Petition."

The submission of Citizen Petitions to FDA has increased dramatically in recent years. This is attributable to a combination of creative new uses of Citizen Petitions by submitters and the realization that the submission to FDA of a well-researched, well-drafted, and well-timed Citizen Petition can provide competitive advantage and bottom-line benefits to regulated companies. With many Citizen Petitions, the bottom-line benefits to a submitter are achieved when FDA delays taking action on the request (i.e., the delay occasioned by FDA having to act on the Citizen Petition may benefit one company at the expense of another).

In late 1999, FDA issued a proposed regulation that, if finalized without change, would severely curtail the types and forms of relief that can be requested in a Citizen Petition. No one should begin the process of preparing a petition without checking on the status of that rulemaking. With that in mind, the following discussion puts forward some ideas for success in strategizing, researching, preparing, submitting, and following up a Citizen Petition.

The filing of a Citizen Petition may lead to litigation. It is wise to utilize legal resources from the outset. Petitions typically raise a host of administrative law issues, including exhaustion of administrative remedies and final agency action. Also, because many Citizen Petitions request FDA to take action that could have implications on competitors, antitrust legal review is a prerequisite.

II. Scope

A Citizen Petition is only one of a number of submissions to FDA that include in their title the word "petition." For example, food additive petitions, GRAS affirmation petitions, and many other forms of petitions are subject to FDA regulations that are separate and distinct from those applicable to Citizen Petitions. They have different content, must be formatted and submitted differently, and are subject to strategies unique to the specific form of petition.

On the other hand, FDA's regulation that defines and establishes the rules for submitting a Citizen Petition is cited in about twenty other FDA rules and regulations that contemplate submissions being made to FDA. A submission to FDA pursuant to their terms must be submitted as a Citizen Petition. Some examples of this include a challenge to the determination of the regulatory review period for patent term extension; an exemption from the pregnancy/nursing warning requirement in drug labeling; and a request to establish, amend, or revoke a device performance standard. The substantive rules that apply to the format, content, and submission requirements of Citizen Petitions can be found in section 10.30 of title 21 of the *Code of Federal Regulations.*

III. When to Consider Submitting a Citizen Petition

Currently, there are no limits on what a Citizen Petition can and cannot request. Therefore, whenever an issue arises with FDA, or an opportunity exists if FDA were to take or not take certain action, a Citizen Petition should be on the list of options to consider. Obvious practical limitations exist as to what FDA can and cannot do, so there are some reasons why a Citizen Petition should be rejected as an alternative in certain circumstances. Also, a Citizen Petition that requests FDA to take an action that the agency lacks legal authority to perform wastes the time of both the submitter and FDA.

IV. Preparing the Citizen Petition

A. Pre-Filing

Before preparing and filing a Citizen Petition, analyze fully whether other means exist to achieve your regulatory objective. Ask whether FDA may be inclined to do what you want to achieve without a Citizen Petition's formality and exposure to public scrutiny. No regulation or other restriction exists against talking or meeting with FDA officials. Therefore, when an issue arises or a situation exists when you want FDA to take or not take certain action, determine what officials at FDA may be in a position to help you achieve that objective. Request and pursue a meeting with those officials. Then, prepare fully for that meeting, and enter fully armed with arguments in support of your request and responses to agency questions that you have anticipated. While FDA may not agree to what you are requesting, a major part of the work of preparing the Citizen Petition will be complete, and issues that you had not previously considered or had overlooked may be raised in the meeting. You would be advised to address these in your petition.

B. Strategy Development

When a Citizen Petition is being considered and strategies are being developed, always keep in mind that FDA is an agency whose foremost objective is the protection of the public health and safety. Therefore, every argument in support of your request should be framed persuasively, as much as possible, to convince FDA that acting as requested in the Citizen Petition will advance the public health. As tempting as it may be to focus on the importance of the issue to your company, you should avoid that emphasis in your discussion. First, the importance of the matter to you will be obvious to those within FDA; second, the more universally applicable your request appears, the more favorably it will be perceived by those who are assigned to review it.

Ask yourself whether the Citizen Petition you are contemplating might be better received if filed by someone other than yourself. Company-filed Citizen Petitions immediately raise suspicions of self-interest; the same petition filed by a trade association or medical association is less likely to be received with that immediate reaction. Also consider whether the substantive aspects of the petition are such that it would be wise to have the Citizen Petition filed by someone else. For instance, if the request involves substantive legal issues, the Citizen Petition might best be filed by outside regulatory counsel.

C. Researching

The wide breadth of potential subject matter in a Citizen Petition makes a specific discussion of research techniques impracticable here. To avoid making the mistakes others before you have made, however, time spent reviewing Citizen Petitions filed by others on matters similar to yours will be time well spent. All Citizen Petitions, and comments filed in opposition, in support, etc., are kept on file with the FDA Docket Clerk and are available for public review.

A day or more spent in that office will yield discernable benefit both to your research efforts and to your end product. Going to that office blind, however, could waste several hours while you try to locate Citizen Petitions relevant to your intended filing. It will come as no surprise that the solution lies on the Internet. FDA's excellent and constantly expanding website includes a Docket icon, and on that site a great many Citizen Petitions, responses, etc. are posted. Those documents are in Adobe™ .pdf format, but they are searchable by key words, making it easy to identify documents with potential relevance and precedential value to your contemplated Citizen Petition. A visit to this website prior to an actual visit to the FDA Docket Room will help you identify relevant material that you want to review, and may even eliminate the need to make the latter visit in-person.

D. Writing the Citizen Petition

Basic rules applicable to any document intended to persuade a neutral arbiter should be followed. Although the document must contain a full statement of the factual grounds on which the petitioner relies, do everything you can to make the document concise and to the point. Be absolutely sure not to include any information that is erroneous, obsolete, or irrelevant. If, despite your best efforts, the document is lengthy, include an executive summary to let reviewers know what they will be reading and their supervisors know what it is about without having to read the entire document. Ask others with whom you work to give the document a critical review, and accept that review by disowning any pride of authorship.

E. Final Review and Submission

Review the regulations to confirm that all requirements regarding the content of the Citizen Petition have been met, as well as that requirements about how to address the petition, method of filing, number of copies, etc. are understood and followed to the letter. Upon receipt, FDA's initial review is not substantive, rather it is a review to make sure that the minimum requirements specified in the regulation have been met. The Citizen Petition will be deemed "filed" only after that initial review; if the petition is found deficient, it will be returned. You may want to make up a checklist of the basic requirements and include it as an attachment to your cover letter.

In addition to the multiple copies that must be filed with FDA's Dockets Management office, consider whether any FDA officials whom you have talked to or met with about the issues (or those who may be involved in the substantive review of the Citizen Petition), should be sent courtesy copies of the Citizen Petition. Courtesy copies make the review easier for the reviewer and will be appreciated.

F. Follow-up

When all the research and background work necessary for the Citizen Petition are done, and the Citizen Petition has been written, reviewed, and officially submitted, the temptation exists to sit back and wait for the agency to take action. Other priorities may have suffered at the expense of preparing the Citizen Petition, and many overdue projects may beg for attention. While moving on to new challenges is a temptation, it is one that must be rejected. Many things can still be done to improve your chances of success.

Your research should have led you to develop a good idea of those within FDA who would be responsible for the review of your Citizen Petition at the working level. A week or so after submission, if you have not heard anything, start calling those people to confirm receipt and inquire where things stand. If calls go unreturned for several days, place new ones. Also send e-mails; they are easier to avoid than phone calls, but they leave a form of paper trail that may later work to your benefit. Your task after filing the Citizen Petition is to make sure that it receives the attention that it deserves. As the person who filed it and who is the most interested in its success, you do not want to let FDA think that it can sit on a desk and be ignored without anyone raising an objection. There are instances when a Citizen Petition does languish, despite a petitioner's best efforts to shake it loose. Whether you take your case up the chain of authority within the agency, and possibly threaten legal action in that circumstance is a difficult decision that potentially has major implications for the company. Generalizations of how to react to such frustrations are simply not possible.

You will also know from your research what administrative procedure FDA must follow to take or refrain from taking the requested action. Your follow-up should include periodic checks to see if that procedure is being followed, and if not, why not. If publication in the *Federal Register* is a prerequisite to FDA taking action on your Petition, you will want to follow that on a daily basis, or set up an automatic notification system with one of the many services that provide such notification. If your Petition is assigned a docket number, you will want to check that docket periodically to see what comments are being filed either in support of or in opposition to your Petition. If new issues are raised by opponents, you will need to determine if you need to provide more information.

V. Conclusion

A great deal of the practice of food, drug, and cosmetic law is reacting to events that occur without forewarning. We often do not know when the FDA investigator will arrive, when the agency will commence an enforcement action, or when a company's product will have a problem requiring a recall. The filing of a Citizen Petition is typically an exception to the reactive nature of the practice of this law. It is one of the few occasions in the practice where the Petitioner fires the first volley. When researched thoroughly, written persuasively, and pursued doggedly, a Citizen Petition can be an extremely effective tool to achieve regulatory objectives.

William W. Vodra

Arnold & Porter

CHAPTER 13

 ow to Write Letters to FDA

I. Introduction

"What we have here is a failure to communicate." That famous line from the movie *Cool Hand Luke* explained, ostensibly, why the prison inmate was going to be punished. It also explains many of the situations in which the regulators and the regulated are at odds. To be sure, the obligations and interests of each side may compel disagreement. But more frequently, disagreements seem to emerge from misunderstandings and a failure to communicate.

This problem is not one-sided. The language of any government agency is frequently opaque and indirect. Messages issued from different parts of a bureaucracy can be conflicting. And even when the message is clear and unequivocal, the government may be diverted from following through by external events having little or nothing to do with the issue at hand. The Food and Drug Administration (FDA) is certainly not unique in having difficulties communicating, despite its best efforts.

The challenge for regulated companies is to help themselves and FDA avoid and overcome misunderstandings in communications. Meeting that challenge is the focus of this chapter.

II. The Importance of Written Communications

"An oral contract is not worth the paper it is written on." The late movie producer Samuel Goldwyn summarized the fundamental deficiency in face-to-face and telephonic dialogues with FDA.

Companies put great stock in meetings with FDA, perhaps hoping that, by demonstrating sincerity and good faith in person, they will be more likely to prevail in persuading the agency to accept the company's position than if communication were solely in writing. And, in fact, meetings are very important and often the best way to reach a common understanding. FDA works hard to make meetings successful, generally holding an internal pre-meeting to identify and reach a consensus on the issues to be discussed.

Meetings, however, have significant limitations and, in any event, must be preceded and followed by written communications. FDA generally requests a written agenda, together with a list of the company attendees, prior to arranging a meeting. This submission permits FDA to hold its internal pre-meeting. After the meeting, the conclusions must be memorialized in order to create a permanent record. Otherwise, one is left with the oral contract of which Mr. Goldwyn complained.

Of course, neither FDA nor industry can reasonably expect to conduct all business via meetings and telephone conferences. In fact, probably the vast majority of all communications is through submissions and responses, rather than oral dialogue. These writings create the record on which any meeting or institutional decision will be based.

In short, the written record is a most important aspect of the dialogue between a company and FDA.

III. Routine Correspondence

"Reference is made to the submissions of January 30, 1999, June 15, 1999, October 12, 1999, December 20, 1999, January 12, 2000, February 9, 2000, and March 6, 2000. Reference is also made to meetings on June 22, 1999, October 20, 1999, January 20, 2000, and March 10, 2000." So begins the opening paragraph of many letters to and from FDA. What is going on? What are the issues? Why should anyone read the next paragraph of this letter? Would you write a member of your family in this way?

The format for official correspondence seems to have been selected by people who are interested in archival history rather than active communication. Later generations have accepted it with little protest. The result is that the formbooks may not present options that the writer really wants. At a "go away" for management of the drug review process in the Center for Drug Evaluation and Research a few years ago, a division director complained that industry would not engage in meaningful dialogue. He gave as an example his desire to discuss a particular research protocol; he was worried that some elements of the study might not succeed, and he thought an open discussion with the company scientists would educate him and resolve his doubts. But instead of dialogue, the company simply revised the protocol. I asked him whether his letter to the company said, "Hey, I have some questions; can we talk?" Or did it say, "Please submit a revised protocol that assures…." His expression answered the question; the division had followed the formbook, and the book did not contain an invitation just to talk.

Industry has its version of these formbooks, although not always written. They contain additional instructions, such as "Do not tell FDA more than you have to" and "Keep control of the issues."

As a result of each side's formbook restrictions, misunderstandings can occur. We have a failure to communicate. No one need be trapped by these historic forms, especially when they interfere with — instead of advancing — effective communications. Here are some suggestions:

Write a clear opening paragraph explaining the purpose of the submission. FDA staff receives an unbelievable volume of material every day from industry. Submissions rarely are as short as three to five pages; frequently they contain numerous attachments and exhibits. You should tell the reader in the opening paragraph what the company wants from this submission, so that the reader knows what to do with it. For example:

- "This submission is for FDA's information and does not require any action."

- "This submission seeks FDA permission to change product labeling."

- "This submission seeks answers from FDA to two questions."

If the company has a deadline, advise the agency in the opening paragraph. Telling the agency you want a reply by a certain date does not guarantee a timely response, but it does set forth the company's desires and expectations. If the deadline is imposed by external events, such as the need to commence printing of a label for the next product manufacturing cycle, inform FDA of the reason for the deadline. If a response is urgent, justify that fact and then orally reinforce the request for a rapid response. Be realistic as well; FDA has many stakeholders clamoring for its attention.

Do not assume that FDA knows your product and your regulatory history as well as you do. Barrett Scoville, an FDA medical officer and division director in the 1970s, described the intellectual excitement of his job as "playing 100 chess games at the same time, with 100 experts." Each unit of FDA faces a staggering multitude of issues on any given day, and the array changes like a kaleidoscope each subsequent day. To expect FDA personnel to recall the specifics of your situation after a three- or six-month hiatus is unrealistic and dangerous. You should assist the reader in getting to the heart of the issue. For example:

- Instead of simply listing referenced submissions and meetings, explain the relevancy of each item being referenced to the issue being presented.

- Remind the reader what the product is and its current regulatory status.

- Provide a succinct regulatory history of the issue.

- Point out any prior precedent that might be consistent or inconsistent with the present issue.

Never ask FDA a question when your company cannot accept whatever answer FDA gives. If you seek an FDA answer on a matter, you must be prepared to live with it. You may not be able to change FDA's mind, once the answer is given, and FDA does not look favorably on having its positions ignored. The best illustration of this principle relates to preclearance of advertising or labeling claims, when preclearance is not legally required. If the company simply made the claim in the ordinary course of business, FDA might not learn of it, or upon learning of it, might not take any adverse action because of other priorities. On the other hand, when a company asks FDA whether it can use the claim, the agency is now in the position of having to take a position. If FDA rejects the claim, the company runs a real risk of adverse action by the agency, not because it otherwise is a priority matter, but because the company has now appeared to challenge directly FDA's position.

Do not assume that FDA will answer the question as you phrase it. This advice falls under the category of never underestimating the people on the other side of the table. FDA will attempt to understand the issue and will, if necessary, do additional homework to develop the facts needed to make a decision. Insofar as it relates to your product, the information already may exist in agency files. Hence, the notion of "not giving FDA more information than necessary to decide in your favor" may not prevent the agency from ferreting out other relevant information that is less favorable to you. Furthermore, the issue you raise may have broader policy implications to which you are not sensitive. As a result, FDA may not be "trapped" into the issue as you present it.

Never omit or misstate material facts. Your credibility — personally and as a company — rests on honesty and candor. FDA does not look kindly on being treated as a fool or lied to; enough said.

IV. Requesting a Meeting

The first order of business is to decide why the company wants a meeting. Usually, this question is answered before a meeting is proposed. Unfortunately, firms occasionally request a meeting before determining if there is anything to be said!

A. Meetings on Enforcement Matters

The practice of requesting a meeting without having something to say is most common when the company fears an FDA enforcement action. The firm's motivation appears to be that, after seeing real people and hearing their sincere protestations of good faith, the agency will elect not to proceed with sanctions. This reaction is human and natural; it is also of limited efficacy. Just as attempting to talk a traffic cop out of a speeding ticket is often fruitless and can backfire, so also is meeting with FDA just to show goodwill. FDA personnel are professionals and do not generally act out of malice or to retaliate. Rather, if the agency concludes that official action is needed under the circumstances, it will proceed, notwithstanding kindly personal feelings toward the company or individuals.

If one does have a meeting under these circumstances, however, here are a few "do's and don'ts":

Demonstrate that the problem is already solved. If FDA enforcement action will not remediate the situation any further, the agency may choose to stop.

Do not try to demonstrate simply that you are now committed to solving the problem. The agency will conclude that it was only the threat of enforcement action that brought management to this point, and that removal of the threat will result in no change. Serious enforcement actions — seizures, injunctions, shutdowns, recalls, and embargoes — are considered when FDA has lost faith in the firm's ability to comply voluntarily with regulatory requirements. Multiple inspections or communications often precede the agency's decision to take such actions. Thus, protestations that the firm now "gets it" will be greeted skeptically. Consider the following dialogue, which is based on several real experiences:

- Company: "These products are vital to the public health."

  FDA: "We agree. That is why you have an obligation to comply with the law and we have an obligation to enforce it."

- Company: "But our checkbook is opened. We have brought in the best consultants and placed no limits on the resources to get into compliance."

  FDA: "That is good news. But why did this not happen before, for example, following any of the last four FDA inspections?"

- Company: "Consumers, patients, employees, and other companies, will be adversely affected through no fault of theirs. It is not fair to them."

  FDA: "Consumers and patients are adversely affected by products that do not comply with the law. Employees and other companies are relying on your management to run a compliant business. Any unfairness results from your noncompliance. And we are willing, as FDA, to take any heat, because we will tell people why they are being hurt."

Do argue that enforcement would be inconsistent with agency or public policy. FDA is concerned about its actions' implications for its larger mission.

Do not argue that all of your competitors are doing the same thing without FDA enforcement, or that you are the industry leader (i.e., that you have a state-of-the art product), unless you know it to be true. FDA usually has assessed where a company is vis-à-vis its competitors and others in the same area of regulation. Although it is natural for each company to believe in itself, benchmarking studies and current metrics are not so reliable as FDA's own internal scorecards based on inspections, mandatory reports from all firms, and other databases. Suggesting that you are being singled out is another way of accusing FDA employees of being arbitrary, vindictive, and unfair. Although you may believe all of those things, you are not likely to be very persuasive throwing this belief into FDA's collective and institutional face without ironclad proof. Finally, bear in mind that FDA does single out some firms as bellwethers for their industry, in order to ratchet up regulatory standards. As an FDA psychiatrist once explained to me, "In FDA regulation, paranoia may merely represent being reality-oriented."

Do not plead with FDA simply to "drop the case." The only thing FDA can do in this situation is to proceed. Otherwise, it will be subject to criticism from all sides for having "sold out to industry."

B. Meetings on Nonenforcement Matters

As stated earlier, meetings with FDA are important to industry and the agency. FDA works hard to make them productive, especially through internal pre-meetings.

These pre-meetings frequently last longer than the industry meeting itself, depending on the number of questions to be answered. In one case, the pre-meeting lasted for over five hours; the actual meeting lasted ten minutes, as FDA responded to each question presented, and each answer was satisfactory to the company involved. This successful dialogue was possible because of written communications prior to the meeting.

The submission requesting the meeting should contain several key elements:

Clearly state each question to be discussed. This advice merely repeats what is proposed above for routine correspondence. But in the context of a meeting, it goes beyond an agenda item to identify the issue and choices as the company sees it.

- In the judicial system, appellate briefs always start with the "Question Presented," which is usually stated in a manner that can be answered "yes" or "no." For example, "Does the First Amendment apply to FDA regulation of advertising?" or "Did the defendant get a fair trial when the jury was asleep?"

- If you cannot present the issue that way, identify the options in another way that makes your proposed choices plain. For example, "What is the appropriate length for follow-up in this study — three months, six months, or twelve months?" or "What evidence is needed to show that a dietary supplement was sold as such prior to 1994 — shipping invoices, advertisements, or market research reports?"

- Do not ask FDA a question if you cannot live with one of its possible answers, and do not assume that FDA will confine itself to the question as you asked it. This advice was discussed above. In addition, however, do not ask FDA a question that you are not prepared to discuss and answer yourself. FDA may well ask, "What is the company's position on this issue?" If you are not prepared to supply it, you may be forced into taking a stand that has not been considered fully.

- Do not assume that FDA is a free consultant. The agency will expect that you will have thought about the issue and have some idea about the "right" answer.

Summarize objectively the history and facts surrounding the question. The FDA employees involved will not recall the events and facts nearly as well as you. In addition, there may be participants for whom this letter is their first exposure to the product and the issues.

Supply the relevant earlier documents. Instead of simply listing the attachments, however, guide the reader to understand what specific part of each document is considered relevant to the question under discussion. Again, you should bear in mind how busy FDA employees are; they will not have the time to read everything you submit, let alone try to guess why you submitted it.

Present the answer that the company prefers to hear, if there is one. Do not be afraid of advocating a certain outcome.

V. Writing to Appeal FDA Decisions

Among the more delicate letters to write FDA is one challenging the decision of an FDA official to agency superiors. This process seems to intimidate many in industry, who fear damage to the relations with the official involved, or futility because FDA will routinely support subordinates, or even retaliation from the agency. These fears usually are exaggerated, but are not totally invalid. And under some circumstances, a company must seek to reverse a decision that adversely affects its business. Accordingly, appeals will be taken. To address the concerns, here are some ideas:

Use a civil and respectful tone. Disagreements on scientific issues or procedural matters are natural and legitimate. There is no need to disparage the official whose decision is being challenged.

Describe the issue fairly and with balance. The person whose decision is being challenged probably will be given an opportunity to present the other side. If you have omitted material information, or misrepresented the basis for the decision, it will soon become obvious.

Give a copy of your letter asking for supervisory review to the employee whose decision is being challenged. Attempts to overturn a decision in secret are always fraught with peril. You should assume that the person who made the initial decision in question will see your letter. You should have nothing to be ashamed about or hide.

File an appeal to the proper person. Taking appeals from a medical officer or field inspector immediately to the Office of the Commissioner is not merely fruitless, but is counterproductive. As in any organization, the management hierarchy is intended to resolve easier problems at lower levels before burdening more senior management. By going over middle management's head, the appealing party will offend a number of people who are made to look to their superiors as ignorant of disputes within their purview.

VI. Memorializing the Results of Meetings

After any meeting, FDA and the company usually exchange minutes shortly after the event. This is an excellent practice and should be encouraged. Once in a while, however, comparing these minutes suggests that the writers were at two different meetings. Why?

The most dangerous reason is that the industry participants are attempting to rewrite history and put FDA into positions that it did not necessarily agree to take. If the minutes are shared promptly with FDA, this practice is dangerous because FDA will see the attempt and take offense. If the minutes are not exchanged, the practice is even more dangerous because company employees not at the meeting will act in reliance on incorrect information. Months or years later, a problem may emerge when FDA advises the company that the position was not that of the agency.

Industry minutes are meant also for company management. This fact is another cause for inconsistency between corporate and FDA minutes. If a meeting did not go well, the company representatives may want to soften the situation rather than upset their bosses. The techniques include omitting reference to points of disagreement, presenting an issue on which FDA has taken a firm stand as still being open for discussion, and phrasing the issue in a manner to downplay the importance of the outcome. Unfortunately, if management is banking on a new product's approval for $1 billion in annual sales, and FDA is advising that the drug may never get approved, the miscommunication can have devastating consequences.

VII. General Writing Tips

It may be too late to get adults to study Strunk & White's *The Elements of Style*, although it is the best short guide to clear writing that exists. In lieu of that, consider these three thoughts:

Use the active voice. This recommendation is not merely to enhance readability. The passive voice conveys a sense that events happen independent of the writer's or company's control. That may be true in some situations, but when the company is making commitments or describing actions it has taken, the passive voice communicates a lack of accountability. "People were appointed, new procedures were written, and submissions will be made." Who is responsible for these matters?

Be specific on key details. Events do not simply happen; they happen at points in time, at locations, to people or things. One does not have to overwhelm with extraneous detail, but should provide FDA with the critical specifics.

Keep concepts clear and precise. Ambiguity is perhaps the greatest single cause for miscommunication. Describing things in general terms, or using vague terms, can lead to misunderstandings. For example, the process for revising a standard operating procedure (SOP) involves many steps: drafting, formal approval, training, and an effective date for implementation. If a company writes FDA that a certain SOP was "changed," which of these steps have occurred?

VIII. Conclusion

Members of the regulated industry need to ensure effective communications between themselves and FDA. Although FDA certainly shares in this responsibility, the adverse consequences for confusion seem to fall disproportionately on companies. As in *Cool Hand Luke*, the failure to communicate results in more pain for one party than the other. Writing clear and useful letters to FDA may reduce the risk of miscommunication. It takes hard work, but it is worth it.

Michael R. McConnell

National Notification Center

14

How to Deal With a Recall

Working with the Food and Drug Administration (FDA) on recalls and withdrawals can be least painful if manufacturers try to understand what FDA is concerned about, and act accordingly. The basic regulations governing how food and drug recalls should be conducted are found in 21 C.F.R. section 7.40 through 7.59, and in part 5 of the *Regulatory Procedures Manual*. They have changed little or not at all since they were first published in 1978. Over the years, additional laws and regulations affecting recalls have been enacted, but they mostly address overriding legal authority for FDA to mandate recalls of certain products (e.g., medical devices, certain biologics, infant formulas, etc.).

There are four guiding principles and two courses of action on how to work with FDA in recall situations. The following observations are gleaned from experience, and are important for understanding the underlying motivations of FDA during a recall.

I. Four Guiding Principles

It is generally fair to say that FDA is concerned with the following subjects as they relate to product recalls, in order of importance:

(1) degree of health hazard that a recalled product may inflict on the public;

(2) compliance with regulations;

(3) degree of disruption a recall will cause the general public and/or the healthcare community; and

(4) degree of disruption a recall will cause a manufacturer.

A. What Is the Degree of Health Hazard?

All recall actions of FDA and manufacturers should, and generally do, stem from this question. How quickly should the recall notice be disseminated (e.g., via press release, broadcast voice/fax, e-mail, overnight letter, or regulation mail)? To what depth/level should the recall be conducted (e.g., wholesalers/distributors only, all hospitals, all pharmacies/retailers, nursing homes, physicians, or patients/consumers)? For those questions and others about how a recall should be conducted, FDA will judge a manufacturer's proposed actions as acceptable or unacceptable based primarily on the degree of health hazard.

A seemingly-correct action might be interpreted by FDA as the wrong way to approach a recall issue, an example of which may be found in the facet of recall "depth" or "level" (defined in the regulations at section 7 of 21 C.F.R.). A narrow, but perhaps perfectly valid, interpretation of some C.F.R. statements on recall depth could lead one to believe that the manufacturer's only responsibility is to notify, and then recall the product from, their "affected direct accounts." It becomes the "direct account's" (e.g., the wholesaler's) responsibility to notify and recall the product from their accounts. This is referred to in the regulations as a sub-recall. Other C.F.R. statements on recall level could be interpreted such that the manufacturer's responsibility is broader and that the manufacturer must notify and recall from "anyone who has received, purchased, or used the product being recalled."

These are the kind of legal wrestling matches that attorneys may find interesting, and differing interpretations would probably be decided in court. Regarding a present recall, if FDA thinks that a manufacturer is engaging in hair-splitting or foot-dragging when the public health is at risk, then that is the kind of situation that may prompt the agency to use its ultimate practical weapon: the press release. This would be the kind of press release in which FDA warns the public of an "imminent health hazard" or "preventable patient injury" or some other such unwelcome phrasing.

Guiding Principle #1 — Make sure your proposed actions convey to FDA your concern about the public health hazard, and that you are not simply complying with a conservative interpretation of the law.

B. Complying With Regulations

Compliance with regulations becomes the driving force behind a recall when the issue of health hazard has been settled; it is especially important when the degree of health hazard is low. It can be extremely frustrating for a manufacturer in a situation where FDA agrees that there is little or no health hazard, but still insists on a recall. Some personnel within the manufacturing firm, especially those for whom regulatory matters are not their primary responsibility, may conclude that a recall is not necessary and attempt to oppose the recall.

All actors must try to understand that FDA essentially is governed by the regulations almost as much as the manufacturer. If a manufacturer's product is deemed "violative," even in the smallest way, then it will probably have to be recalled. Following are some examples of seemingly trivial problems that could lead to recall. If rayon is used to top off a bottle of tablets, instead of the cotton that is specified in a particular product's manufacturing procedures, then technically the product is in violation and should be recalled. If the lower potency limit for a 100 mg tablet is 90 mg, and the product is testing at 89 mg, then technically the product is out of specs and should be recalled. If the font size for the expiration date on a product label is not large enough, then the product is technically misbranded and must be recalled. While all parties concerned may agree that there is no health hazard, the prescribed action in these situations is to recall, and there is not much equivocation on that point.

Some cynics might suggest that FDA plays a numbers game by trying to get many recalls "under its [administrative] belt." An alternative suggestion is that FDA wants to avoid a potential scenario that might play out as follows: a recalled product causes serious health problems, and the FDA Commissioner is called before a congressional committee, at which past instances where regulations were violated but a recall was not conducted are paraded out as evidence that FDA is not doing its job. Certainly that is the kind of situation FDA wants to avoid.

Having said all of the above, however, FDA-ers are not without a sense of proportionality and they may treat nonhealth hazard situations with some leniency. Firms should first accept the fact that retrieval of the product from the marketplace most probably will be necessary. Second, firms can propose to FDA that the situation be considered a "minor violation" (see definitions in section 7.3 of 21 C.F.R.) and that the action be classified a withdrawal instead of a recall; they also should be prepared to accept FDA's ruling that it be termed a recall, not a withdrawal. Whether it is a recall or withdrawal, propose to FDA that your recall actions (urgency of notification, level of recall, etc.) be limited in scope, based on Principles #3 and #4 below.

Guiding Principle #2 — Any violation, no matter how small, probably will result in a recall. But if FDA agrees that there is no health hazard, now is the time to propose actions that simply comply with the letter of the law, but may not go much further.

C. Disruption to Public or Healthcare Community

Once FDA has settled the two issues of health hazard and regulatory compliance, the agency will take into account whether a recall will unduly disrupt the delivery of healthcare. Examples of disruption can be either short supply of a medically necessary product, or fear of misinformation about medical therapy.

Short supply is fairly self-evident. A product may be recalled, and then there may not be sufficient re-supply, especially if there may not be a therapeutic alternative. FDA may be reluctant to force a broad and extensive recall over a truly minor violation if it creates a shortage of a medically necessary therapy. The agency will consider, even if there are other products available on the market, whether competitors can supply enough product to meet demand in a short timeframe.

Misinformation could happen when therapy with a recalled product should not be interrupted unless the patient is able to see a physician and the patient's therapy is evaluated. It could be the case that an incomplete or poorly communicated recall notification may cause, for example, a patient with epilepsy to overreact and/or to discontinue medication before a physician has arranged for other therapy. Where a recalled product has an identified health hazard, there may be no choice; but if there is no health hazard, then FDA may be amenable to limiting the scope of a recall in order to prevent a misinformation situation.

Guiding Principle #3 — Try to present information about the potential impact of the impending action on the delivery of healthcare.

D. Disruption to a Manufacturer

When making recall decisions, FDA is not supposed to take into account the financial impact that a recall will have on a manufacturer. But, *provided there is no health hazard*, FDA has been known to work with a manufacturer to accomplish the overall goals of the recall without putting the manufacturer out of business. Even if the impact is not as drastic as potentially going out of business, FDAers are human and they do not want to see the waste of disposing of large volumes of otherwise-good product because, for instance, the font on the label is the wrong size.

Guiding Principle #4 — Try to present information on the potential impact of the impending action on the manufacturer. Do not overplay this card. It really only comes into play for minor violations when a firm is trying to limit the scope of the potential recall.

II. Two Courses of Action

A. Keep FDA Informed

Share information with FDA as soon as you have it. It does not have to be complete and it does not have to be conclusive, but it is important to share the information you have when it is first available. Something that will almost always cause a strained and adversarial relationship is for FDA to find out about a recall situation at the last minute, or even worse, to find out from a source other than the manufacturer. It can cast a pall over all subsequent interactions between that manufacturer and the agency.

Some manufacturers have expressed concern over maintaining the confidentiality of shared information, and that early communication, no matter how preliminary, will lead to a recall even if it may not be fully warranted. This is not so. FDA learns about many potential recall situations where the early information eventually is overridden and a recall is not necessary. Agency personnel are as pleased as anyone when a recall is not necessary, and they keep those situations confidential every day.

Also, share all the other information you have about the recall situation. FDA probably does not have the resources or the information that a manufacturer does about potential health hazards, e.g., of rayon versus cotton packing, or of subtherapeutic doses of a product. You probably know the manufacturing capacity of your competitors, and you may have research on the concerns of wholesalers, hospitals, pharmacies, and patients. If FDA is short on data, they have to err on the safe side, so the agency will tend to overclassify a recall and require a broader scope of implementation. Information can help to shape the pending recall event, but only if it is shared with FDA.

B. Don't Ask; Tell

When you are communicating with FDA about recall actions, tell them how you intend to proceed. FDA prefers to see a manufacturer present a solid plan for how it intends to conduct the recall, not that a plan will necessarily be perfect, or that a firm will know more about recalls than the Recall Coordinator in the agency's district office or Center. If something in the plan is not adequate, FDA will suggest an alternative. But again, if you ask the Recall and Emergency Coordinator (REC) how to do everything, he or she may err on the safe side and suggest a broader scope than might be necessary.

As the recall progresses *past initial stages*, the manufacturer may not get fast responses to questions or fast approvals for proposed actions. RECs are busy people, and some are not always able to reply to questions or to approve actions immediately. If your recall plan is reasonable (i.e., not just trying to get away with the bare minimum), then send written communication outlining your proposed actions, include timeframes, and politely signal your intention to proceed unless FDA has an objection. Language in this communication may take the form of "We are highly confident in this effectiveness check plan. We welcome your suggestions, but if there are no suggestions or concerns, we will proceed on . . . ." **One note of caution:** while this strategy works well in general, and the manufacturer should take the lead on all aspects of the recall process, it is important *not* to proceed with the initial recall notification plan and the initial recall communication until you receive explicit FDA approval of these items.

In summary, while FDA's interests and a manufacturer's interests may not be in perfect harmony, both parties are made up of reasonable human beings who generally want to protect the public from harm, obey the rules, and not waste time, money, or materials. Recalls are no fun, but they do not have to be as painful as they sometimes are allowed to be.

Arthur N. Levine

Arnold & Porter

How to Deal With Warning Letters

The reason you have received a warning letter is that FDA is not satisfied. In most circumstances, FDA sends a warning letter because the agency believes that your previous communication on the subject discussed in the letter — e.g., your response to a list of inspectional observations (Form 483) or your support for a labeling claim or other promotional activity — is inadequate or unpersuasive. Now what?

The last thing you should do is to start drafting your response to the warning letter. Here are several things you should think about first:

Read the warning letter carefully. Compare it to the FDA-483 or other notice you have received from the agency on the problem addressed in the warning letter. Determine how the warning letter characterizes the problem. If the warning letter follows the submission of your response to an FDA-483, review the way the warning letter relies upon certain of the observations, how it groups those observations, and which observations are not discussed. Pay particular attention to those passages in the warning letter that specify how your response to the FDA-483 was inadequate.

Assess the strength of the agency's position. Look at the language of the warning letter and at those portions in which FDA invokes sanctions, such as announcing that the agency will not issue export certifications or will not review product license applications. These sanctions may have an immediate and significant impact on your business. If they do, you need to consider whether a written response to the warning letter will provide an adequate means for resolution of the enforcement initiatives that the agency has announced. A more immediate communication may be needed to begin a dialogue that could lead to FDA reassessing the sanction or limiting its scope or application.

Do not guess at the meaning of a warning letter. For example, if the agency has rejected some corrective action that you described in a response to an FDA-483, and the reason for its rejection is unclear, you should determine why your position was judged to be inadequate. It may be necessary to call the FDA person designated in the warning letter and explore further the agency's position. You cannot shoot at a target you see only vaguely.

When the warning letter describes with particularity the inadequacies in your previous communication to the agency, it is fairly easy to frame your response. For example, where your previous communication advised the agency of a new standard operating procedure (SOP), but the warning letter notes that you failed to provide a copy of the new SOP, the remedy is reasonably obvious. In many cases, however, the agency's description of the reason why your previous communication was inadequate may not make immediately clear what response the agency is looking for. If you remain uncertain as to why the agency was not satisfied with your previous communication, call the contact person designated in the warning letter to explore whether there may have been a misunderstanding, and to determine why the agency did not credit the changes that the company already has undertaken or the commitments that it already has announced.

Identify your primary audience. It also is important to determine (unless it is clear from the warning letter itself) what part of the agency is primarily responsible for the issuance of the warning letter. Is it the local district office or the Center's Office of Compliance? It is valuable to know what part of the agency will be the primary audience for your response to the warning letter.

Consider both immediate and system-wide enhancements. In issuing a warning letter, the agency usually is seeking an immediate short-term "fix" and a long-term program that will reasonably be expected to prevent the recurrence of the problem. Often, the short-term fix is easy to describe in the response to the warning letter. Long-term actions designed to prevent the recurrence of the problem usually require activities that are ancillary to, and supportive of, the short-term fix, such as documentation, retraining, audit or other verification that the fix is working as desired, and the commitment of the necessary resources.

Often FDA concludes that a company's previous position was too narrow and that the company is not pursuing a sufficiently "system-wide" solution. At that point you should review your earlier assessment of the implications of FDA's concerns beyond the immediate context in which they arose. You may need to apply the "fix" to a larger portion of your operation.

Review your previous improvement efforts critically. Because the issuance of a warning letter means that the company's previous communication with the agency has not been successful, it may be useful to obtain an independent "arm's-length" review of the issues highlighted in the warning letter. An outsider may provide a fresh look as to how the previous communication may have lacked clarity, specificity, or otherwise failed to satisfy the agency. Subject that previous communication to a critical review. Challenge "business-as-usual" assumptions.

Do enough without promising too much. Once you are satisfied that you understand why the agency has issued the warning letter, what part of the agency is primarily responsible for the warning letter, and what, in fact, are the remaining gaps between what the agency desires and what the company is already doing, then you can begin to assess what else the company is prepared to do to try to satisfy the agency. In this assessment, your objective is to overcome the agency's conclusion that your previously announced programs, improvements, and commitments were inadequate. You need to seriously consider what more you can do. At the same time, there is no value in committing to changes or enhanced procedures that you cannot implement. Nor can you commit to quick "band-aid" remedies that disrupt existing practices and procedures, or undercut already validated processes. Any changes or systems enhancements that you initiate in response to a warning letter must be real and achievable.

Your description of these remedial activities should be accurate and complete. Wherever possible, they should include target completion dates. New activities should be integrated into the company's existing quality system in a meaningful sequence. Your response to the warning letter also might explain the rationale for the process by which a new practice or procedure is being implemented. Whatever enhancement you describe in your response to the warning letter, its implementation should be carefully considered and described. This is why most companies do not merely describe an individual remedial action, but rather execute a *plan* to fully effectuate the change. You do not need a "corrective" action plan; an "action plan" to implement a change or a system enhancement is all that is necessary. Such change should be documented and verified.

Because a warning letter already reflects the fact that the agency has found your previous communication inadequate, it is possible that your response to the warning letter may be your last opportunity to communicate with the agency before it decides to escalate its enforcement posture by seeking either an administrative remedy (e.g., a customer notification) or a judicial remedy (e.g., an injunction). Make sure you are going as far as you can, consistent with resource realities.

Consider whether you should rely only on a written reply. You should consider whether a written response to a warning letter is adequate. Depending on the complexity of the issues underlying the warning letter, or the extent to which the agency has found the company's previous communication to be inadequate, a written response, by itself, may not provide enough assurance that the agency will understand what the company is doing and what positive impact the company expects its actions to have.

There is no reason that a response to a warning letter cannot include a request for a meeting with the appropriate agency officials. If such a request is included in the response to the warning letter, you should call the contact person designated in the warning letter to emphasize the fact that the company is seeking a meeting. When the meeting is set, you need to find effective ways of highlighting the actions you have described in your written response. Your primary "message" at the meeting will be to assure the agency that the necessary short-term fixes and long-term preventive actions are in place, or soon will be, and that there is a reasonable expectation that they will fully address the agency's outstanding concerns. A meeting may be particularly appropriate when your response to the warning letter involves highly technical information or where you have a different perspective on essentially the same information that is before the agency. Such a different perspective may be presented, on your behalf, by an outside expert, independent auditor, or third-party supplier of some goods or services. These same people also can play a valuable role in helping the company assess the appropriateness of its written response to the warning letter in the first instance.

Tell FDA when you expect to get the job done. Once you have submitted a response to a warning letter, it is likely that your response will include timeframes for system enhancements and other quality improvements. You should update the agency regularly on your progress respecting these commitments. It is vitally important that you demonstrate to the agency not only your ability to develop the right action plan, but your ability to achieve your implementation schedule. The agency should never be left too long to guess how you are doing. Whether your updates are in writing or by telephone, make sure the agency knows that you are making progress. Should your efforts reach some snag, such as a delay in the delivery of some piece of equipment needed to achieve one of your improvements, you should consider notifying the agency if that snag is likely to have a significant impact on your plan. Keep the lines of communication open. In addition to communicating your progress to the agency, you should also listen carefully to whatever responses you may get from your contacts with the agency. To communicate effectively, you must listen carefully.

Prepare for FDA scrutiny of your response. Finally, determine as quickly as possible FDA's reaction to your response to the warning letter. Agency officials may be reluctant to provide a lot of information about their assessment of your response. There is no harm, however, in asking. You should be attuned particularly to indications from the agency that it plans to verify your response to a warning letter by a further inspection, product sampling, contacts with suppliers or customers, review of adverse reaction reports, and similar activities. Particularly where your response to the warning letter is an action plan that involves more than one product or more than one facility, the agency may be tempted to verify your commitment by assessing your compliance for that other product or facility.

It is important to remember that a warning letter usually represents the agency's last effort to obtain voluntary compliance from a company. After it has issued a warning letter, FDA believes that it has done everything it can to get a company's attention. Continuing dissatisfaction with a company's performance after the issuance of a warning letter is likely to lead to more aggressive enforcement action. Thus, the response to the warning letter should be viewed as your last clear chance to avoid a confrontation with FDA.

C
H
A
P
T
E
R

16

Douglas B. Farquhar

Hyman, Phelps & McNamara, P.C.

Seizures, Injunctions, and Consent Decrees

I. Introduction

Advising you how to deal with the Food and Drug Administration (FDA) after your products are seized or you are threatened with an injunction or consent decree is like telling you to see the mechanic for a tune-up after your car suffers a breakdown; it is too late to try to create a constructive relationship, and the repairs will be more costly than preventive maintenance would have been.

In theory, any drug or medical device company in the country is subject to any of these civil enforcement actions. A drug or medical device is considered adulterated if it has not been produced in conformance with current good manufacturing practices (cGMPs). No company in the world can function in complete compliance with cGMPs at all times. The government is empowered to institute a seizure by establishing probable cause that drugs or medical devices are adulterated, and to secure a court order (injunction) by showing that a company will distribute adulterated drugs or medical devices in the absence of an injunction. FDA has jurisdiction over any regulated article that is shipped in interstate commerce, is held for shipment in interstate commerce, has traveled in interstate commerce, or contains a component that has traveled in interstate commerce.

Realistically, FDA has jurisdiction over every drug or medical device in the country. It is impossible for companies to function in complete compliance with the law. But, if companies do not function in complete compliance with the law, their products are technically subject to seizure or they can be enjoined from producing further noncompliant goods.

Government regulators maintain that they seek these drastic remedies only when violations of cGMPs or sections of the Federal Food, Drug, and Cosmetic Act (FDCA) pose significant threats to public health or safety, or when other equally alarming consequences could follow in the absence of civil enforcement sanctions. Even for an agency as large as FDA, there is a limit as to how many companies can be litigated against or credibly threatened with civil sanctions. As a result, the numbers of consent decrees entered, seizures instituted, and injunctions sought nationwide are not overwhelming. At a recent FDLI seminar, FDA reported that there were only eleven injunctions entered at the request of the agency in fiscal year 1998, and thirty-five seizures of products. Still, if you are the subject of one of these civil enforcement measures, you and the agency probably have a very different perspective on whether serious violations occurred or enforcement action was warranted.

Your situation is not as completely hopeless as this discussion might indicate. Companies willing to stand up to the agency can be comforted by the fact that, in a disputed proceeding, FDA will be granted permanent powers over a company and/or its goods only if a federal judge is convinced that the agency is entitled to that relief. And federal judges, busy with many matters, do occasionally see the agency as overbearing and unreasonable.

II. A Primer on Civil Enforcement Actions

An explanation of procedures and terms may be helpful.

A. Seizure

Seizure of products occurs when FDA secures a seizure warrant (called a "warrant for arrest of property") from a judge or magistrate in a U.S. federal court. Goods occasionally may be subject to seizure under state laws, pursuant to warrants issued by state courts, but those types of seizures usually are not initiated by FDA and are beyond the scope of this discussion. The agency is required to present a sworn affidavit and other pleadings that establish probable cause that a violation of the FDCA has been committed and that the items produced as "fruit" of those violations will be held or distributed unless a seizure warrant is granted.

You and your company do not have a chance to argue, before a warrant is granted, that the agency is wrong. Indeed, a company is unlikely to have any notice that the agency is seeking the warrant, or that the warrant is about to be executed. Unlike other civil enforcement proceedings, the agency is not required to secure approval of reviewing authorities (e.g., the U.S. Department of Justice's (DOJ's) Office of Consumer Litigation (OCL)) before seeking a seizure warrant. Most warrants are sought based on an affidavit of an inspector with an FDA District Office, with the assistance and approval of an attorney from FDA's Office of Chief Counsel, and with the cooperation of an Assistant U.S. Attorney. The latter may be unfamiliar with the FDCA, and may not be (or may not feel) empowered to challenge the agency's expressed desire to seek a warrant.

Once a warrant is granted (if sought, a warrant almost always will be granted), goods will be seized by U.S. Marshals, accompanied by FDA agents or investigators. Other federal law enforcement agents may participate in the seizure, as well. Once seized, the goods technically are under federal court jurisdiction and cannot be released either to the company or to FDA without a court order. Easily transportable products may be removed by the marshals and placed in a commercial warehouse. If the goods cannot be readily removed (e.g., where the seized goods are large tanks of medical gases), the goods will remain at the company site, secured in some manner to ensure that they are not tampered with or removed.

If you file a claim for the goods, and the goods ultimately are condemned (i.e., a court finds that they were properly seized) and forfeited to the government (i.e., the government can dispose of the goods), you will be held responsible for the government's costs, which include the costs of marshals and FDA personnel seizing and transporting the goods, the storage costs of the goods, FDA's court costs, and any disposal costs.

Once goods are seized, subsequent legal proceedings are a rather archaic series of events based partially on the Rules of Admiralty, which have developed over the last thousand years to resolve maritime disputes over goods or vessels. Extensive discussion of these procedures in this forum would not be particularly helpful; suffice to say that generally companies can continue to manufacture and distribute product if they can do so without disturbing the seized goods. Be aware that, in many seizure cases, FDA seeks to use its leverage to force the owner or manufacturer of the seized goods to enter into a consent decree, which is likely to contain terms that most businesses will find burdensome. A seizure, then, is extremely bad news.

B. Injunctions

Injunctions are even worse news. A seizure of products freezes only the products that are physically seized (i.e., secured or removed by the marshals). An injunction can affect an entire company or, more likely, an entire manufacturing facility.

An injunction is a court order that commands (or enjoins) a company to do something or to stop doing something. FDA can seek injunctions only with the approval of the OCL, a branch of the DOJ located in Washington, D.C. OCL lawyers do, occasionally, reject agency requests to seek injunctions. Once such a request is approved, OCL lawyers, usually working with local investigators, a lawyer from FDA's Office of Chief Counsel, and an Assistant U.S. Attorney in the district where the company plant or warehouse is located, will file a lawsuit in the federal district court with jurisdiction over the facility.

If the agency believes that emergency relief is necessary, and if the evidence supporting the government's case is relatively recent, the government may seek an immediate court order, called a temporary restraining order (TRO). The government also may seek less immediate — but still accelerated — relief, called a preliminary injunction. Except in extremely unusual circumstances, companies will receive advance notice of the government's request, and will be able to argue to a federal judge that the relief should not be granted. Indeed, an Executive Order signed by President Bush in 1991 requires the government, in most circumstances, to contact an affected party in advance of filing litigation in court. You must, however, act very quickly (sometimes, literally within minutes of being notified) to secure legal representation and to notify the judge that you contest the proceeding, if the government seeks a TRO.

The government, in all these cases, seeks a permanent injunction instead of, or in addition to, the temporary or permanent relief. Judges will grant such relief if they are convinced that an injunction is necessary and that the agency has established by a preponderance of the evidence (i.e., that it is more likely than not) that a violation of federal law is occurring and is likely to continue in the absence of a court order.

Injunctions can and usually are extremely burdensome — even fatal, on occasion — to drug, food, and medical device companies. Injunctions usually give FDA the power to inspect your facilities whenever the agency wants, at your expense, and to shut down operations and order the disposal of goods. The agency's power over business normally is subject only to judicial review, and judicial review usually is rendered practically meaningless by the standard of review that the agency will ask the judge to insert in the injunction. Injunctions frequently require immediate shutdown of manufacturing and halt of shipping, until and unless the agency approves of resuming operations. Usually required are a review of operations by independent expert[s] and certification by the expert of substantial cGMP compliance before the agency will approve. In other words, the agency assumes control of your company, and you have to pay FDA to tell you what to do.

When threatened with an injunction, you should not assume that all is as dark as it may seem. If a company chooses to contest a requested injunction, the terms of the injunction will be granted only if a federal judge considering the case determines that the injunction is appropriate; and federal judges generally will grant a fair hearing.

When an injunction is entered, it cannot be ignored or treated lightly. Violation of the terms of a consent decree or an injunction can result in civil or criminal contempt proceedings against companies or individuals named in the lawsuit or acting as agents of the companies.

In almost all cases, negotiations between the government and parties threatened with injunction actions are able to achieve agreement and entry of a court order that is more or less acceptable to all parties. Most cases settle because the government has a great deal of power over companies as proceedings begin; it is too difficult for most companies to face the uncertainty and expense of protracted litigation over these issues. Creditors and investors become nervous about a company that is faced with a pending injunction request. And most companies feel that the agency will move against them in an aggressive and overwhelming manner unless the companies work out an agreement. At any rate, an agreed-upon court order resolving threatened or actual court proceedings is called a consent decree.

C. Consent Decree

A consent decree is simply a court order agreeable to both parties (the company and FDA) and submitted to the court for its approval. Depending on its terms, a consent decree may be permanent or limited; it may be precise or broad; and it may provide only limited judicial review of agency action or it may be silent on that point. Usually, the agency seeks to include specific individual defendants within the coverage of the consent decree. Even individuals who are not named as defendants can be punished — severely, in some cases — if they act as agents of the company and knowingly disobey the consent decree.

III. Plan of Action

A. Hire a Lawyer

If confronted with the prospect of civil enforcement proceedings (seizure, injunction, or consent decree), a company must have a lawyer. Most federal courts do not permit organizations to be represented by anybody but a lawyer. In-house counsel sometimes do not have the experience necessary to deal with agency and DOJ lawyers at the levels involved here. Risking criticism for a self-serving statement, I strongly recommend hiring a lawyer who is familiar with FDA civil enforcement proceedings. If, as is usually the case, the government wants to name individuals as defendants, it may be appropriate to secure independent legal representation for the individuals, as well. Indeed, it is best to hire outside counsel as soon as the company is aware that the agency may be contemplating these types of proceedings, to be as well-prepared as possible.

B. Stand Up for Your Rights

Most regulated companies find it difficult to stand up to FDA when the agency threatens to institute the type of proceedings discussed here. Regulated industries tend to believe that their long-term interests are best served if they can maintain an accommodating and harmonious relationship with their regulators. If the agency believes, however, that seizure, injunction, or consent decree is warranted, the agency is well beyond ascribing to that company any faith, credit, or goodwill. Being nasty with the agency is uncalled for and probably will be counterproductive, and usually it is advisable to see if a mutually acceptable resolution can be achieved. Still, companies are best advised not to simply acquiesce to unreasonable agency demands. The agency frequently seeks much more stringent provisions than a court has ever granted in a contested proceeding. The agency can, and frequently does, back down from insisting on some of its more onerous demands if the company asserts its rights and demonstrates that it is prepared to challenge the agency in court.

C. Retain Outside Experts

In almost all civil enforcement proceedings it is advisable to retain qualified outside experts who are knowledgeable in the field that forms the basis of FDA's contentions. These experts can determine that products are not adulterated, for example, because they were produced in substantial compliance with cGMPs. They can perform independent audits that either confirm or refute FDA's findings about manufacturing or storage practices. They can suggest remedial action plans. Sometimes, companies can live with a consultant's suggested action plan and the plan also is acceptable to FDA, obviating the need for further litigation and stemming the severity of FDA's demands (Sometimes, however, the agency will not consider a proposed action plan until after a consent decree is signed). It can happen that a company will unilaterally institute remedial action plans, leading a judge to determine that court action is unnecessary. It is important that companies secure independent, qualified advice to determine whether significant or health-threatening violations have occurred, and to suggest appropriate measures to address perceived problems.

D. Limit the Scope of Relief

The consent decree that FDA will propose to resolve seizure actions or to preclude or resolve injunction actions usually is very burdensome. Experience has demonstrated that, in most circumstances, the agency will back down on some areas if the company does not capitulate immediately. In seizure cases, try to determine if some products that have been, or are about to be, seized can be released back to the company. For example, recently a drug company avoided the seizure of a particular product when they were able to demonstrate a compelling need for the availability of the drug. In injunction cases, defendants have been able to secure sunset provisions; to limit the scope of the injunction to one site; or to re-open after providing advance notice to FDA, even if FDA does not approve the re-opening in writing.

E. Specific Advice in Seizure Cases

Do not impede law enforcement officers who are serving the seizure warrant, but request to accompany them to carefully document what items they take and to ensure that no safety violations occur. Ask to see credentials, and record the names and agency affiliations of all those who participate in the seizure. Ask for a copy of the seizure warrant. Ask for a copy of the affidavit supporting the seizure warrant; this may or may not be given to you.

Try to have an employee in every area of the facility with the seizing agents. If the agents refuse this accompaniment, indicate to them that you will not try to impede them, but only wish to advise them as to potential threats to their safety (e.g., if dangerous compounds are stored in the area where they will be located) or to the safety of the products or the manufacturing processes (e.g., if sterility or contamination issues may be involved). You also might tell the agents that you may be able to help them determine whether certain items fall within the description of the seized goods contained in the warrant. Try to determine the name or names of the lawyers who are involved from FDA or from the U.S. Attorney's Office, and provide that information to your attorneys as soon as possible.

If goods are secured and sealed at your facility, attempt to verify the accuracy of the inventory that will be made of those goods. Do not touch or disturb the goods under any circumstances. If you believe that the conditions in the location where the goods are seized pose a threat to safety or to the stability of the goods, do not hesitate to convey that message to the law enforcement agents.

If goods are to be removed from your facility, determine where seized goods will be stored, and ensure that relevant environmental conditions (e.g., temperature and humidity) will be adequate at that location.

Sometimes, there are strong reasons *not* to seize drugs or medical devices; threats to the company's financial stability or to continued employment of company workers generally will not be sufficient. Tell the seizing agents these reasons, but do not exaggerate or fabricate the circumstances. (Note: False statements to federal officials can, and sometimes do, result in criminal prosecution.) Factors that militate against seizure may include: that a seized product is required in the manufacturing process (e.g., to clean or purge equipment) and the inability to use that product could create safety hazards; if medical devices or drugs are urgently needed for imminent surgery, and suitable replacements cannot be found in time; or that seizure of an entire inventory of a certain product would deprive patients of vital products for which there will be no available substitutes. Do not be surprised if the seizing agents will not exclude products from seizure without first consulting with lawyers from FDA or the DOJ.

F. Specific Advice in Injunction Cases

It is difficult to provide much guidance for injunction cases because these proceedings will be so heavily dependent on the specific factual circumstances and the allegations presented. Furthermore, legal advice tailored to your situation will be absolutely essential. With those caveats in mind, there are several features that are common to most injunction proceedings.

If the government is seeking immediate relief in the form of a TRO, a firm may have only minutes, or hours at most, to respond, unless the government has presented you, in advance, with a proposed consent decree. The government's request may be filed and assigned to a particular judge, and the news may come immediately before a court hearing that the government is seeking to shut the company down. The hearing may be extremely informal — for example, by conference call with the judge's chambers — and the judge will be expected to make a decision almost instantaneously.

When the judge considers a TRO, he or she will consider the balance of the hardships. If the TRO would cause your company immediate and irreparable damage, that will be a strong factor against granting a TRO, unless the judge is convinced that there is a more serious immediate threat to public health and safety. Another argument that sometimes can be raised by TRO targets is that the government delayed in seeking the TRO; this may be characterized as an indication that there is no threat to public health and safety because, if there was, the agency would have moved much more quickly.

If a TRO is granted, remember that it is only *temporary*. In very unusual cases where notice is not given before the TRO is sought, the TRO will last no more than ten days, and a defendant can move for a quick hearing to convince the judge to revoke the TRO. In most cases, notice is granted before the TRO is sought, and the TRO will be valid until a judge issues a ruling on a request for a preliminary injunction. A preliminary injunction hearing usually will be held within twenty to thirty days after the TRO is granted, or, in the absence of a TRO, within a like amount of time after FDA files for a preliminary injunction.

Many of the same arguments that can be raised against a TRO can be raised against a preliminary injunction. The judge must balance the hardships to your company if a preliminary injunction is granted against the hardships to the public and the agency if the injunction is not issued. If FDA has delayed seeking the injunction, this might indicate that there is no immediate public health or safety threat.

Moreover, before most preliminary injunction proceedings, the company's lawyer will be permitted to take expedited discovery. This could require FDA to turn over the documents on which it bases its case, and also could permit the lawyer[s] to question FDA investigators and experts under oath in deposition proceedings. These discovery tools can be very valuable in revealing weaknesses in the government's case, and in influencing FDA to enter into a consent decree that is not as burdensome as otherwise insisted on by the agency.

Preliminary injunction and permanent injunction proceedings are sometimes merged into one proceeding, under the Federal Rules of Civil Procedure. Company lawyers should examine carefully the relief that FDA is seeking in either a preliminary or permanent injunction, because the agency frequently seeks injunction provisions to which the agency may not be entitled by statutes or by precedent (i.e., prior court decisions).

G. Consent Decrees — Some Basics

The scope of this article does not permit extensive discussion of the many provisions that FDA routinely seeks to include, but may not be entitled to, in consent decrees. However, you and your lawyers should be aware that FDA's first draft of a consent decree submitted for your consideration is not a final document that cannot be altered. Terms are negotiable, and you and your lawyer should keep in mind that one option is to present agreed-upon facts to a federal judge and have the judge determine what consent decree provisions are appropriate. In many cases, it is unlikely that a judge will impose terms as severe as those the agency has sought in a consent decree. Once an item is agreed to in a consent decree, it will be binding; a judge usually cannot and will not alter it. Companies should proceed with caution before agreeing to terms that may become quite burdensome.

Lawyers specializing in this area can make valuable contributions, because they can foresee problems that others may not. For instance, sometimes the agency insists that a company shut down operations and requires a consent decree provision that the company will not recommence manufacturing until FDA has re-inspected the premises and issued written approval. In those cases, your lawyer may be able to secure commitments from federal lawyers that they will intercede, if necessary, to encourage FDA to schedule re-inspections expeditiously. Occasionally, companies have secured prompt re-inspections only through the use of this influence.

IV. Conclusion

If you are faced with an imminent seizure, injunction, or consent decree, do not panic, but do take the matter seriously, and try to ensure that health, safety, and product integrity are protected until you can get professional outside help.

Steven M. Kowal

Bell, Boyd & Lloyd

CHAPTER 17

Criminal Investigations

I. Introduction

Executives who manage companies under the Food and Drug Administration's (FDA's) jurisdiction generally have fairly predictable reactions to a discussion of the government's criminal enforcement activity. Some assume that prosecution is directed only against the "bad actors" of the industry and conclude it will never happen to them. Others are shocked they could be the target of such an investigation, and implement policies and procedures to enhance compliance and prepare for the possibility that government agents will arrive at the door. In the current environment, it is the latter who are more likely to avoid, or survive, an investigation.

FDA possesses substantial criminal enforcement power and authority. This includes the "responsible relation" theory that was articulated in the *Park* and *Dotterweich* decisions, and can result in a type of strict criminal liability for companies and individuals in misdemeanor cases. It extends to more serious felony charges related to conduct that was based on an intent to defraud or mislead. But prosecution is not limited to the criminal provisions of the Federal Food, Drug, and Cosmetic Act (FDCA). Many felony cases also allege violations of general criminal statutes such as mail and wire fraud, false statement, and conspiracy.

The exercise of this enforcement power has changed over time. Until the late 1980s, most FDA criminal cases were misdemeanors, often focusing on insanitary conditions in food warehouses. The disclosures and revelations of the generic drug scandal, however, altered FDA's enforcement direction, and since then most cases have involved felony charges. Also, this era spawned a new office of experienced criminal investigators, who ensure a continuing agency emphasis on felony prosecution.

This chapter is not conceived as a general description of substantive criminal law and FDA's enforcement power and program. Rather, it is intended to focus on the less formal, but equally important, area of dealing with the government during a criminal investigation. These communications, if handled properly, can reduce the burden that will be imposed and can, in certain instances, persuade the government to terminate the investigation and decline prosecution.

Communications with the government during a criminal investigation are fundamentally different from most regulatory, compliance, and administrative matters. First, the government's players are different. Those being investigated will have very little contact with FDA. The investigation will be conducted and the decision to prosecute will be made by lawyers in the Department of Justice (DOJ) — usually from the Office of Consumer Litigation (OCL), which somewhat paradoxically is in the Civil Division. Although FDA's Office of General Counsel will be involved, and FDA investigators will do much of the leg work, the crucial decisions will be made by DOJ.

Second, unlike many other types of communication with FDA, there is a substantial adversarial component. The government possesses extensive investigative power that will be exercised aggressively. Dealing with the government in this environment, and protecting the rights of those under investigation, often requires opposition or a negative response to the government's exercise of that authority. This is not an example of "partnering" with the government.

Third, communications designed to reduce the impact of a criminal investigation should not be confined to the government. Corporate managers and employees must understand their legal rights and obligations. The government will employ investigative techniques that could confront individuals with the need to make immediate decisions on important issues without the assistance of legal counsel. Uncertainty often results in acquiescence — a decision that could increase the risk of prosecution for both the company and the individual. Preparation is the only effective response to this type of encounter. In many instances, the most important communication concerning a criminal investigation occurs within a company, long before there is any reason to suspect an investigation has been commenced.

Thus, this chapter will focus on the different types of communications related to a criminal investigation. Some will be directed to the government, while others will be internal and intended for a company's managers and employees.

II. Communication With the Investigators

A decade ago, the investigation of suspected criminal conduct was relatively straightforward. Most cases were misdemeanors, and the agents' observations and the documents gathered during an administrative inspection usually were enough to support a case. The relatively few cases that involved more complex situations — and possibly felony charges — were investigated through a grand jury with an FDA inspector assigned as case agent.

This structure permitted effective communication through the local FDA District Office. A company under investigation could use the same approach as that employed in responding to Form 483 Inspectional Observations. There was some possibility, at least, of relatively open discussion during the investigative stage.

This case development pattern was fundamentally altered by the extensive series of investigations related to the generic drug industry. FDA's emphasis shifted from misdemeanor to felony prosecution. Inevitably this involved complex factual inquiry relating to proof of surreptitious conduct and fraudulent intent.

FDA's change in enforcement philosophy caused it to reevaluate its investigative procedures. Although the government compiled an impressive series of successes in the generic drug cases, some in FDA believed there was a need for an office comprised of experienced criminal investigators who would concentrate only on the development of cases for prosecution. The Office of Criminal Investigations (OCI) emerged from this perceived need for greater expertise. The office was conceived as a specialized investigative unit composed of experienced investigators; it is charged with responsibility to investigate suspected criminal violations of all statutes administered by FDA.

OCI became operational in 1992. It was assembled from investigators drawn from numerous governmental agencies (e.g., the Federal Bureau of Investigation, the Customs Service, and the Drug Enforcement Administration), and operates as a relatively autonomous unit. Currently, there are approximately 130 agents dispersed in six regional offices. These offices do not report to either FDA district or regional offices. Rather, OCI reports directly to the Associate Commissioner for Regulatory Affairs.

FDA's redirection of criminal investigations to OCI also has substantially altered the response of a potential target. There no longer is any prospect of effective communication through the local FDA district office. Any discussion of the issues must be directed either to the agent conducting the investigation or to a supervising attorney. Telephone calls should be documented in immediate follow-up letters. This will help to eliminate confusion over agreements and commitments, and will produce a paper trail if the course of communications needs to be reconstructed for a court. It is best to maintain a courteous and professional relationship while complying with all legal obligations, but note that volunteered assistance that streamlines the government's job seldom results in avoidance of a charge.

Experience demonstrates that OCI agents often will not be very responsive to direct communication. If issues arise that are not addressed promptly, then communications should be directed to the attorney in charge of the investigation — who might be more concerned with the potential reaction of a judge in the event of litigation. Also, it is inevitable that OCI agents will employ investigative methods that are far more intrusive than would have been the case a decade ago. An effective response requires preparation.

III. Investigation and Effective Preparation

Investigations by FDA of potential violations have moved far beyond the traditional issuance of grand jury subpoenas. Now, there is a substantial possibility that the government will conduct a covert investigation, and rely on cooperating insiders and informants to provide information and perhaps record conversations with corporate representatives. Also, the government will pursue "surprise" interviews of managers and employees, and has begun to execute search warrants in a significant number of investigations. Both of these methods are employed at the very beginning of the overt stage of the investigation, and often before the company has an opportunity to consult with legal counsel. A company's preparation and communication of legal rights and responsibilities to employees could be critical, and may be the only really effective response.

A. Surprise Interviews

Interviews of potential targets are pursued actively. Executives often are confronted by prosecutors and agents who arrive without prior arrangement, earnestly solicit cooperation, and request answers to "a few questions." These encounters usually are timed to reduce the possibility that legal counsel will be available, and to frustrate consultation with business colleagues. In some instances, the executive will be contacted in the office during normal business hours. More often, however, the agents will arrive at the executive's home during the evening or on a weekend.

Immediate interviews provide the government with enormous psychological advantages. The executive will be caught by surprise but usually will feel some pressure to cooperate and be responsive. There will not be an opportunity for preparation or reflection, which is most important if the questions focus on activity that has faded in the executive's memory, or was not deemed very significant when it occurred. These advantages are multiplied if the interview occurs in the executive's home with the family present. Questions about the business life of the executive, particularly if criminal violations are asserted or implied, likely will cause embarrassment and humiliation. Unfortunately, this pressure can result in answers that are ill-considered and that later can be construed as incriminating or misleading.

Perhaps most significantly, the executive will almost certainly be required to deal with the government agents without the benefit of legal counsel. Few caught in this situation, however, understand their legal rights and obligations, or the scope of the government's power and authority. Ignorance breeds uncertainty, which the government can exploit to obtain answers that ordinarily might not be forthcoming.

The agents also might try to persuade the witness to sign a statement or affidavit, which will be prepared to support the government's case. A variety of techniques will be used to attempt to overcome any reluctance.

Perhaps the best defense response to the possibility of a surprise interview is preparation and a corporate educational program. Most companies prepare manuals for management and statements of internal policy and recommended procedure. These documents should include a section discussing direct government inquiries. Executives must be informed that such contacts are possible — many will assume mistakenly that the corporation insulates them from such direct communication — and that they can occur almost anywhere and at anytime. A description of the government's investigative tactics and techniques also should be included. It is imperative that corporate representatives understand that the information conveyed during an interview can be used later against the company and the executive individually at a trial. The executive's statements are not "off the record." Some who are interviewed mistakenly conclude that the information cannot be used in a legal proceeding because of the informal nature of the meeting.

This information and the procedures to be followed should be included in the description of the response to an FDA regulatory inspection. Also, the information could be summarized on a wallet-sized card that the executive could carry for ready reference. At the very least, the following points should be conveyed:

Executive's Rights and Obligations

- Interview is entirely voluntary.
- Each person can decide to consent, decline or postpone the interview.
- If commenced, the interview can be terminated at any time.
- The interview cannot be compelled.
- There is no legal obligation to sign any statement or affirm the accuracy of any recitation.
- Any information provided must be accurate and truthful.
- The witness should not guess or speculate.
- No matter what is said by the government, the interview will not be "off the record."

Government's Power and Authority

- Interviews can be sought anywhere and at any time.
- A subpoena cannot be used to compel interviews.
- A search warrant cannot be used to compel interviews.
- The government can and will use any information provided against the individual, and perhaps against a corporation in a criminal proceeding.
- Agents do not have authority to bind the government with promises of immunity or leniency.

If executives are armed with this information, then at least they will not acquiesce in the government's demands merely because they are uncertain of the types of responses that are legally appropriate.

B. Execution of Search Warrants

In a typical investigation of potentially criminal business conduct, such as that initiated by FDA, the use of a search warrant is unusual and probably unnecessary. The search warrant procedure, however, sends a very strong message that, in essence, FDA intends to treat the suspected activity in the same manner as more traditional forms of criminal conduct. It has been stated that the use of a search warrant in a white collar criminal case is the "corporate equivalent of throwing the suspect against the wall."

The use of a search warrant in the early stages of an investigation accords the government significant advantages. It allows the immediate seizure of documents when a grand jury subpoena might not secure full compliance for several months. It entitles the agents to enter the facility without warning, and provides them an opportunity to attempt to interview managers and employees before legal counsel has been secured. Also, it provides justification to seize product that is believed to be in violation of the FDCA. This seizure has the same effect as one that is carried out under a civil seizure complaint, but without any of the usual judicial or litigation safeguards.

A warrant almost always is executed without warning. Management will be required to respond instantly to this unique challenge. The agents will not wait until senior management and attorneys are consulted, and it may be difficult to locate an attorney on short notice who is familiar with a search warrant and the related criminal law. In most instances, management officials will be required to respond without the benefit of outside guidance and assistance. This is a situation that invites acquiescence to government activity that could have significant ramifications.

The level of anxiety and confusion can be reduced somewhat if company officials can consult written guidelines. Most companies have prepared procedures for their response to an FDA inspection. These procedures could be expanded to encompass the execution of a search warrant.

Company procedures in the event of a search warrant should address the following points:

- Review the warrant carefully to identify the areas the agents are authorized to enter.

- Contact senior management and in-house attorneys immediately.

- Monitor the activity of the agents closely, but do not hinder, impede, assist, explain, or answer questions.

- Interviews are voluntary and there is no legal obligation to sign statements or affidavits.

- Send home nonessential employees.

- Discuss a reduction in the disruption to the company with the government's team leader.

- Prepare a specific inventory of the documents and items seized, to supplement the general inventory that will be provided by the government.

- Debrief all corporate representatives who have been involved in the search immediately after its conclusion.

- Consider contacting a public relations firm in the event of public disclosure of the execution of the warrant.

- Identify a criminal lawyer who can be contacted to help during the course of the execution of the warrant.

Written procedures that can be consulted in the event a search warrant is executed may reduce some of the harsher effects and help sustain the company. They also can direct activity that will provide a foundation for whatever attempt is made to gain access to, and perhaps the return of, the items that are seized.

IV. Pre-Indictment Discussions With the Government

Throughout the investigation, defense attorneys should pursue a dialog with prosecutors and agents. These discussions, which usually are informal and impromptu, can reveal the direction of the investigation, the potential targets, and the evidence that supports a possible charge. In many instances, this discussion should benefit both sides. If the case is strong, the defense might decide to seek an early and favorable resolution. Conversely, if the premise of the investigation is wrong, then perhaps it could be terminated efficiently and economically — and with a minimum of anxiety for those who might be targeted.

Often, however, this dialog does not occur, or it might not be pursued effectively by defense counsel. Frequently, it is rebuffed by the prosecutor, who fears that early disclosure could result in obstruction of the investigation.

This concern is reduced substantially once the investigation has been completed. The government usually is willing to talk before an indictment is returned, and a target potentially can participate in a series of meetings — with the government's staff attorneys, supervisory attorneys in the DOJ's Office of Consumer Litigation (OCL), possibly a member of the Office of the Assistant Attorney General, and perhaps even the U.S. Attorney for the district where the case will be brought.

Each of these meetings should be pursued vigorously. They provide an opportunity to persuade the government to drop the case or narrow the charges. At the very least, the possibility of an acceptable resolution can be explored. Experience indicates that the supervisory attorneys in the OCL usually are willing to consider reasonable arguments. This is not necessarily the case with all branches of the DOJ. We have represented several companies and individuals in FDA cases who were fortunate enough to terminate investigations at this stage.

Benefits can be derived from the process of preparing for these meetings. The available information can be reviewed in context, and the viability of a defense can be assessed realistically. If there is little to be said, then perhaps the meetings should turn to plea negotiations.

The initial meeting will be with the government's investigative staff of lawyers and agents. Usually, this will be a relatively informal discussion of the evidence and other relevant issues. The staff's recommendation is important. If they conclude the case is not prosecutable, then it probably will be closed. Even if the case is not dropped, the staff might include defense arguments in the memorandum recommending an indictment.

The meeting with supervisory attorneys in the OCL is much more formal. By this time, the staff's written recommendation will have been reviewed, and there is at least a tentative decision to proceed with the prosecution. Obviously, at this point it is an uphill battle, but certainly worth fighting. There probably should be separate presentations for each targeted company or individual. Serious consideration should be given to a written presentation that should be delivered to the government a few days prior to the meeting. This will enhance the government's understanding of the defense arguments. Particularly relevant documents should be attached — although some caution should be exercised if the disclosure includes material protected by the attorney/client or work product privileges. Despite the government's contrary agreement, a court could determine later that this disclosure constituted a waiver of the privilege and could order production of the material to plaintiffs in civil litigation.

Whatever the specific focus of the investigation is, there are several general considerations for these meetings:

- Candor is important. Do not lose credibility by misrepresenting evidence or overstating a position.

- Discuss legal deficiencies in the government's theory. Some unsavory conduct simply is not a crime.

- Highlight factual weaknesses. This works better if there is a failure of proof on an issue rather than a credibility contest between witnesses.

- Demonstrate that the sentence for conviction will be light. Sometimes the "bang" to be produced does not justify the expenditure of the government's buck.

- Document and discuss extraordinary personal or family problems. Perhaps this is not supposed to make a difference, but government lawyers are people too.

- Stress inequitable treatment. If similar conduct by a competitor brought only a warning letter, then perhaps prosecutorial discretion could be exercised more evenhandedly.

Just as these factors should be considered for every pre-indictment meeting, there are several things that should never be done:

- Do not bring your client. Invariably, the client will say or do something that makes the case worse.

- Do not try to intimidate or insult government lawyers. Telling them how badly you will beat them at trial will not redound to your client's benefit.

- Do not blame the government agents for the client's problems. Even if this is true — and in some instances it is — it might force the government to proceed aggressively to vindicate the conduct of its agents.

- Do not bring an army of lawyers for each client. Somehow, the persuasive force of the argument seems to be inversely proportional to the number of defense lawyers who attend the meeting but say nothing.

If the government is unmoved by the force of the defense argument, then some attempt should be made to determine the outline of a potential negotiated plea. This type of resolution may not be possible, but certainly it is something a client should know and understand before an indictment is returned. If nothing else, it conveys graphically what is at stake in the litigation.

V.   What About Section 305 Hearings?

Although they have not been used frequently over the course of the last decade, section 305 hearings are not yet extinct. It is possible that you may have to deal with this precursor to a criminal prosecution. Section 305 of the FDCA provides that a potential target "shall" be given an opportunity to attempt to persuade FDA not to pursue a criminal investigation. This provision recognizes that an investigation — even without a prosecution — can devastate a company or an individual. Unfortunately, the Supreme Court has watered down this minimal protection. In *Dotterweich,* the Court held that a notice under section 305 of potential charges is not a criminal case. FDA usually conducts a 305 hearing when it is considering a misdemeanor prosecution. The hearing itself is quite informal and can follow several different patterns at the discretion of the respondent. Information can be submitted orally or in writing, and either form can be accompanied by exhibits. If the presentation is oral, consideration should be given to the preparation of a stenographic transcript. If one is not prepared, the hearing officer will prepare a Record of Hearing from the notes taken during the presentation.

The 305 hearing response should be made by an attorney on behalf of the respondent. A direct presentation by the respondent could result in an inadvertent waiver of the Fifth Amendment privilege against self-incrimination that would adversely affect the future defense strategy.

The respondent should be mindful of the various levels of review in FDA, and the 305 hearing presentation should include arguments for those levels. There can be technical arguments intended for the District Office and the appropriate FDA Center; policy arguments intended for the Commissioner's Office; and legal arguments intended for the lawyers in FDA's Office of General Counsel. Based on the government's own investigation and the information presented at the hearing, a decision will be made as to whether the matter should be referred to the DOJ for prosecution.

The traditional response to a section 305 hearing notice has been a full and complete exposition of the facts, circumstances, and beliefs relating to each specification on FDA's charge sheet. It was hoped that this type of response would be most effective in dissuading the government from prosecution; presumably, if those named in the notice did nothing wrong, then they have nothing to hide. Under this approach, the more complete the disclosure, the better the possibility that the government would conclude a prosecution was not warranted.

On many occasions, this approach succeeded in averting a prosecution. One commentator has stated, however, that approximately eighty percent of all section 305 hearing notices result in a referral to the DOJ. In those instances when FDA decided that a criminal case should be pursued, a substantial problem was created. The government had received at least a preview, or perhaps a complete presentation, of the defense case

— and this occurred even before the government had initiated its formal investigation. The government is thus afforded a substantial advantage; it can seek information during its investigation not only to support its own case, but to undermine the defense theory. It can alter the eventual charge to delete those that are weak or ill-considered, and hone its case to strike at the most vulnerable and least-defensible activity. In essence, the government has the advantage of knowing the full defense theory, even before it must commit to a formal theory of prosecution.

The response to a section 305 hearing notice should be considered in light of the reasonable prospects of success at that stage and the government's more aggressive prosecutorial approach. Certainly, there are instances where an issue of technology must be resolved or the feasibility of particular conduct is in question. These decisions clearly benefit from a complete presentation of the facts and information that tends to refute the government's belief. There would be no reason to withhold information at an early stage only to demonstrate to the government at trial that its case was premised on an assertion of fact that could be demonstrated conclusively to be erroneous.

If, however, the defense presentation at the hearing relies on arguments concerning the weight that should be given to the evidence, issues of credibility, or the state of mind or motivation of particular actors, then perhaps it would be better not to present this information. In essence, these types of arguments invite the government to decline prosecution where there is probable cause to believe some violation has occurred, and this invitation depends on an acceptance of defense information that probably conflicts with the inferences the government seeks to draw from the evidence. This is the type of fact-oriented decision that is usually relegated to a jury for determination, and it seldom persuades the government to terminate the investigation. A full presentation of this type of defense evidence is unlikely to accomplish anything more than an early disclosure to the prosecution.

This is not to say that no defense presentation should be made. Information can be presented to demonstrate that an individual did not exercise responsibility for certain activity, or that social, family, and financial considerations should be considered as mitigating factors. A company can present evidence of its compliance policies that were disregarded by the allegedly offensive conduct, its exemplary history of regulatory compliance and cooperation with FDA, and its adherence to industry standards. Essentially, mitigating information that does not require the government to weigh evidence or engage in credibility decisions should be presented.

VI. Conclusion

Communication during a criminal investigation is not open and unfettered — it is adversarial. Nevertheless, there are opportunities throughout the process when effective communication can reduce the effects of the investigation and perhaps persuade the government to terminate its inquiry. Conversely, ill-advised communication can generate evidence that the government might not have obtained otherwise, and fuel the prosecution.

Anthony C. Celeste

AAC Consulting Group Inc.

CHAPTER 18

How to Prepare for an FDA Inspection

I. Introduction

The arrival of a Food and Drug Administration (FDA) investigator is, for some, a very intimidating experience. It has been compared to the same trauma one may go through when undergoing an Internal Revenue Service tax audit. The inspection can be much less traumatic if the facility and its personnel are properly prepared for the inspection and the investigator. There are many things that can be done to prepare for the inspection that will minimize trauma, disruption, and any misunderstandings by the investigator during the inspection. Some of these may be obvious, while others may be just common sense. Undergoing an inspection is, however, the surest way to gain helpful experiences in making preparations.

Under a pilot program, except for food and blood products, all FDA routine inspections are pre-announced. A firm's initial awareness of an inspection will come via a telephone call from an agency representative — usually an investigator from a local district office — with the information that FDA has scheduled an inspection of the establishment. The caller generally will give a firm about five days' advance notice of the actual inspection, explain what areas are to be covered, estimate how long the inspection may last, and advise as to the number of inspection team members. The agency also may request the presence or availability of specific individuals, records, and documents. It is important to recognize that this advance notice will be the norm for almost all pre-approval inspections and good manufacturing practice (GMP) inspections. This effectively works to the firm's benefit in planning and scheduling for an FDA inspection.

While this program provides prior notice of an FDA inspection, firms with compliance problems certainly will not be able to change their situation before the arrival of FDA, five days after the notification. For those firms that are prepared, however, the notification can facilitate the inspection and make it much less time consuming and imposing.

II. Preliminary Preparation

FDA investigators are considered the "eyes and ears" of the agency. In years past, many FDA investigators were considered "generalists." In today's highly scientific and technical world of medical devices, pharmaceuticals, biologics, and computer-run systems, many investigators have specialized earlier in their FDA careers.

The agency continues to use some basic tools to provide inspection and program uniformity in carrying out its various compliance programs. It is critical for the industry to prepare for FDA, and understand the standards under which it will be inspected. In this regard it is important for an establishment to know where it fits in the FDA enforcement and inspection programs. The establishment should be cognizant of all the programs, guidances, and regulations that are applicable to its products and to the manufacturing procedures utilized to market those products.

There are many sources of information available to assist a firm in determining the areas that a FDA investigator will be covering. It is important for a company to have copies of the programs and guidance that will be used by FDA and to utilize these documents to set the standards under which the facility will operate. These documents should be used to develop and implement training programs for the responsible personnel, to develop and implement internal auditing programs by the quality unit, and to measure how well one is complying with the FDA requirements.

Although an entire book could be written on the FDA material available to the industry, some of the more significant ones will be highlighted here.

FDA Compliance Program Guidance Manual

Prepared by headquarters offices, this manual is the field compliance/enforcement instruction and work planning guidance document. It provides a uniform and convenient system of categorizing the various FDA field-related program activities. These programs provide guidance to the FDA field offices in the various industry/product categories. Each program usually includes a description of the problem or activity, information to be gathered or issue(s) to be addressed, and guidance to the investigator on how to conduct the inspection. Also discussed, if appropriate, is the process of sample collection and guidance to laboratories on the analysis of samples that includes a reference to the method of analysis and regulatory guidance on the actions to be taken as a result of the program activities. This manual provides a great deal of insight into the FDA inspection and enforcement process.

FDA Investigations Operations Manual

Designed to provide to investigators national standard operating procedures on how to conduct day-to-day business, this manual is a basic tool for personnel in the practical aspects of conducting inspections and investigations for foods, cosmetics, human drugs, biologics, veterinary medicine, medical devices, and radiological health. Because this manual provides FDA investigators with overall policy and procedures on how to conduct inspections, it is important for any establishment that will be inspected by FDA to become familiar with its contents. It will provide the inspected facility with information on how the investigator must conduct him/herself during an inspection. The chapters on specific establishment inspections and inspection methods provide valuable insight into what the investigator will be covering during the inspection. This information is essential in preparing your establishment for an FDA inspection.

FDA Compliance Policy Guides

FDA has been publishing compliance policy statements in one form or another since it came into existence. The current manual and format were instituted in 1968, and represent an orderly method for assembling and maintaining statements of FDA policy. This manual should be reviewed to determine FDA policy on the processes, systems, and equipment utilized, as well as the products manufactured in an establishment. By doing this, management can prepare themselves for an inspection by determining if the products they manufacture are complying with agency expectations.

Code of Federal Regulations — Title 21

An establishment cannot be prepared for an FDA inspection if it does not know and understand the FDA requirements and standards for compliance. Each regulated establishment should have a system in place that requires responsible individuals to know what sections of title 21 of the *Code of Federal Regulations* apply to their facility and the products that are manufactured, processed, packed, or stored there. This information, along with other guidance, should be used for the development and execution of internal quality programs.

FDA Inspection Guides

FDA has published specific inspection guides for distribution to its field staff. They cover a number of technical areas and are used by FDA investigators during inspections of the areas that are addressed in the guide. For example, the "Guide to the Inspection of High Purity Water Systems" provides significant and substantial information on FDA's expectations concerning the installation, validation, and performance of such systems. Other guides are more general, such as the "Guide to the Inspections of Pharmaceutical Quality Control Laboratories." The inspection guides, which pertain to the establishment to be inspected, should be made available to personnel who will be involved in the inspection. They can use this information, along with other material, to prepare for FDA.

This listing represents only a fraction of the available guidance from FDA. Firms should require that any establishment that will be inspected by FDA should gather and use all the applicable FDA regulations and guidance in preparation for an inspection.

III. Establishment of Internal Procedures

A. Audit Program

In FDA-regulated industries it can be argued that internal audit programs are current good practice. Companies should include in this process a review of all previous FDA inspections and internal audits; the findings from these inspections and audits should be checked when conducting internal audits. Action plans and corrections of previous deficiencies should be evaluated. The program can be used to assure facility and upper management that they are in compliance and are ready for an FDA inspection.

Auditing programs should take into account corporate quality standards in addition to regulatory requirements. In the food industry, the term "quality assurance" generally implies conformity with commercial quality or grade. The term "safety assurance" generally means a more rigorous quality system is required. In the medical products industries, quality assurance is associated with much broader prevention systems to ensure product effectiveness, safety, and conformity with all procedures and specifications. FDA is most concerned with compliance with agency rules, which are tailored to each of the industries regulated.

Do internal audits make a difference? Most companies that have trouble with approvals, and those faced with enforcement actions, have badly flawed audit programs or no programs at all. Rehabilitation programs implemented by some firms to achieve compliance after FDA inspection(s) are far more costly than maintaining a quality system that includes an effective internal audit component.

Audit findings need to be supported by facts, and the site audited must be given the opportunity to respond to any deficiencies observed. Operational managers and their staffs generally have both a good understanding of the rules and policies that govern their operations and, technical knowledge superior to that of the auditor. The auditors bring different perspective or "outside eyes" to an operation, and they should be expected to probe systems and question whether they are functioning as designed.

Occasionally, an FDA manager may be heard to say that corporate audit programs should be patterned after the FDA inspection program. In fact, corporate programs should be superior in many respects to the FDA inspection program. Because of its law enforcement responsibilities, FDA cannot engage in the sort of partnership that is necessary for a successful internal program. Corporate audits should be more efficiently managed, as to frequency and depth of scrutiny, because the audit staff has one "master" to serve rather than the White House, Congress, consumer groups, etc., as does FDA. FDA investigators often are required to cover a number of industries and processes, and have developed skills in performing their inspections. By design, however, the investigators generally do not have in-depth technical knowledge or expertise about a firm's internal system. Corporate auditors may be selected from personnel with superior technical skills relating to the corporations' functions, and these auditors also should be able to access company information more easily. Audit follow-up and problem solving should be better focused and more timely when legal constraints are removed.

Routine internal audit reports should be provided to the management of the units audited, and assistance should be provided, if necessary, for those managers to develop corrective action plans. Should there be an irresolvable disagreement between a site and the corporate audit group, the manager of the operating division (not the audit group) should elevate the issue to corporate management.

Audit groups need to be kept informed of all decisions relating to their findings so they might effectively monitor corrective actions. An audit group would report a specific issue to executive management only if it believes an uncorrected finding presents a potential liability for the company and/or the division has inappropriately represented the matter to management. In such an instance, the division should be informed in advance of the audit group's decision to make a report.

The primary objective of an audit program must be broadly understood by all parties, as it is a system to work together to identify areas for improvement (rather than finding fault or engaging in autocratic criticism). Corporate auditors should be viewed as staff available to help line managers do their jobs better. The audit group should be an extension of executive management leadership and should not diminish the responsibility and authority of division managers. Based on our survey, we believe some companies may need to rethink their approach to auditing to ensure that their programs function in a cooperative, constructive manner and remain viable.

B. Company Policies and Procedures for the Handling of FDA Inspections

A number of significant areas must be addressed when developing a policy on how to handle FDA inspections. Many of these require company decisions at the highest management levels, and not too infrequently these decisions should involve corporate or outside legal counsel. Some of the more controversial and significant questions to answer before the arrival of the investigator are:

- Who should greet the investigator?
- Who should be notified of the investigator's arrival?
- Who should accompany the investigator during the inspection?
- Where will the investigator be provided space to work?
- What employees will the investigator be allowed to speak with, and who will answer their questions?
- What is your policy on the taking of photographs in the plant during the inspection?
- Will anyone be assigned to keep notes during the inspection, and will they be required to provide daily reports?
- If the investigator collects samples, will you also collect equivalent samples?
- Will you charge the agency for the samples they collect, and at what rate?
- What is your policy regarding internal audits? Will you provide copies?

Individuals and organizations responsible for dealing with FDA investigators also should be provided with the same information that is available to the investigators so that they are as fully prepared as possible for the inspection. This information should include:

- The company's standard operating procedures for handling FDA inspections.
- Appropriate sections of the *FDA Inspection Operations Manual*. This will provide the facility with information on how the investigator should conduct her/himself during the inspection.
- The particular Compliance Program that covers the program area for which the investigator may be conducting the inspection. For example: the pre-approval programs (for drugs, devices, and veterinary medicine) provide guidance on the areas FDA will cover during these inspections; the drug quality assurance programs (for finished pharmaceuticals, bulk drugs, and sterile drugs) cover the type of products manufactured; and the compliance programs in the bioresearch monitoring area provide substantial guidance on the significant issues on which FDA investigators will focus.
- If available, copies of previous inspection reports and FDA-483s (notice of observation forms from prior inspections), and company responses thereto, should be included and reviewed.
- All applicable FDA reference documents.

It is extremely important that FDA inspections proceed as smoothly as possible with a minimum of disruption and delay for both the company and the investigators. If company representatives are well-prepared for the inspection, understand the investigators' role, and are familiar with both company and agency policies, they will get the inspection off on the right foot. This, in turn, will allow the inspection to proceed efficiently.

IV. Summary

Undergoing an FDA inspection can be a harrowing experience for company management and personnel. It is therefore appropriate to be as ready as possible. If your establishment is so fortunate as to be provided with advance notice that an inspection is scheduled, you have the opportunity to alert the staff and perhaps gather up in one place significant documents and files that the investigator may need to conduct his/her inspection. All of the techniques discussed above should be utilized to prepare the establishment for FDA. Because you may not know when FDA will be arriving, it is critical that facilities adhere to a policy to always be prepared.

The following "Draft Corporation FDA Inspection Policies and Procedures" is provided as a model for establishing uniform policies and procedures for handling FDA inspections. It should be modified to incorporate company policy and handle any variations necessary.

CORPORATION FDA INSPECTION POLICIES AND PROCEDURES

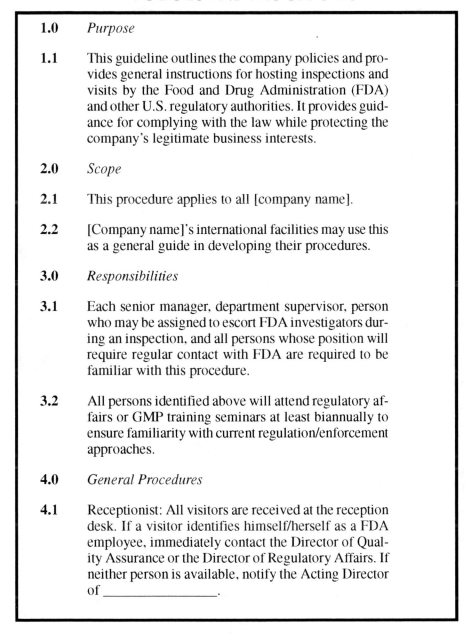

1.0   *Purpose*

1.1   This guideline outlines the company policies and provides general instructions for hosting inspections and visits by the Food and Drug Administration (FDA) and other U.S. regulatory authorities. It provides guidance for complying with the law while protecting the company's legitimate business interests.

2.0   *Scope*

2.1   This procedure applies to all [company name].

2.2   [Company name]'s international facilities may use this as a general guide in developing their procedures.

3.0   *Responsibilities*

3.1   Each senior manager, department supervisor, person who may be assigned to escort FDA investigators during an inspection, and all persons whose position will require regular contact with FDA are required to be familiar with this procedure.

3.2   All persons identified above will attend regulatory affairs or GMP training seminars at least biannually to ensure familiarity with current regulation/enforcement approaches.

4.0   *General Procedures*

4.1   Receptionist: All visitors are received at the reception desk. If a visitor identifies himself/herself as a FDA employee, immediately contact the Director of Quality Assurance or the Director of Regulatory Affairs. If neither person is available, notify the Acting Director of _____.

4.2 The receiving company official will ask about the purpose of the visit, examine the investigator's credentials (to see they are not expired), record the investigator's name, credential or badge number, and the stated purpose of the visit.

4.3 If the visit is for inspection of the facility, the investigator(s) will issue a Notice of Inspection (form FD-482).

4.4 If a Notice of Inspection is issued, notify investigators of the company Policy Statement (see below) and provide them a copy of same.

4.5 After determining why the investigators have come, notify the company legal counsel of their presence, stated purpose, and whether or not a FD-482 was issued. Company legal counsel will be available for consultation during the inspection should this be required.

4.6 Discuss the reason for the visit so appropriate areas, records, and perhaps persons can be made available.

4.7 If the visit is to extend more than three days, explore the possibility of an agenda to facilitate the availability of the appropriate personnel during the visit.

4.8 An escort will be designated to accompany the investigators during the entire visit. Should the visit consist of an inspection team (more than one person), additional escorts will be assigned to ensure that no member of the FDA team is without an escort while on the premises.

4.9 Request that investigator(s) direct all questions to the escort(s).

4.10 If it is necessary for more than one escort to accompany the FDA team, a lead escort will be designated.

5.0 *Duties of the Company Escorts*

FDA Investigators sometimes wish to interview operational employees to determine whether training is effective or whether a procedure is being followed properly. This is an area that escorts should be prepared to forthrightly discuss with the investigator. Because operators frequently have limited responsibilities, they may not appear responsive. Also, a government investigator intimidates some employees to the extent that they appear halting or not fully aware of their responsibilities. When the escort or management concludes that employee interviews are necessary, it may be helpful if they ensure that employees have applicable written procedures in-hand for ready reference.

5.1 The company escort(s) will accompany the FDA investigator/team during the entire period of time they are on site.

5.2 Answer questions to the extent the escort is knowledgeable.

5.3 Decide whether other company personnel should interact with the FDA investigators.

5.4 Take detailed notes during the visit.

5.5 Make a detailed listing and, if necessary, copies of all documents reviewed by FDA.

5.6 Keep track of items that require follow-up during the inspection.

5.7 Release a single copy of documents to the FDA team, after ascertaining that the provisions of policy regarding release of documents have been complied with.

5.8 Record a complete description (including lot number) of any finished product collected as a sample during the inspection. Report if the sample was randomly collected or the investigator sought a particular lot. If a component or in-process material is to be collected during an inspection, an identical sample should be collected by the company at the same time.

5.9 Seek counsel with senior management and/or legal counsel if sensitive or unusual matters arise or if there is a conflict between the FDA investigation(s) and the company's Policy Statement.

6.0 *Discussions and Personal Decorum*

6.1 Display a positive attitude, and be cooperative within the bounds of this SOP.

6.2 Avoid conflict or the appearance of hostility, evasiveness, or condescension.

6.3 Do not leave the investigator(s) alone in the storage areas, the manufacturing areas of the plant, or with open file cabinets. Investigators may be left alone to examine files that have been collected for their review, but an escort must remain nearby.

6.4 Before answering a question, be sure you understand what is being asked.

6.5 Never lie to the investigator(s).

6.6 Avoid (while in the plant) having anyone other than the supervisor drawn into conversations, unless specifically requested by the supervisor.

6.7 Never state that a particular event or situation (e.g., a problem or violation) is impossible with company product(s).

6.8 Never threaten to call the investigator's supervisor.

6.9 Never try to compromise the compliance role of the investigator.

6.10 Do not volunteer information.

7.0 *Dealing with the Inspection, Note Taking, and Apprising Management of Developments*

7.1 The receiving company official/escort will escort the investigator(s) to a vacant conference room or office (free of company information). This room will serve to minimize disruption to normal business activities during the inspection.

7.2 The investigator(s) should be given time to review documents, but every document (or file) presented for inspection should be listed by the escort.

7.3 The FDA investigator(s) may physically observe any area, equipment, or process related to the manufacture of a regulated product. This includes component, raw material, and final product storage; labeling and packaging operations; testing and recordkeeping areas.

7.4   When requested, manufacturing processes, equipment, and materials may be identified and explained. This may be done in general terms. If more detailed information is sought or questions go beyond the escort's knowledge, the area supervisor should reply.

7.5   During the inspection the FDA investigator will be taking notes. The escort(s) should be alert for issues that attract attention and take notes themselves regarding these matters, including any unusual questions or volunteered comments. All notes taken by the escort during the inspection should be factual; avoid opinions.

7.6   If, during an inspection the investigator(s) identifies a condition that merits correction and the proper correction can be made promptly, remedial action should be taken during the inspection. This will not preclude its mention on the FDA-483, but the inspection report should then take note of the correction.

7.7   The investigator(s) may request documents related to the facility that are not routinely available at the facility. The escort should inform the investigator(s) of the location of the documents. If the investigator(s) insists on viewing the documents, and the request appears reasonable within the context of the inspection, offer to obtain them by fax or overnight delivery.

7.8   All documents should be released in accord with paragraph 8.0 herein.

7.9   If FDA collects samples of components, in-process materials and/or finished products during an inspection, the investigator is required to leave a Receipt for Samples (form FD-484).

7.10   FDA may legally collect exhibits of labels and labeling. Copies of product labels, inserts, customer promotional literature, and advertising materials may be released. A second set should be retained, however. FDA will not leave a form FD-484 for these materials, as they are not regarded as samples.

7.11 Regulated companies are not obligated to sign affidavits. Should an affidavit be presented during an inspection, do not sign it, read it, or listen to it being read. If it is read and you are asked about its content, reply, "No comment." No further comments should be elicited by succeeding questions on this matter.

7.12 The closing meeting of an inspection may result in the FDA investigator(s) presenting a Notice of Observations (form FDA-483). If an FDA 483 is presented, read every item carefully. If a comment is not understood, ask what it is based on. Do not argue, but if there is a misunderstanding or the investigator(s) is in factual error, explain and provide any practicable documentary evidence as to why the observation is in error. The investigator is unlikely to delete an item from the FDA-483, however, this is the opportune time to determine the investigator's basis for listing the item.

8.0 *Release of Documents*

8.1 Good business judgment must be applied when releasing documents to regulatory authorities. Refusal to provide FDA with information to which it is entitled may constitute a violation of the Federal Food, Drug, and Cosmetic Act (FDCA). Before refusing to provide specific information (except as exempted), the lead escort must consult the Director of Regulatory Affairs and company legal counsel.

8.2 Information and documents exempt from release, by statute or FDA regulatory policy are:

8.2.1 financial data,

8.2.2 sales data (other than shipment data),

8.2.3 pricing data,

8.2.4 personnel data (other than data as to qualifications of technical and professional personnel),

8.2.5 medical device research data (other data subject to reporting provisions of section 519 or 520(g) of the FDCA), and

8.2.6 quality assurance audit records.

8.3 While FDA is responsible for maintaining security of all documents it receives, it also releases copies of some documents under the Freedom of Information Act. To ensure that FDA recognizes the proprietary value a company places on its documents, all documents released to FDA shall be stamped with the following confidentiality and issuance stamps: "[Company Name] Issued Confidential Information MTH, DA, YEAR."

8.4 Two identical sets of all documents being released to FDA will be made. After both sets are identically prepared, one set will be released to FDA and the second will be given to Regulatory Affairs.

Sample

Policy Statement for Protection of Proprietary Property and Privacy Information

It is [company name] policy to deny the use of cameras and electronic recording equipment during inspections of [company name] premises by visitors to [company name] including all state and federal authorities.

During the inspection of [company name] premises, only [company name] copying equipment may be used to copy documents. Unless the number of pages copied becomes burdensome, there shall be no charge for making copies. Should it become burdensome, a charge will be made. The charge will be 15 cents per page.

There will be no charge for samples, unless the cost of the materials exceeds $[amount to be entered].

Ronald M. Johnson

Quintiles Consulting

CHAPTER 19

How to Handle an FDA Inspection

I. Introduction

What does it mean to "handle" a Food and Drug Administration (FDA) inspection? To some companies it means that an FDA-483 (List of Inspectional Observations) was avoided. To others it means the investigator did not find any serious violations, or that no company employees committed any gaffs that led FDA into weak areas of the operation. To others, it means that the company successfully confused the neophyte investigator so as to obscure his/her recognition of a production flaw. Some companies even talk in terms of "managing" an FDA inspection. Of course, FDA would bristle at the thought that the inspection could be "handled," let alone managed, by anyone other than FDA personnel.

Firms should accept that FDA has the upper hand in inspection situations; for the most part, agency personnel are in control during an inspection. Setting out to "handle" or "manage" an FDA inspection inappropriately directs the company's attention to power dynamics; this should not be the primary aim of the company. One should not conclude from this that planning and preparation for an inspection are not essential … clearly, they are. The roles and responsibilities of company employees as well as company "do's and don'ts" during an inspection should be established well before an inspection takes place.

With these necessary mechanics in place, the company needs to think more broadly as to what it hopes to achieve during the actual inspection process; that should be the focus of its efforts during the inspection. Emphasis on the mechanics at the expense of this broader objective can have disastrous consequences. For example, such inappropriate focus has bred company managers who might religiously accompany the investigator even to the restroom yet fail to ensure that the investigator has a clear understanding of the company's rationale for not submitting a particular supplement. Making sure the latter is achieved can make the difference between a company not receiving any criticism from FDA and receiving a warning letter, or worse.

II. A Successful Inspection

What is a reasonable objective of the inspection process from a company perspective? The objective should be a successful inspection … meaning that during the conduct of the inspection:

- the company made certain the information obtained by FDA was accurate;

- any concerns or questions the investigator had were addressed and resolved;

- the company's logic and rationale for any action in dispute were communicated and understood by the investigator; and

- the company knows any residual issues or concerns of the investigator.

Achieving a successful inspection can prevent the regulatory escalation of insignificant issues, enhance the credibility of the company, result in timely correction of problems, and avoid regulatory conflict between the company and FDA.

A company can enhance its prospects for a successful inspection by:

- establishing a constructive relationship with the investigator(s);

- ensuring that potential problems are brought to the company's attention as they are encountered by the investigator(s);

- ensuring these problems or issues are clearly understood not only by the company, but also, importantly, by the investigator(s); and

- ensuring an effective response is made to identified issues as rapidly as possible.

A. Investigator Relations

The FDA investigator is key to the outcome of an inspection. A company's ability to communicate with that individual is essential to achieving its objectives for the inspection process. Care must be taken to avoid any situations or circumstances that might interfere with good communication with the investigator.

The best time to articulate the company's communication objectives and establish procedures to accomplish them is at the beginning of the inspection. It is then that the company can request ongoing communications during the inspection and, at minimum, a daily briefing about the investigator's observations, concerns, or questions. Today the FDA investigator will most likely cooperate with such requests. If there is reluctance, the company should persist. Even an unwilling investigator can be encouraged to share information.

When I had occasion to make speeches during my FDA tenure, I always asked the FDA investigators in the audience to stand and be recognized. I commented that many people in the industry believed FDA investigators were Neanderthals, or some other primitive form of human. My point was that FDA investigators are human beings just like those in the industry; they have personalities, emotions, quirks, good days, and bad days. I believe most investigators share a somewhat unique characteristic of FDA employees in general, which is the passion they have for their jobs. They take their role of public health protection very seriously. This mind-set of FDA employees sometimes affects the manner in which they interact with the industry, such that they approach industry as if it were untrustworthy. Any industry effort to develop a constructive relationship with FDA investigators must recognize, and perhaps accommodate, these factors.

FDA investigators expect to be treated with respect, courtesy, and professionalism; most react positively to such treatment. Most companies have mastered the basics of this treatment of investigators, but being courteous and respectful does not mean that a company must sacrifice its rights or comply with every whim of the investigator. There are instances of investigators who seem to thrive on making unreasonable and inappropriate demands of company officials (e.g., demands that specific company officials report to the investigator for interview at a certain time/place, with the threat that failure to comply will be regarded as a refusal of inspection, and investigators who literally track the time it takes the company to respond to a request or retrieve a record). FDA investigators will lose respect for a company who allows itself to be bullied during the investigation.

It is important for a company to obtain and maintain the respect of the investigator so that communications can occur at a common level. If the investigator has no respect for the company spokesperson(s), communication invariably will break down. The inability to communicate effectively will only harm the company. In one situation, an investigator simply covered her ears, shook her head, and told the company she did not want to hear any of their explanations; at the time, company managers were trying to provide the basis for a decision with which the investigator disagreed. The investigator's lack of respect for anything the company had to say obviously compromised the company's ability to communicate its position.

Sometimes, a company official can innocently or unknowingly offend the investigator. For example, the investigator should not be addressed as "inspector." There is a class system in FDA, and inspectors are technicians at a lower level than investigators in the FDA hierarchy. Even if it is obvious that an investigator is not familiar with the technology, process, or product on-site, they should not be asked, "Is this the first time you have inspected a facility like this?" Some investigators may not be affected by such a question, but others may feel they are being challenged and may be motivated to demonstrate their investigational prowess notwithstanding their unfamiliarity with your process.

Another *faux pas* that companies frequently commit is senior management failing to at least introduce him/herself to the investigator. This failure may be perceived as disrespectful of both the investigator and the process (i.e., senior management did not take the inspection seriously). During an inspection, company personnel should not "drop" the names of FDAers they know or have met, nor should they identify former FDAers who have served as consultants to the company. At minimum, the investigator will disregard your comments but another possibility may arise if the investigator "has issues" with some of the people mentioned.

The objective is not to become friends with the investigator, rather it is to establish a rapport that will facilitate and permit the level of communication that is vital to the company's interest. While the investigator is part of the relationship, attention also must be given to the other half of the communication equation ... the company spokesperson(s). Company employees also have human frailties, so care needs to be taken when selecting those who will interface with the investigator. Poor choices as a spokesperson, for example, would be someone who is outspoken on his/her views about a government bureaucracy bloated with inane regulations, or someone whose mother died because a potential treatment of choice was bogged down in FDA review. For the most part FDA investigators do not appreciate such opinions, and hearing them may provide motivation for the investigators to use the inspection to demonstrate the importance of regulatory requirements. The investigator's motivation for conducting the inspection should not be adversely influenced or inappropriately redirected as a result of the personality of the company spokesperson(s).

B. The Bad Seed

What can a company do if they are visited by "the investigator from Hell"? First, this assessment of an investigator should not be made too hastily. Preceding such a conclusion, firms should ensure that the company spokesperson(s) has conducted her/himself appropriately and has not caused or contributed to the aberrant behavior. In this process, companies must be objective, and be able to demonstrate that their concerns are materially affecting the outcome of the inspection, or at least have the potential of doing so. Disliking the investigator is not enough; companies have to be prepared to demonstrate how the investigator's actions 1) have interfered with the ability to provide information, 2) reflect his/her loss of objectivity, or 3) demonstrate conduct that is unprofessional or unethical.

If, in the final analysis, a company determines that the investigator's actions are unacceptable, there is another decision to make regarding whether to take the next step. That next step is communicating company concerns to management of the local FDA district office.

In my view, the district director of the local office is the most appropriate person with whom to raise such inspection concerns, this contact will provide some assurance that your concerns will be fairly considered. FDA is fairly protective of its investigators. FDA, however, does not want its investigators conducting themselves in other than a professional manner. There will not be much feedback from FDA on what the agency has done in response to a company's complaint. FDA may say that the matter will be, or is being, looked into, or that the agency believes the investigator acted appropriately. If FDA does believe the investigator was at fault, there will be little information relayed to the company about that, nor about what actions may be taken to correct the problem. FDA does use valid industry complaints in investigator performance appraisals. After making a credible complaint, what a company can reasonably hope for is that a different investigator will be assigned for their next agency inspection.

The reality is that FDA does not do a good job of containing the behaviors of its investigators, in large part because industry is afraid to complain. Many companies are afraid to express their concerns about investigator deportment for fear of retaliation or retribution from FDA. In my experience as a manager in FDA, I took complaints about investigator behavior very seriously and conscientiously investigated them. The majority of FDA managers, are sensitive to the industry's concern about retaliation, and take precautions to avoid the appearance of such. Often, the best way to do this is to reassign another investigator to avoid the appearance of a biased inspection following a complaint.

III. Timely Awareness and Understanding of Potential Problems

Most companies make efforts to learn of investigator concerns in a timely manner. A first step in these efforts is to obtain a commitment from the investigator that perceived problems will be pointed out to the company as they are encountered during the inspection or, at minimum, provided in a daily briefing. A successful inspection requires more, however, in that there must be a clear understanding of the problem by the investigator and the company. More than one company has invested enormous amounts of energy and resources to solve what they thought was the problem, only to find out later that it was not the same problem identified by FDA.

This situation causes serious upheaval in any case, but when it occurs at a critical point in the regulatory history of a company, it can be devastating. Several injunction actions resulted when companies simply solved the wrong problem post-inspection. FDA's view in those cases was that the company may have been well-intended in its efforts, but was incompetent. The time and place to avoid this kind of misunderstanding is *during* the inspection. It is incumbent upon the company to make sure the investigator understands what he/she is seeing and the company understands the investigator's concerns, namely, why a particular point is perceived as a problem and the degree to which it may adversely impact product. This requires effective communication between the investigator and the company.

The company should explore with the investigator the factual basis for his/her concern, the impact it may have on the finished product, and the specific violation it represents. The investigator should be able to cite a specific regulation or statutory requirement as the basis for any concern he/she has; the inability to do so brings into question the validity of the observation. Thereafter, the company should investigate the matter to ensure that all pertinent facts are known to the agency, and that any ameliorating facts have been identified and considered. If appropriate, the company should develop a proposed resolution. This information should be shared with the investigator(s), and the proposed resolution should be discussed with the aim of obtaining agreement from the investigator as to its propriety.

IV. Timely Response to Investigator's Observations

At the conclusion of the inspection, the investigator will present his/her observations on the form FDA-483 (Inspectional Observations) and will offer to discuss them with the company. This is the next best time to ensure clear understanding of the issues and should be regarded by the company as the last effective opportunity, because attempts to do so after the inspection are much more difficult.

The investigator is required to discuss his/her observations and to record any response made by the company. This is the only time that the FDA-483 can be changed. Once issued, it becomes a permanent document that cannot be modified even if it contains erroneous information. Current agency initiatives also require the investigator to annotate the FDA-483 observations with corrections made or promised by the company. In the ideal situation, when the FDA-483 is issued it will contain known observations and the company will have conducted necessary investigations and developed acceptable resolutions that can be provided to the investigator. In some cases, it may be appropriate to show the investigator the corrective action that has been taken (e.g., the write-ups of documents or physical plant/equipment modifications). The company should solicit a reaction from the investigator to obtain some sense as to whether the response is regarded as adequate. The investigator may be reluctant to commit, but frequently will give some indication that his/her concerns have been addressed. Certainly, the investigator should tell the company at this point if the problem has been misinterpreted or misunderstood.

Today, most companies wisely provide a written response to the FDA-483. Ideally, this response should be confirmation of what occurred during the inspection, should be directed to the district director with a copy to the investigator, and should be signed by a senior management official of the company. Some may argue that senior management puts itself at jeopardy by signing such a letter, but from FDA's perspective, the response has greater credibility and impact if signed by a senior official. It conveys to FDA that the company has taken the matter seriously and thus, FDA can rely on the representations expressed and commitments made. If FDA has confidence in the company's willingness and ability to correct the problems, it will be less inclined to feel the need to intervene.

One of the major benefits of satisfactorily responding to the issues raised during an inspection (during, at the conclusion of, or after the inspection) is the chance that a more serious communication from FDA may be averted. There currently is a pilot underway in FDA that will allow companies to avoid a warning letter if a satisfactory response to the FDA-483 is made. Although it was not official agency policy before, many districts, as a matter of practice, did not issue warning letters when the issues were resolved during or following the inspection.

V. An FDA Inspection Can Have a Successful Outcome

Having the right focus during an FDA inspection can help determine the outcome of the inspection. Rather than concentrating on the mechanics of handling or managing the inspection, a focus on a desired outcome will produce superior results. A successful inspection, meaning that the information obtained by FDA is complete, is understood, and represents the pertinent aspects of the issue(s) for both the company and FDA is a reasonable expectation. All company participants should share the objective of a successful inspection. A successful inspection can:

- avoid inappropriate or erroneous observations on the FDA-483;

- permit the company to be responsive to valid observations in a timely manner so as to be reflected in annotations to the FDA-483 or investigator's report;

- establish the company's credibility with the agency; and

- prevent further regulatory action.

20

Alan H. Kaplan
Stacy L. Ehrlich

Kleinfeld, Kaplan and Becker

After the Inspection: Addressing the 483 and the Establishment Inspection Report

I. List of Inspectional Observations - The 483

Upon their completion of an inspection, Food and Drug Administration (FDA) investigators issue to the operator of the facility a form, namely an FDA-483 (List of Inspectional Observations), addressing "significant objectionable conditions" observed in the inspected premises. The investigators are not to classify such conditions as violations of the Federal Food, Drug, and Cosmetic Act (FDCA); determination of whether any violations exist will be made at higher levels of the agency. While issue is frequently taken by representatives of the inspected facility as to the validity of some of the observations, each must be taken seriously, as the failure to respond to all of them adequately may lead to a warning letter, the initiation of an injunction, the seizure of merchandise, or even criminal prosecution.

The investigators' assignment is to assess deviations from the standards of current good manufacturing practice (cGMPs) and other regulatory obligations. While an inspection should not be viewed necessarily as a cat-and-mouse encounter, neither should it be approached with the naive attitude expressed in the statement, "They are from the government and they must be here to help me." FDA investigators are no different than the people who operate the facilities being investigated; they run the gamut from constructive to antagonistic. It is the obligation of the operator of the establishment to conform to legal standards, and it is the responsibility of investigators to determine whether those obligations are in fact being met.

For instance, about three years after the 1962 Drug Amendments were enacted, a small generic manufacturer was the subject of repeated inspections with what appeared to be changing points of focus by the investigator. The investigator would point out alleged deficiencies and, when the manufacturer inquired how these could best be remedied, the inspector would respond, "That is your obligation; mine is to find them." In an attempt to resolve his dilemma, the manufacturer followed a suggestion that he might offer the investigator a full-time position at the firm and thereby obtain constructive advice from the very person who had found the deficiencies. Before doing so, the manufacturer contacted the director of the FDA District and informed him that he was contemplating offering the investigator the position of Head of Compliance at his firm. The District Director had no objections. Thereafter, a job offer was tendered to the investigator and he accepted. Unfortunately, however, the ex-investigator was even more difficult to deal with as an employee than as an investigator. The lesson ultimately learned by the manufacturer was to let the FDA investigators do their job; the manufacturer has the responsibility to make sure that the facility has competent employees and independent consultants who are able to exercise their skills to avoid significant deficiencies in operations.

During the inspection, company managers should discuss with the investigators all inspectional observations on a daily basis to minimize errors and misunderstandings. Based on these discussions, the establishment should be aware of the inspectors' concerns and should take steps to address them right away. Based on a program formally adopted for medical devices in 1997 and a pilot program initiated in January 1, 1999, for other program areas, FDA investigators will annotate the 483 at the time of issuance if the firm has promised or completed corrective action of a particular observation. Investigators are encouraged to verify the establishment's corrective actions and will note in the 483 whether the corrective action has in fact been verified. The inspectors will not, however, delete a reportable observation simply because the firm has corrected or promised to correct it. Observations that were made in error, on the other hand, are to be deleted.

Occasionally, 483 observations sound more serious than the inspectors intended. Under such circumstances, it is important to obtain clarification from the inspectors at the earliest possible time. Sometimes, there is no question as to the import of an observation. In one inspection of a drug manufacturer in the 1970s, there was an observation that the establishment had run out of toilet paper in the men's room. The manufacturer immediately rectified that issue.

483 observations that reflect verifiable, clear-cut deficiencies in a facility, process, or product may range from those that have no adverse health implications (e.g. deviations from type-size or placement requirements under the provisions of the Fair Packaging and Labeling Act) to those that present a risk of serious injury or death (e.g., food, drug, device, or cosmetic contamination). In between these extremes, particularly for drugs and devices, are conditions that can be classified as deviations from the standards of current good manufacturing practices. These deviations, of course, can have effects that range from minor to catastrophic risks. With respect to the latter, chances are that FDA will descend on a firm before they have any opportunity to respond to the 483. Thus, it is best for the operator of the establishment to assess, and then address, deficiencies in descending order of significance.

If an adequate written response to the 483 is made in a timely fashion in conjunction with prompt corrections, follow-up FDA inspections may be scheduled to determine that the alleged deficiencies have in fact been remedied. If no response is submitted, such inspections become more likely; even then, corrections and remedial action in the intervening period will minimize the potential of regulatory consequences. In other words, while there is no obligation to respond to a 483, a timely and adequate response often will achieve a better relationship between the firm and the agency.

All firms subject to FDA inspection should have written procedures in place so that the observations in a 483 can be addressed efficiently, effectively, and promptly. While issue may be taken with the accuracy of certain observations, no response should ever be antagonistic or belittling. It is important that FDA be recognized as the authority it is, and that responses to all observations, valid or otherwise, be framed in a professional manner. There is no reason to admit that any observation is correct, but responses must not be misleading in any way.

Misrepresentation in responding to a 483 can create more difficult problems than will silence on the part of the firm. Remember, it is FDA's burden to establish a violation; an admission can relieve the government of that obligation. Of course, the establishment must be able to fully document everything it says in a response. Expert consultants should be available to help assess the validity of the inspectors' observations and, where they are valid, to advise as to how they can best be addressed. Where observations are not considered valid, an explanation should be provided in the response setting forth the basis for such a position. If the firm and its consultants believe that, irrespective of the validity of the inspector's observations, the 483 raises a serious challenge to the integrity of the product or processes, the firm should consult with an attorney knowledgeable in the law and the ways of the FDA. Once a draft response to the 483 has been prepared, it should be reviewed and corroborated by the relevant consultants and legal counsel.

If the observations in the 483 appear minor and easily correctable, and the establishment is confident that there is no need to bring in any consultant or attorney, the company can respond reasonably to the 483 using in-house expertise. Under such circumstances , however, it is important to make certain that all of the responses are accurate and that action is taken promptly to correct the points raised by the inspector.

483s generally are available to the public shortly after an inspection is completed. This means that, aside from considering the observations made by the inspectors, the establishment should consider whether the 483 reveals any information that it views as subject to trade secret status. Before the inspectors leave, they will have a closing interview with company management and will provide the 483.

During the closing interview, in addition to reviewing the accuracy and validity of the observations, management also should address any trade secret issues. If trade secrets are revealed in the 483, management should advise the inspectors that such information must be deleted before the 483 is made available to the public and that the firm must be notified if the trade secret information becomes the subject of a Freedom of Information request. This will be important in protecting the confidentiality of information that FDA may believe does not constitute trade secrets. If a firm's request for deletion has been made but FDA does not agree, the agency nevertheless is required to advise the firm of the submission of an FOI request, after which the firm is provided a brief opportunity to seek a court order requiring FDA to withhold specific items.

Depending on the seriousness of the observations, a written response to the 483 may not be a sufficient response. The most important task is for the firm to address the observations by correcting them adequately and expeditiously, and not waiting for further agency action. Additionally, consideration should be given to meeting with the District Office for the purpose of demonstrating the firm's full commitment to adherence to all relevant regulatory standards. In this process, however, firms should never cry "*mea culpa.*" This is an issue that is best left open.

At a meeting with the District Office, it may be useful to have the relevant consultants and legal counsel present. It is important to have a dry-run with any company advisors before meeting with the District, to be sure that the presentation will be credible and constructive. If it is not, it may be best to hold off on any meeting. Either way, firms should not delay in making appropriate correction of the circumstances that gave rise to the observations.

II. The Establishment Inspection Report

At the conclusion of their inspection, FDA investigators, in addition to providing form FDA-483, will prepare an Establishment Inspection Report (EIR) that sets forth information derived from the inspection in greater detail and broader scope than is contained in the 483. While a copy of the 483 generally will be provided to the "Responsible Head" of the inspected facility at the close of the inspection, the EIR will not.

The EIR covers more about the firm than reports of deficiencies and takes much longer for the investigators to prepare. The EIR will include: the firm's regulatory history; the officers and operating manager (persons involved and their responsibilities); FDA personnel who were involved in the inspection; the sources of ingredients and components; how the products are manufactured and stored; quality control practices; the facts underlying the 483 observations; consumer complaints; recall procedures; promotional practices; refusals to provide requested information and documents; and sample collections and results. It also will contain relevant exhibits to support the findings, such as photographs and copies of production and control documents. Where an observation noted by the investigator was corrected by the firm during the course of the inspection, the observation and corrective action will be discussed in detail in the EIR.

The EIR is reviewed by the district office. If it reflects a violation of the FDCA, it will be referred to higher agency levels for a decision regarding compliance action. The report also may be referred to the appropriate FDA headquarters Center for final review and disposition.

As part of a program formally adopted for medical device inspections in 1997 and a pilot program initiated in January 1, 1999, for other program areas, once the EIR has been completed and evaluated, the District Director routinely will send the firm a letter about its compliance status. (In the past, following evaluation of an EIR, it was FDA's practice to send a letter to the firm only to request correction of problems or to issue a warning.) If no regulatory action is planned by the agency, the letter will show that the firm's compliance status falls into one of two categories: no action indicated (NAI) or voluntary action indicated (VAI).

A compliance status of NAI means no 483 was issued or no significant violations observed. A compliance status of VAI means that a 483 was issued describing practices that the agency believes should be addressed by management, but that there is minimal likelihood that product integrity will be compromised. In such cases, the agency will follow up during the next inspection to determine if the described practices have been corrected. Under either category, at least until there has been follow up, the operations inspected at the facility will not be the subject of regulatory action.

A firm should review the EIR in detail for outstanding issues that merit attention, even if it believes that all of the observations set forth in the 483 have been addressed adequately. In at least one situation involving the inspection of a medical device manufacturer, the firm was surprised to find that an FDA seizure action had been initiated based, in part, on deficient good manufacturing practice allegations that were never listed on the 483, but had been described in the EIR. If the firm had reviewed the EIR, which had been received and which referenced the deviation, the seizure action may have been avoided.

Because the EIR is a more comprehensive document than is the 483, it presents far greater prospects of containing trade-secret or other confidential information. To guard against such information being inadvertently disclosed by FDA (particularly in situations where an affirmative request for the EIR must be made by the operator of the establishment), at the close of the inspection when the 483 is provided the inspector should be requested to inform the company when the EIR has been prepared. At that time, a request for the EIR should be made (probably under the Freedom of Information Act regulations) together with a request that the EIR not be provided to outsiders until there has been a reasonable opportunity for the inspected company to review the report to determine if it contains trade secret or other confidential information.

FDA's unwillingness to release an EIR is suggestive of other unresolved problems; even if released, the EIR may contain information that points to the possibility of enforcement action. Discussions with FDA should be initiated promptly by the firm to attempt to resolve such concerns.

It is obvious, perhaps, that in order to minimize risks of enforcement action, an establishment must be operated under tight controls that ensure compliance. The firm's employees, working in conjunction with independent experts, are best suited to guard against a situation in which FDA will have valid grounds for challenging any firm practices. The costs of such pro-active operations will be far less than the costs associated with the correction and defense of matters that are unearthed by FDA.

Minnie V. Baylor-Henry
Janet L. "Lucy" Rose

The R.W. Johnson Pharmaceutical
Research Institute
Lucy Rose and Associates

21

Communicating With FDA's Advertising Groups

I. Introduction

This is an uncertain time for the regulation of medical products. The *Washington Legal Foundation* case, the explosion of prescription drug information on the Internet, and the release of the Food and Drug Administration's (FDA's) final guidance on direct-to-consumer (DTC) broadcast advertisements have provided new challenges and opportunities for industry, as well as many legal and logistical challenges for FDA. Strong FDA/industry communications are more important than ever to enable maximum understanding of all viewpoints, create the best decisions as they impact patient care, and provide the industry with the information it needs to create and implement marketing programs that meet FDA expectations.

FDA has specific groups in each medical products Center assigned to regulate promotion. The groups range in size from one person to over thirty-two people, depending upon the size of the promotional market they regulate. For example, the Center for Drug Evaluation and Research (CDER), which regulates several hundred thousand promotional pieces a year, has the largest group, the Division of Drug Marketing, Advertising and Communications (DDMAC), located in the Office of Medical Policy. On the other hand, the Center for Biologics Evaluation and Research's (CBER's) review group, Advertising Promotion and Labeling Staff (APLS), located in the Office of Compliance, is comprised of three to four reviewers. The Center for Devices and Radiological Health (CDRH) and the Center for Veterinary Medicine (CVM) also have staffs that regulate their industry's promotional activities.

In general, manufacturers are not required to submit promotional material prior to publication or dissemination. Regulations promulgated in the 1960s require that drug and biologics manufacturers — but not device or veterinary drug manufacturers — submit promotional materials for agency review at the time of initial publication or dissemination. There are exceptions for promotional material for drugs approved under Subpart H and those requiring preapproval subsequent to FDA regulatory action. All of FDA's review groups are willing to provide regulatory comments to manufacturers prior to material being used. Companies need to be aware that it often takes a considerable amount of time for FDA to provide comments because of limited resources and a large number of industry requests. Additionally, DDMAC prioritizes its work, with launch campaign requests representing the highest priority, followed by requests for comments on direct-to-consumer broadcast advertisements. Other requests represent lower priorities.

DDMAC is by far the largest group in FDA that regulates promotional materials. It is organized into four branches, each with a branch chief reporting to the Division Director and Deputy Division Director. There are two review branches, composed of approximately six to seven reviewers in each branch, responsible for the primary review of promotional materials, including advisory comments requested by manufacturers and enforcement actions. Each reviewer is assigned to a group of drugs corresponding to a medical review division with the goal being to promote review consistency within therapeutic classes, as well as the development of technical expertise.

Additionally, there are two research and review branches. Branch III is responsible for patient/consumer labeling, medication guides, Internet and direct-to-consumer promotion. Branch IV is responsible for quality-of-life and pharmacoeconomics policies and promotional claims, patient satisfaction and compliance claims, managed care issues, and other related issues. It is important to understand this organizational structure and the corresponding responsibilities in order to maximize and facilitate effective communication.

FDA groups responsible for regulating promotional materials have increased workloads coupled with limited resources. Industry and FDA's response to the Prescription Drug User Fee Act (PDUFA) has resulted in an increasing number of new product launches. Most prescription drug manufacturers request FDA's advisory comments on launch campaigns prior to the initial use. The result has been a very challenging strain on FDA's limited resources and has slowed FDA's response time for getting comments to industry. The bottom line is a delayed launch campaign, which is a major concern to the industry.

Another challenge, in light of FDA's resource constraints and the goal of successful industry/FDA communications, is the large number of requests for comments prior to manufacturer's use of direct-to-consumer advertising and labeling pieces, as well as the large interest in Internet promotion. FDA has not issued guidance for Internet promotion, and announced that it will not issue such guidance because of the ever-evolving issues in this area. Because FDA promotional regulatory organizations are not likely to find significant new resources, it is important for these groups to organize and operate as efficiently as possible to maintain their regulatory effectiveness.

From an industry perspective, it is important to work as effectively as possible with FDA. These interactions can be improved by providing appropriate supporting documentation when required; learning from public regulatory actions; having an effective regulatory professional interacting with FDA; and staying abreast of any new guidances or other information issued by FDA.

In this chapter, DDMAC is used as the primary model for interaction between industry and FDA. Promotional regulatory groups in other Centers may have somewhat different processes and should be consulted directly with any questions.

II. Launch Campaigns

FDA and industry both agree that the most important time in a product's lifecycle is the introduction of the product to the market. This is important because the product's initial marketing impression to health care professionals and consumers is usually the lasting one. DDMAC has made industry requests for advisory comments on launch campaigns its first priority.

It is important to re-emphasize here that, generally speaking, FDA does not *require* submission of launch campaigns for advisory opinions prior to initial use of the materials. For business reasons, however, many prescription drug manufacturers routinely submit at least the core pieces for initial comments. The review process will be greatly slowed by submitting materials with claims that are clearly inconsistent with the approved product labeling or in violation of the Federal Food, Drug, and Cosmetic Act (FDCA). Manufacturers can expect at least three weeks for review and initial response to requests for launch advisory opinions.

The following recommendations may help facilitate DDMAC's review of launch campaign material:

- establish rapport with the DDMAC promotional reviewer during the product medical review;

- submit materials immediately upon product approval with a letter requesting launch comments; DDMAC generally cannot provide comments until the labeling negotiations have concluded;

- call the promotional reviewer to alert him/her that materials have been sent and provide information about any unusual materials;

- submit only core materials, such as the primary visual aid, primary journal ad, most important DTC pieces (television advertisement, magazine/newspaper advertisement), product monograph, or file card; these pieces should be nearly identical to the actual final pieces;

- provide all supporting materials and annotate all claims to supporting materials;

- provide final labeling in large, readable type;

- expect at least three weeks for initial comments;

- respond immediately to reviewer questions/letters;

- after receipt of initial comments, make edits as appropriate, and request a teleconference or meeting, if necessary, to clarify or negotiate comments; it is recommended that marketing personnel be included in these discussions; and

- if the company decides to print and distribute materials prior to receiving "final" DDMAC comments, the materials should be consistent with the law and there should be substantial support for all claims. DDMAC has asked that it be notified if a company is not going to resubmit a piece, so that the reviewer can close the launch project.

III. Direct-to-Consumer Promotion

Just as FDA considers launch campaign requests for advisory opinions extremely important to its mission, it also considers requests for advisory opinions for DTC broadcast advertisements extremely important. In fact, DDMAC considers industry advisory opinion requests for DTC broadcast advertisements its number two priority. Requests for advisory opinions for other DTC promotional pieces are given less priority.

FDA finalized the DTC Broadcast Guidance in August 1999. This guidance provides assistance in preparing consumer-directed broadcast advertisements. DDMAC advises manufacturers to expect three to four weeks for initial comments on DTC broadcast advertisements submitted for advisory opinions. It is important for manufacturers to note that, although the regulations do not require submission of DTC promotional materials (including DTC broadcast advertisements), prior to use, on occasion, television networks have asked manufacturers about the status of FDA review.

Manufacturers should submit requests for DTC advisory opinions to the promotional reviewer responsible for the advertised product. The product reviewer will involve the DTC specialist reviewers as appropriate. DTC broadcast advertisements are reviewed by a DDMAC team, including DTC specialists, the product reviewer, branch chiefs, often the review division medical reviewer, and the DDMAC deputy director or director. If there are questions following the initial comments on a proposed broadcast advertisement, it is appropriate to request a teleconference or in-person meeting to finalize materials. It is helpful to have a marketing person and an advertising agency representative attend this meeting.

The following items are recommended to facilitate review of DTC broadcast advertisements when they are submitted for advisory opinions:

- current, readable product labeling;

- storyboard and/or script with video, with "supers" in approximate placement (oversize storyboards are nice, but legible letter size also is helpful);

- clear label on both video and box that includes MACMIS # (for revisions) and/or submission date;

- a cover letter that clearly states the scope of what is being requested; and

- substantiation, with annotation, for claims not in the labeling.

The most common reasons for DDMAC to raise concerns when issuing an advisory opinion include:

- inadequate safety information or appropriate balancing information;

- language not adequately "user friendly";

- competing background (e.g., background music too loud, or too much movement in visual background) during safety information;

- inadequate attention to regulatory "details" (e.g., generic name too small or not on screen long enough, or failure to inform consumers that the drug is available by prescription only);

- inadequate reference to a healthcare professional as the ultimate decision maker;

- implication of indication broadening, through text or graphics; and

- insufficient provision for disseminating product labeling.

IV. Competitor Complaints

FDA does not have the resources to effectively monitor all advertising and promotional labeling activities. Therefore, the agency depends on receiving information from stakeholders about the promotional activities. The information usually is forwarded to FDA in the form of a complaint letter, although it may be a telephone call on occasion. These complaints may come from multiple sources, including, but not limited to, healthcare professionals, consumers, advocacy groups, law firms, and the regulated industry.

There are many considerations when one decides to forward a complaint to FDA. If there is no tangible evidence of the alleged violative activity, it is difficult for FDA to pursue an enforcement action. Therefore, strong consideration should be given to whether it is a good use of FDA's and the company's time when there is little or no substantiation.

If there is sufficient evidence and a company forwards a complaint to FDA, the package should have several components. There should be a cover letter that clearly states the alleged violation(s), the citation to the FDCA section and implementing regulations that support the allegation, and samples the pieces that are the subject of the complaint. To the extent possible, FDA would prefer original pieces, rather than photocopies of the pieces.

If the alleged violation is based on detailing, there should be a list of names, addresses, and phone numbers of healthcare professionals who are willing to speak to FDA and, if necessary, to sign an affidavit. There also should be included a complete explanation of the detailing activity. While many companies include a recommendation about the type of action that FDA should pursue (e.g., a warning letter), this is not necessary and is seldom persuasive.

The agency will attempt to review the complaint package within sixty days, and will acknowledge, in writing, receipt of the documents. In that letter, the agency will generally indicate whether the complaint appears to have merit. After this letter, the complainant will receive no other direct information from the agency. The status of a possible regulatory action must be obtained through a Freedom of Information Act request or by checking the FDA website. It is not advisable for complainants to call FDA in an attempt to learn the status of an enforcement action against a competitor.

After the acknowledgment letter, FDA will independently evaluate the evidence that has been submitted and will, in some instances, seek additional evidence from the company that is the target of the complaint. After carefully evaluating the entire package, the agency will make a decision about whether to pursue an enforcement action and what type of action is appropriate under the circumstances. The fact that FDA has indicated that a complaint has merit does not mean that an enforcement action will result. Because there are competing priorities, it may be determined that undertaking an enforcement action is not the most efficient use of the agency's resources.

V. DDMAC Regulatory Letters

If FDA decides to take an enforcement action because it believes advertising or promotional labeling pieces violate the FDCA or implementing regulations, there are several regulatory options, including injunctions, product seizures, and criminal charges. The agency most commonly will send either a warning letter or an untitled letter.

A warning letter is sent to a company for a violation that the agency considers to be of regulatory significance, i.e., the violations may lead to an enforcement action if not promptly and adequately corrected. A warning letter generally is addressed to the company's president or CEO, and states the agency's position regarding a particular piece, but does not commit the agency to taking further action. Warning letters generally are issued under the following circumstances:

- the promotional piece raises safety concerns that present a reasonable possibility of injury or death;

- the violation represents a repetitive course of conduct that DDMAC has discussed previously with the company;

- the violative claims were broadly disseminated;

- DDMAC believes that the dissemination of a corrective message is necessary to protect and promote the public health; or

- the violation is intentional and flagrant.

Under certain circumstances, DDMAC may issue an untitled letter, sometimes referred to as a notice of violation (NOV), to the company's regulatory professional. Untitled letters are issued when the violative conduct does not meet the threshold for a warning letter. In general, FDA will not ask for a corrective action with an untitled letter, but will require that any further dissemination of the piece or similar pieces be stopped.

Often companies are uncertain about the appropriate response when an untitled letter or warning letter is issued by DDMAC. Is it better to call DDMAC and acknowledge receipt or just respond in accordance with the instructions in the letter? In the case of an untitled letter, it is appropriate to respond by the stated date and to provide — in writing — the requested information. If there is disagreement regarding the facts, the company should telephone the DDMAC reviewer and advise him/her of this difference of opinion. These issues should be negotiated during a meeting with DDMAC, either by phone or in person. The company also should telephone DDMAC for clarification, if there are any portions of the letter that are unclear.

Warning letters should be handled differently than untitled letters. The company should call DDMAC to acknowledge receipt of the letter and indicate whether it intends to request a meeting. This is important because there are usually numerous attendees at a meeting regarding a warning letter, and it is logistically challenging to schedule such a meeting. It is still important to send a formal meeting request in accordance with the procedures outlined by CDER. Because corrective actions usually are requested when warning letters are issued, it is important that a company meet with FDA to negotiate not only the allegations raised in the letter, but also the language and scope of the corrective campaign.

VI. Non-Launch Advisory Requests

Often companies seek comments from FDA on promotional materials other than launch pieces or consumer-directed broadcast advertisements. These pieces may be consumer-directed print material, press releases, or health professional pieces. Companies frequently have questions about DDMAC's priorities in reviewing such pieces. There also may be some confusion about what should be included in these requests for advisory comments and what a company can expect in terms of DDMAC's review.

DDMAC has stated publicly in numerous speeches and other discussions that providing comments on non-launch and consumer-directed pieces, other than broadcast, is a low priority. While the agency has always expressed a willingness to evaluate these pieces, there are competing priorities and limited resources. With this in mind, a company should not expect advisory comments on non-launch pieces any sooner than sixty days from the date that DDMAC receives the submission. The timeframe is not mandated and may be sooner, but frequently it will take longer.

With the sixty-day or longer timeframe in mind, if a company still desires comments from DDMAC, there should be careful consideration given to the selection of pieces that are submitted. Some companies submit all promotional pieces, regardless of the similarity of the claims. Obviously, the more pieces that are sent in, the longer it will take DDMAC to evaluate the material. It is probably more prudent to select for submission a representative piece that contains the claims in question (e.g., a brochure or multiple-page advertisement).

Once comments are received from FDA, they should be used as a guide in modifying related pieces, if necessary. If there is some doubt about whether a derivative piece deviates to the extent that DDMAC would have concerns, it is probably wise to submit this piece to the agency. The submission should include a cover letter addressed to the reviewer, the proposed promotional material, and the annotated references. While DDMAC has stated clearly that companies should plan accordingly for the time that it will take the agency to review proposed pieces, on occasion it may be helpful to include information about proposed utilization dates in the cover letter. This is particularly useful if such a timeframe is far enough in the future to permit the reviewer adequate time to meet the proposed date.

While many companies realize that non-launch advisories are a low priority for DDMAC, there is still a certain level of anxiety that prevails when a company is waiting for the agency's comments. Many company representatives will call DDMAC to ascertain the status of the review. If DDMAC provides a target date, a company should refrain from making multiple calls with the hope that the reviewer will expedite the review. The outcome of such calling is usually further delay, because the reviewer must stop the review to take the phone call and make a record of same through a memorandum to the file.

The important message here is that, in most instances, there is no regulatory mandate to get comments from FDA prior to disseminating promotional labeling or advertising. If a company does decide to solicit comments from the agency before disseminating material, it should factor in the delay that will occur while waiting for the comments. If a company decides that it cannot afford to wait after submitting a proposed piece to FDA, the agency asks that the company notify FDA so that the reviewer does not continue to spend time reviewing a piece that will be disseminated without agency comments.

CHAPTER 22

Douglas B. Farquhar

Hyman, Phelps & McNamara, P.C.

Reporting Stolen or Lost Drug Samples

I. Introduction

Manufacturers and wholesalers of prescription drugs — and their agents and representatives — are required under the Prescription Drug Marketing Act to report to the Food and Drug Administration (FDA) "any significant loss of drug samples and any known theft of drug samples." How do you do that? How quickly do you have to file your report? What are you required to report? What is a "significant loss"? Answers to these questions were provided in a regulation that was finalized as this publication was prepared. The advice set forth below is based on that regulation, which was issued December 3, 1999.

II. Avoid Reportable Events

If you are reading this chapter because you want to know what will happen if you experience a reportable event in the future, your best course of action is to carefully control prescription drug samples so that none will be lost or stolen.

If you are reading this chapter because you have discovered a significant loss or theft of prescription drug samples, this advice may seem too late. But FDA likely will want to know how drug samples were lost or stolen, and why it took the company so long to find out about the loss or theft. Systems for accountability will be measured by FDA against what the agency considers to be required systems for inventory and reconciliation.

In either case, it makes sense to know what FDA expects from your control systems.

Prescription drug manufacturers and their distributors must have control systems in place. Prescription drug samples must be maintained in a secure place, and may be distributed only under very restricted conditions. When drug samples are distributed by sales representatives (or other employees or representatives) of a manufacturer or authorized wholesaler, inventories of the drugs under the control of sales representatives shall be conducted by the manufacturer or wholesaler at least annually, as required by statute.

The regulation expands this requirement, requiring that the results of the physical inventory be "recorded in an inventory record and random audits conducted of sales representatives' inventories." A reconciliation report must be created that includes the physical count of the "most recently completed prior inventory"; records of shipments received (including the sender, date of shipment, name of the drug, dosage strength, and number of samples); records of distributions (including name and address of recipient, date, name of drug, dosage strength, lot or control number, and number of sample units delivered); and an "explanation for any significant loss."

In the proposed rule, which was superseded by the final rule, physical counts of samples remaining in the possession of sales representatives were required to be conducted by employees who work outside the sales representatives' department or division, and who are not in their "direct line of supervision or command." Before finalizing the regulation, FDA changed that requirement, recognizing that there may be "less burdensome" procedures. The finalized rule requires manufacturers to "take appropriate internal control measures to guard against error and possible fraud." The commentary to the final regulation still stresses that a security and audit system must be "controlled by independent personnel, i.e., personnel other than the representatives, their supervisors or managers or others in their direct line of command." In other words, unless there are strong reasons against it, manufacturers would be well advised to follow the original guidance and to ensure that employees or contractors independent of the sales division conduct the physical counts.

Manufacturers and distributors "must have written policies and procedures detailing. . . methodology for reconciling sample requests and receipts and for determining if patterns of nonresponse exist that may indicate sample diversion," according to the preamble to the regulation. A company's standard operating procedures (SOPs) should require that inventories and reconciliation reports be conducted at least annually, and should assign specific responsibility for the physical counts. SOPs should also assign specific responsibility for determining and documenting whether discrepancies constitute significant losses, and for investigating discrepancies and significant losses. It also is advisable to establish procedures for determining what quantities of specific drug losses will be considered significant, and to standardize the company's loss investigations. Indeed, the regulation specifically requires a company to establish "written policies and procedures describing its administrative systems" for conducting random and for-cause audits, for auditing drug sample records, for identifying significant losses and notifying FDA of the losses, for monitoring loss or thefts of drug samples, and for storing drug samples by representatives.

Furthermore, a specific procedure should be in place to inventory, reconcile, and return drug samples when a representative leaves employment with the company, whether because of resignation, contract termination, or firing.

III. The Reporting Process

A. When Do You Report?

FDA would say that a significant loss or theft of drug samples should be reported as quickly as possible after discovery. The statute says nothing about a reporting deadline; the regulation is quite specific. FDA recognizes that an investigation will have to be undertaken when a manufacturer or distributor has "reason to believe that any person has falsified drug sample requests, receipts, or records," but the agency will not accept delayed notification while the company completes that investigation. Likewise, where a company has reason to believe that any person is diverting prescription drug samples, a report must be filed. Companies are required, under the regulation, to provide FDA an initial notification within five working days of "learning of the falsification" or within five working days of "becoming aware" of a significant loss of drug samples or any theft of drug samples. The initial notification may be by telephone or in writing, and a "complete written report" is required not later than thirty days following initial notification.

B. How Do You Report?

Initially, report by telephone. Companies rarely will wish to convey to FDA their suspicions about diversion based merely on a report from a source of unknown reliability; they usually will want to investigate rapidly to determine as many facts as possible. FDA and your company may well disagree about the date the investigation ripened from a mere suspicion into a reportable event. To delay notification of FDA until a written report was prepared would likely lead the agency to believe that a company did not move as quickly as possible to disclose to the agency. FDA prefers not to be kept waiting on diversion investigations — so *call* the agency.

Once the telephone call has been placed to the agency — even if it only alerts the agency to an ongoing investigation — the FDA generally will be more understanding about the delays required to prepare a written report.

C. To Whom Do You Report?

Reports should be submitted to the Prescription Drug Compliance and Surveillance Division of FDA's Center for Drug Evaluation and Research. If controlled substances are involved, the Drug Enforcement Administration's (DEA's) district office should also be notified immediately, and state authorities may have to be notified as well.

> As this publication was being prepared, Margaret M. O'Rourke (301-827-7296) was the FDA official responsible for handling reports that rise to the level of possible criminal behavior; she identified Donna Stewart as the person who handles reports of noncriminal matters.

If the product involved is a biological prescription drug product, the report should be directed to the Division of Inspections and Surveillance at FDA's Center for Biologics Evaluation and Research.

D. When Do You Investigate?

All discrepancies have to be "evaluated." Where a discrepancy cannot be "justified," an investigation is required.

E. What Is a "Significant Loss"?

All thefts must be reported. Only *significant* losses must be reported. FDA has been "mindful of the difficulty of establishing a threshold for significant loss," but urges each manufacturer or distributor "to establish its own threshold for determining when inventory not accounted for is significant." By way of example, the regulation notes that a "small discrepancy in the total inventory of a multimillion dollar company may not be significant," but "the loss of a hundred tablets of a particular drug by one sales representative in one quarter might be significant." This explanation from FDA probably is not very helpful in a determination as to whether a loss is significant.

FDA "does not seek to receive reports concerning minor mathematical errors that are caught and corrected in the normal case of business." If discrepancies do not exceed a company's historical shrinkage due to "routine accounting errors, mistakes or losses," a report need not be filed.

Unfortunately, similar language in regulations enforced by the DEA is likewise unhelpful. Registered distributors of *controlled* substances must report to DEA "any theft or significant loss of any controlled substances upon discovery of such theft or loss." But there is no definition of "significant loss."

Companies should establish thresholds for each prescription drug, and should have a reasoned explanation for why that threshold is appropriate. If in doubt, *report*.

F. What Do You Report?

The report should begin by identifying the drug, with a description of what the drug is used for and whether it is controlled. Discuss the quantity that is not accounted for, and whether loss or theft is suspected. Then outline the facts that are known or that have been reported to you. Be prepared to answer questions about the names and phone numbers of those whom the agency may want to interview or who you feel may be culpable. Anticipate questions from the agency about when the loss was discovered, what steps have been taken to investigate the discrepancy since discovery of the loss, how your company monitors its inventories of prescription drug samples, and how your company maintains drug sample inventory and reconciliation reports. If you have identified any individual suspects as being involved in the loss or theft, be prepared to fully answer questions about their training, education, background, and job history; their responsibilities with your company and length of employment; their job performance; and names and phone numbers of their contacts or coworkers at your company. Discuss what job actions have been taken, or can be taken, against the suspects.

It usually will be the case that the investigation will be ongoing. Determine whether the agency has any objection to the remaining investigative steps you intend to perform. For example, if the suspect is a former employee, the agency may have reservations about your contacting that individual before law enforcement does.

Thoroughly and carefully document your contact with the agency, and draft a memorandum shortly thereafter to ensure a good record as to precisely what was communicated to the agency, as well as the agency's instructions, if any, as to further investigative steps.

Begin preparing the written report for FDA immediately. The report may contain some confidential or sensitive information, so it must be carefully drafted. Getting a head start on preparing a draft of your report will ensure that you become aware of issues in time to resolve any questions about releasing that sensitive information to FDA. Preparing, and sharing with responsible company officials, the written report also may reveal what documents need to be located or what additional investigative steps need to be performed before the report is filed with FDA.

IV. What Happens If You Do Not Report?

Federal law makes it illegal to fail to file a report of a significant loss or theft of prescription drug samples. The penalty for failing to report is a maximum of one year incarceration and a fine of $100,000 for an individual and $200,000 for an organization. If a defendant fails to file a report with "intent to defraud" or after a prior conviction for a violation of the Federal Food, Drug, and Cosmetic Act, the penalties rise to as much as three years incarceration and a fine of $250,000 for an individual and $500,000 for an organization. It is difficult to imagine what circumstances would show an intent to defraud in such a violation, but it is likely that if, for instance, the failure to file a report was designed to conceal an ongoing, wide-ranging, sample-selling racket, intent to defraud would be presumed.

If company employees or agents have unlawfully sold or traded drug samples, that company could be susceptible to significant criminal sanctions and civil money penalties. If you have voluntarily reported the activity to FDA before learning of an investigation into your employee's conduct, the fact that you reported the activity can be immensely helpful in reducing or avoiding liability for the company.

CHAPTER

23

David L. West

Quintiles Consulting

Combination Products

I.   Introduction

The thought of having a product regulated by the Food and Drug Administration (FDA) as a combination product has caused many company managers to cringe with apprehension. This results from fear that timeliness of product development and agency review will be thwarted by uncertainties of how to proceed — uncertainties on the part of the company and on the part of FDA. Since company and agency managers, from their respective positions, strive to minimize uncertainty over issues that arise with a new product, a company's natural anxiety associated with the development of a novel technology is exacerbated when the product is deemed a combination product. When encountering this special situation, one can maintain self-confidence by attending to the basics: manage the situation. The product jurisdiction regulations (21 C.F.R. part 3) provide a decision framework that can be used, directly and indirectly, for situation management.

From the time of enactment of the Medical Device Amendments of 1976 through 1990, there was no framework within FDA for deciding which Center of the agency would have jurisdiction over innovative products that did not fit clearly within statutory definitions of drug, biologic, or device. Without a framework, agency jurisdictional decisions were made on an *ad hoc* basis and usually reflected the provincial views or interests of the agency staff who initially dealt with the product. Industry experienced, and then came to expect, lengthy delays and inconsistent or even conflicting requirements as agency components debated among themselves the issues of jurisdiction and the applicability of drug, biologic, or device statutory requirements.

Congress intervened by including in the Safe Medical Devices Act of 1990 a provision that required FDA to designate an agency component to have primary jurisdiction for the premarket review and regulation of a product that constitutes a "combination product." The product jurisdiction regulations implement this provision and also apply to circumstances where primary jurisdiction is unclear or in dispute. It is important to note, however, that the scope of these regulations is limited to settling issues of agency component jurisdiction and does not extend to deciding the applicability of statutory requirements and associated regulations. Thus, to effectively manage situations involving combination products a company should understand how to use the product jurisdiction regulations for dealing with jurisdictional issues and how to use the "spirit" of these regulations for managing other regulatory issues.

II. Product Jurisdiction Regulations: Their Utility and Limitations

A. When Jurisdiction Is in Doubt, Go to the Highest Authority

For products meeting one of the regulations' definitions of a combination product, or in circumstances where the agency component with jurisdiction is unclear or in dispute, the product jurisdiction regulations provide that primary jurisdiction shall be based on the primary mode of action of the product.

The regulations envision a company referring to the three "Intercenter Agreements," which provide nonbinding guidance on assignment of primary jurisdiction for categories of products. These regulations also envision that a company will contact the Center it believes to have jurisdiction to receive that Center's confirmation. Supposedly, only where there is uncertainty or dispute should a company need to submit a Request for Designation to the FDA Ombudsman. The FDA Ombudsman is designated in the regulations as the Product Jurisdiction Officer. Operating at the Commissioner's level, this Officer has higher authority than the centers in matters of jurisdiction; the relative level of authority is extremely important.

In cases where a request to a Center raises any degree of uncertainty, before the Center confirms that it has jurisdiction, it is supposed to confer with the other Center(s) in question, so that the confirmation reflects a consensus of the Centers potentially involved. It is important, however, to realize:

- such a confirmation letter issued by a Center rests on nonbinding guidance (e.g., the Intercenter Agreements);

- even though the letter reflects a consensus of the potentially involved Center(s), it does not convey the authority of the FDA Product Jurisdiction Officer; and

- a Letter of Designation from the FDA Product Jurisdiction Officer can overturn a letter from a Center on matters of jurisdiction.

Consider the situation where a company consults with staff and managers within a Center's office and subsequently is sent a letter from an Office Director confirming that the combination product at issue would be regulated in that Center and office, and that a specific guidance document would be applicable. Consider further the delay and disruption that could be caused by an FDA reviewer who, late in the review cycle of the company's marketing application, challenges the office- and center-level jurisdictional decision and gets the issue referred to the FDA Product Jurisdiction Officer for resolution. This is not a purely hypothetical situation! To avoid being caught in this kind of predicament, companies should submit a Request for Designation to the FDA Product Jurisdiction Officer. Letters of Designation are binding, unless changes are needed to "protect the public health or for other compelling reasons."

B. Realize That It Is More Than a Matter of Jurisdiction

Sometimes, the most vexing questions are how a combination product should be evaluated for safety and effectiveness, and specifically which regulations should be applicable, notwithstanding who has jurisdiction. This is true especially when the combination product is one entity comprised of multiple attributes (e.g., hormone-producing cells housed in an implant). While the product jurisdiction regulations do not provide explicit direction, they do provide a basis for a company to articulate and propose a rationale approach.

The product jurisdiction regulations define four kinds of combination products. Shorthand definitions and examples are:

- Two or more regulated components physically, chemically, or otherwise mixed and produced as a single entity.
    Example: antibiotic-impregnated in-dwelling catheter.
    Example: hormone-producing cells housed in an implant.

- Two or more separate products packaged together in a single package or unit.
    Example: fibrin tissue sealant packaged with dedicated, unfilled administration device.

- An investigational product intended for use solely with a separately-packaged and approved specified product, where both are required to achieve the intended use, eventually leading to relabeling the approved product.
    Example: investigational photo-activated drug studied with a marketed laser.

- An investigational product intended for use solely with another separately-packaged specified investigational product, where both are required to achieve the intended use.
    Example: investigational photo-activated drug studied with an investigational laser.

From these definitions it is clear that combination products include not only products in which attributes of drug, biologic, and/or device are incorporated into one entity, but also include products comprised of individual, discretely-identifiable entities that, considered alone, could be a drug, biologic, or device. These regulations do not specify, nor constrain, the designated center with regard to which regulatory requirements could be applied to the combination.

In fact, a companion set of regulations (21 C.F.R. part 5) delegates to each of the centers all the respective statutory and regulatory authorities for drugs, biologics, and devices. Furthermore, part 3 allows the designated Center to consult with other agency components. Thus, taken together, part 3 and part 5 envision that under the authority of the designated Center, the agency can choose to apply in selective and focused manner drug, biologic, or device requirements to respective entities or attributes of the combination product.

Photo-Dynamic Therapy (PDT), involving the combination product of photo-active drug and laser, provides a good example. Here the agency decided that jurisdiction is with the Center for Drug Evaluation and Research (CDER). The lead center, in consultation with the Center for Devices and Radiological Health (CDRH), requires that clinical studies of unapproved PDT combination products be conducted under the investigational new drug (IND) regulations, and that market access be through the new drug approval (NDA) process. The marketing application must fulfill all the NDA requirements for the drug component as well as all the premarket approval (PMA) requirements for the laser. The clinical data acquired under the IND is used to fulfill simultaneously both NDA and PMA requirements for data.

While these agency decisions for PDT are available to the public and generally would be applicable to any sponsor of PDT, what remains unclear are agency decisions on obligations and mechanisms for postmarket surveillance and reporting, as well as for submitting supplemental applications. The details of fulfilling postmarket requirements probably could be negotiated between FDA and the owner of the application. If the component parts of the combination product are manufactured by separate companies, ownership of the application and the right to deal with FDA on any matter should be addressed very early in the partnership.

PDT is a simple example because the drug and device components are readily recognized. Other examples, such as hormone-producing cells housed in an implant, are not so simple because the demarcation between one component (or attribute) and another might not be clear. While the issue of fundamental evaluation of this latter product probably would be as a biologic, there are many other issues that might be raised. These others would be subordinate to statutory requirements for marketing of the product as a biologic, but are important nonetheless. Success in managing subordinate regulatory issues involving a combination product lies in the ability to segment and define discrete bounds for issues that otherwise would appear to be intertwined or convoluted.

The process of segmenting and defining issues should be guided by identifying attributes or components of the combination product that can be argued to conform to the statutory definitions of drug, biologic, or device. This in turn requires the ability to clearly articulate the role, mode of action, sequence of action (if applicable), and relative contribution to the overall diagnostic or therapeutic effect.

C. Do Not Overlook Manufacturing

From the statement of purpose of the product jurisdiction regulations and from the definitions of combination products, it is apparent that the scope of the regulations is for the assignment of primary jurisdiction to an agency component and that this process explicitly includes investigational and premarket approval aspects of agency regulation. These regulations are silent on issues of the applicability of the various regulations governing manufacturing, or on how FDA field offices should conduct manufacturing inspections. Moreover, at this writing, there are no publicly available FDA policy statements or guidance documents on this matter.

Traditionally, FDA field inspectors are to determine what manufacturing regulations are applicable to the product being inspected. When the product being inspected is clearly a drug, biologic, or device, no uncertainties of inspection requirements arise. Generally, the inspector and the company each know what inspection criteria will be applied.

For a combination product, however, a company should not leave inspection criteria to the sole determination of the local inspector. Here again, the company should articulate a rational approach and propose it — to both the review staff of the lead Center as well as to the FDA field office. These discussions should occur early in the product development cycle so that design verification and validation, as well as documentation of manufacturing and control processes, will not be impeded by uncertainty of the applicability of FDA's manufacturing regulations and inspection criteria.

III. Recommendations

A company should utilize best practices with regard to managing its interactions with FDA so that regulatory uncertainties can be resolved without delaying critical development milestones. While this is important for the development of any product regulated by FDA, it is especially important for combination products that are fraught with uncertainties. Before interacting with the agency, a company should determine its preference on how to proceed. Such a determination entails establishing a company position on how to deal with potential business partners, and understanding how FDA's statutes and regulations might apply and where advantages might lie if regulatory options are available.

With these issues in mind, for each combination product under consideration, a company should tend to the following details (in approximate order):

- *Partnerships.* If partnerships are envisioned, decide on the assignment of regulatory responsibilities or obligations to respective partners. Consider all regulatory requirements for all phases of product development and marketing.

- *Fundamental Evaluation for Market Access.* Examine the involved technologies and explore options, implications, and rationales for having primary jurisdiction assigned to one agency component or another. Postulate data requirements for approval and devise a tentative plan for product development and testing. Devise and articulate a rationale for applying one set or another of the drug, biologic, or device statutory requirements for market access.

- *Subordinate Issues.* Examine the involved technologies and articulate the role, mode of action, sequence of action (if applicable), and relative contribution to the overall diagnostic or therapeutic effect of the product. Identify attributes or components of the combination product that can be argued to conform to the statutory definitions of drug, biologic, or device. Segment and define discrete bounds for attributes or components that would lend themselves to application of drug-, biologic-, or device-specific regulations. Explore options and evaluate their impact. Devise and articulate a rationale for applying specific regulations to the respective attributes or components.

- *Determine Lead Center Jurisdiction.* Refer to the "Intercenter Agreements" and 21 C.F.R. part 3. Consult with relevant agency staff, and determine lead center jurisdiction through communications with relevant Center(s), if preferred. For highest degree of confidence that a determination will be binding (i.e., lasting), submit a Request for Designation to the FDA Product Jurisdiction Officer.

- *Confirm Applicability of Statutory Authorities.* Communicate with the designated lead center to confirm what statutory authorities will be applied and to determine the agency's expectations for data to support applications for clinical investigation and marketing.

- *Confirm Applicability of Regulations to Attributes or Components (subordinate issues).* Communicate with designated lead center and consultant Center(s) to resolve all subordinate issues, such as design and manufacturing processes and controls, and postmarket surveillance and reporting requirements.

- *Work on Agency Coordination.* Work to foster communication and cooperation between the designated lead Center, the consultant Center(s), and the field office(s).

C
H
A
P
T
E
R

24

Marjorie E. Powell

Pharmaceutical Research
and Manufacturers of America

Working With an Association to Achieve Goals at FDA

I. Introduction

When you have an immediate problem with the Food and Drug Administration (FDA) that you have not been able to resolve, or one you can foresee in the future as a result of your own product development activities or those of another company to create a competing product, consider whether an association can help. While companies frequently work through a trade association (e.g., an association whose members are companies), sometimes a professional association can also be helpful.

II. Association Action

Usually a trade association will not take an action in support of a specific product or a company-specific issue. This reluctance to act on behalf of a single member can be overcome, however, if the member can convince the association that the issue has implications for the entire industry, even though it might be manifested initially in a problem specific to one company. You will need to be prepared to make the argument that the issue has broad implications, and possibly to recruit other members to urge the association to act on the issue. In addition, a trade or professional association is unlikely to take a position on an issue that divides the industry or profession, especially if it is an important issue. Before raising an issue, you might consider whether other members would be on the opposite side of the issue, or whether you can identify a solution that does not disadvantage other members of the association.

Because a trade association is a collection of competitors, its staff may be concerned that association activities do not violate the antitrust laws (i.e., that they not constitute an illegal restraint of trade, division of markets, or sharing of information about prices or methods of setting prices). To avoid any hint of antitrust concerns, and also to protect your company's trade secrets and commercially valuable information, you will need to determine how to raise the issue without revealing proprietary information. Several methods may work, including referring to information that the company already has made public.

You are likely to receive a better initial response if you know the staff of the association, and if they have worked with you in the past. This experience may lead them to accept your indication that a problem for your company has industry-wide implications. Thus, one future advantage of participation in association committees (e.g., helping to draft comments to FDA or organize meetings) may be your ability to recruit the association to support your position in a dispute with FDA.

III. Learning How FDA Is Applying a New Statute, Regulation, Guidance, or Policy

A. Obtaining Information

Following are some avenues to obtain information:

- Ask the association staff whether they have any information about how FDA is applying or will apply the regulation, guidance, or policy. The association staff may have information from conversations with people from other companies or with FDA staff.

- Participate in discussions about the issue during a meeting of an association committee.

- Attend association-sponsored meetings with FDA staff of the relevant agency division or Center.

- Attend an association-sponsored workshop or seminar.

- Participate in the planning of an association workshop or seminar, and offer to invite an FDA speaker. Then ask that FDA speaker to address your concern as well as the concerns of other members of the planning committee.

Example: Pharmaceutical Research and Manufacturers of America (PhRMA) holds periodic dialogues with FDA's Center for Drug Evaluation and Research (CDER) review divisions. Company people attending such sessions may learn how the division is addressing an issue by listening to FDA staff's answers to other people's questions or by directly asking a question of the FDA staff in attendance.

> *Caution: You will need to find a way to ask your question or describe your issue that does not reveal proprietary information to competitors or FDA.*

IV. Resolving a Problem Already Encountered at FDA or One That Is Foreseeable

Identifiable problems may be product- or process-specific, or generally applicable throughout the industry.

A. Obtaining Information

Following are some avenues to obtain information:

- Ask the association staff whether they have heard that other companies have encountered the same problem, or type of problem. If they have, ask if they know how the problem was resolved. Also ask if they are aware of individuals at FDA who might be instrumental in resolving the problem.

- Ask other members of an association committee if they have encountered the same problem and, if so, how the problem was resolved. You may also want to ask if a specific individual at FDA was instrumental in resolving the problem, or if they know a person at FDA who might be helpful.

- Attend an association meeting with FDA and raise the issue in general terms that could apply to multiple members of the industry.

Example: The Animal Health Institute (AHI) staff confer with FDA staff on issue of concern to AHI members and often can identify an FDA staff person to help resolve a member's problem.

Caution: You may need to find ways to describe the problem that do not reveal confidential commercial information to competitors.

B. Shaping an FDA Regulation

If FDA might issue a regulation, an association may be convinced to submit a proposed regulation on behalf of its members. Working with an association committee to develop such a proposed regulation, you might insert regulatory language that would resolve your anticipated problem. Note that the length of time required for FDA to propose and promulgate a regulation usually means there will not be time to use a future regulation to resolve an existing problem. This strategy may be a greater option when a new statute requires, or encourages, FDA to issue a regulation.

Examples: Members of the dairy industry, working through their associations, submit petitions to FDA to establish or modify food standards.

The Association of Disposable Device Manufacturers submitted a proposed guidance for FDA's premarketing review of single-use medical devices that have been reprocessed.

> *Caution: To convince the association to support your position, you will need to convince other members of the association that the position will not disadvantage them and that the issue has broad industry implications.*

C. Convincing FDA to Revise an Existing Regulation

You may be able to convince the trade association to propose to FDA that it revise an existing regulation. This usually will require convincing the association that the problem is wide-spread throughout the industry and is sufficiently important that it is worth the effort involved in convincing FDA to revise its regulation. You may need to convince other companies to raise the issue with the association. In addition, critical comments about the regulation, or its application, in other venues may carry some weight with the association.

Examples: Member companies convinced PhRMA that the application of the Environmental Assessment regulation by chemistry reviewers was imposing an increasing burden on the pharmaceutical industry, a burden that occurred at the very last moment in the new drug application (NDA) review process. Once they convinced PhRMA to act, PhRMA was able to raise the issue with FDA. With support from the Clinton Administration's Reinventing Government Initiative, FDA spent several months revising the regulation, which eventually resulted in lowering the application burden on NDA applicants.

D. Suggesting That FDA Address Your Concerns in Comments Submitted on an Existing Guidance

If an FDA guidance exists, but does not provide the flexibility to enable you to resolve your problem or does not address your problem, you may be able to convince the association to submit comments to FDA urging that the guidance be revised.

Examples: The Animal Health Institute worked with several committees within the FDA Center to establish criteria for environmental assessments for new animal drugs.

E. Using the Flexibility Provided by a Future Guidance Document

Sometimes a principle or goal articulated in an FDA guidance document provides a basis for avoiding a dispute — if a company can demonstrate that its product or method achieves the principle or accomplishes the goal. You may be able to shape the way the principle or goal is stated in the FDA guidance by suggesting language, and arguments to support the language, in comments submitted by a trade association.

Sometimes examples offered by the agency within a guidance document can be used to argue by analogy that a product or procedure meets the goals as set forth in the guidance document. You may be able to include an example in a section of an FDA guidance document by including the example in association comments to FDA. If you include a similar example in company comments you may increase the chances that FDA will use one or another version of the example.

> *Caution: The association likely will submit your suggested language or example for review by other company members of the trade association. Be sure that it does not disadvantage other members of the association, or it is likely to be rejected. Be prepared to provide scientific, medical, legal, or policy justification(s) for your recommendation.*

F. Comments to the Office of Management and Budget

Convince the trade association to submit comments to FDA when it requests comments on a data collection that requires Office of Management and Budget (OMB) approval. If OMB is convinced that the data collection effort outweighs the value of the data being collected, they may require FDA to modify the requirements for data collection.

G. Citizen Petitions

You may be able to convince the association to submit a citizen petition (assuming that the proposed rules allow for a petition to address your problem) to FDA urging the agency to accept a position that will resolve your problem. Note that many trade associations will act only on an issue that has wide industry application. Therefore, you should argue from the start that the problem you have encountered is not specific to your product, process, or company, but that it may occur in multiple other instances. Be prepared to support this argument with examples, either hypothetical or real.

Examples: The Indiana Medical Device Manufacturers Council submitted a citizen petition asking FDA to establish procedures for the initiation, development, issuance, review, and revision of guidance documents. The petition included criteria for determining whether the guidance should be issued in draft with a request for comments or issued as final with comments accepted any time. In 1997, FDA published Good Guidance Practice regulations, after receiving comments on a 1996 draft, in response to the citizen petition.

Prescription drug companies, concerned about how the clinical investigator financial disclosure rule would impact their clinical trial work, convinced PhRMA to file a citizen petition asking FDA to modify the final rule. FDA issued a revision to the final rule limiting the retroactive collection of some types of financial information from clinical investigators for studies completed before the date that FDA issued the revision to the final rule.

> *Caution: You will need to provide enough information about your problem, and the steps you have taken to resolve it, that the association staff will consider bringing the issue to the relevant decisionmaking group for possible association action. You may need to think about how to present that information without revealing proprietary or confidential commercial information.*

H. Litigation

You may be able to convince the association to litigate on your behalf. Note that many trade associations will only litigate about an issue that has important and industry-wide implications.

Examples: The National Food Processors Association, the International Dairy Foods Association, and the Grocery Manufacturers of America successfully challenged a Vermont law that required milk derived from cows treated with the biotechnology drug product rBST to bear a label indicating the use of the rBST even though the milk was indistinguishable from milk derived from untreated cows. The Vermont law was found to be unenforceable as a violation of the First Amendment.

Generic pharmaceutical industry companies convinced their trade associations to sue FDA over implementation of the pediatric provision of the Food and Drug Administration Modernization Act of 1997 (FDAMA). Innovator companies then convinced their trade association to ask the court for permission to intervene. The court allowed the intervention and refused to grant the preliminary injunction sought by the generic companies. The generic associations then asked the court to dismiss the case.

Pharmaceutical companies, concerned that FDA had released or would release confidential commercial information included in NDA advisory committee briefing packets (in response to a suit by Public Citizen), convinced PhRMA to intervene in the litigation and participate in the negotiation of a settlement.

Likewise, pharmaceutical companies with investigational new drugs (INDs) that were "abandoned" according to FDA's definition (and thus subject to release in response to a Freedom of Information Act request), convinced PhRMA to intervene in a suit brought by Public Citizen. Public Citizen filed against FDA, seeking access to several abandoned INDs. The court held that the "exceptional circumstances" provision for release of confidential information did not apply to information in INDs, but only to information in NDAs.

> *Caution: You will need to provide enough information about how the issue affects your company that you can convince the association to act and the court to support your position. You may need to think about how to present the information without revealing proprietary or confidential commercial information*

> *Caution: The association is likely to adopt a position that avoids or resolves a problem for a large number of members, and is likely to take direction from all members. The final solution, therefore, may be one that you would not have chosen for your own product, process, or company.*

I. Legislation

You may be able to convince the association to support legislation that will resolve the problem or establish conditions under which you can resolve the problem.

Examples: Pharmacists with an interest in expanding their compounding of prescription medicines convinced the American Pharmaceutical Association (APhA) to support a provision in FDAMA to allow compounding under conditions established in the provision.

APhA also lobbied Congress to include a prohibition on FDA expending appropriated funds to implement FDA's proposed "MedGuide" plan. That plan would have required prescription drug manufacturers to provide FDA-approved patient labeling for their prescription drugs. The prohibition was contingent on development of a voluntary plan to provide patient information with new prescriptions. FDA is authorized to implement the "MedGuide" plan if the agency finds that the voluntary plan does not meet certain criteria for the percentage of patients receiving written information and the quality of that information. These criteria were established in the legislative provision.

The National Food Processors Association supported provisions in FDAMA that streamlined FDA's procedure for review and approval of claims about the health benefits of foods. The Act now includes a premarket notification system to authorize claims based on an authoritative statement of a federal scientific body such as the Centers for Disease Control and Prevention.

The Cosmetic, Toiletry & Fragrance Association urged Congress to increase funding for FDA's office of cosmetics in 1998, to ensure continued FDA review and regulation of the industry.

V. Conclusion

Companies can work through associations, either trade or professional associations, to resolve problems at FDA. To shape and/or add flexibility to FDA regulations and guidance documents usually requires that company personnel anticipate the potential of a problem. A company's efforts to involve a trade or professional association are more likely to be successful if that company's representatives have participated in association activities.

Peter H. Rheinstein

Cell Works, Inc.

CHAPTER 25

Some Tips on FDA Etiquette I

The Food and Drug Administration (FDA) is an organization of 9000 people, large numbers of whom spend careers of thirty or more years with the agency. Naturally, an organization of such size, and one where people stay together for such lengths of time, will develop a culture all its own.

Many college graduates begin their FDA careers at field offices, learning the ways of the agency through on-the-job training. This is true for inspectors, analytical chemists, public affairs specialists, and other personnel who have contact with industry on a day-to-day basis. Promotions often require moving from one field office to another. After a few field assignments, further promotions often depend on assignment to head-quarters, which is dispersed over thirty or more buildings in the Washington metropolitan area. On coming to headquarters, the field person may go to a compliance office where he or she studies reports from field offices and recommends appropriate regulatory action. This track may lead to permanent work in a Center compliance office; it also may lead to a management position in an FDA field office. The field person also may be assigned to a review division where he or she will work as a consumer safety officer, essentially serving as a project manager in the application review process.

Medical officers and Ph.D.-level reviewers arrive at the agency through a different track. They arrive at headquarters review divisions as fully-trained medical specialists or scientists, and acquire reviewing skills from more senior personnel in their own divisions. The Centers operate staff colleges to teach reviewing skills and to allow reviewers to know one another. Nevertheless, reviewers are likely to spend a career in a single division, or at least in a single Center. Attempts are made to keep requirements uniform across divisions, but from time to time, requirements may vary significantly. The fact that the agency is spread over so many buildings further contributes to this situation.

With people spending so many years in one organization, there are networks extending throughout the agency. Off-the-cuff remarks may be passed on throughout FDA. In fact, there are many FDA employees married to one another, although they may use different surnames.

As of 1999, medical officers are paid from $100,000 to $150,000 annually. Ph.D.-level reviewers receive about $70,000 to $100,000. These somewhat modest salaries are accepted because of the security of government employment and, at least in the case of the medical officers, patient contact is not required.

Many of today's medical reviewers are brilliant, well-trained physicians, who in earlier years might have become full-time academics, but in an era of managed care and shrinking faculties are looking for an experience as close to academia as possible.

Given the comparatively-low levels of government pay, it is probably best for industry personnel not to arrive for an FDA meeting by limousine. Fur coats, ostentatious jewelry, and excessively expensive clothing are similarly out of place. Smoking is not permitted in any FDA building, and the agency is engaged in a campaign to prevent minors from purchasing cigarettes; so a shirt pocket filled with cigars or a pack of cigarettes is also out of place. Fridays are "dressdown" days at FDA, but this applies to FDA employees and not to industry representatives.

A significant number of professional FDA employees belong to the U.S. Public Health Service Commissioned Corps, a uniformed service consisting entirely of officers, and commanded by the Surgeon General. Corps members are encouraged by the Surgeon General to wear their uniforms frequently (essentially naval uniforms with different insignia). Corps members generally are recruited early in their professional careers and frequently have served in a number of different agencies of the Department of Health and Human Services. Pharmacists frequently start in the Indian Health Service, and others have been at the Centers for Disease Control, the National Institutes of Health, the Health Care Financing Administration, and many other agencies. They can retire with twenty years of service, but are divested of all retirement benefits if they leave the Corps before accruing twenty years. Many Corps members retire in their forties and move on to industry positions.

In 1998, FDA's nonsupervisory civilian employees voted to join the National Treasury Employees Union. The first collective bargaining agreement went into effect on October 1, 1999. This bargaining process centers on working conditions, and not wages per se. Physicians with more than ten years of service are guaranteed Physician Special Pay, which keeps their salary on a par with physicians in the Veterans Administration.

There probably is no substitute for company personnel knowing the individuals who will be dealing with a particular product. One place to meet appropriate FDA personnel is an advisory committee meeting at which the committee will be considering the same class of product that the company will be applying to market. Annual meetings and workshops offered by The Food and Drug Law Institute, the Drug Information Association, the Regulatory Affairs Professionals Society, the Pharmaceutical Education and Research Institute, and similar organizations offer excellent opportunities to meet FDA employees who attend both as speakers and as members of the audience. Attendees at such meetings should pay careful attention to speakers who may review product applications; these speakers often will describe what they want to see in a submission. Most of these organizations sell audio tapes of recent meetings, and several have journals that contain edited versions of recent presentations, as well as Websites for additional information.

Chairing a session at one of these meetings provides an opportunity to ask an FDA employee to speak. In most cases, the employee will not be able to accept the invitation until it comes through official channels. Nevertheless, the request is flattering. Meeting speakers also can call an FDA employee as research for suitable background material and preparation for a presentation.

FDA regulations severely limit any entertainment that an FDA employee can accept from regulated industry, so FDAers should not be invited to expensive restaurants. If you go out for a sandwich with an FDA employee, make it a place that anyone easily can afford and do not be offended when he or she asks for separate checks.

Similarly, if an FDA employee visits on-location to talk to an industry group, company meeting planners should resist the temptation to purchase an upgraded room for the FDA traveler. Hotels frequently are willing to give the FDA employee a discounted bill and charge the difference to the company's master account. Even though this may done without the employee's knowledge, the agency may discover this difference, force the employee to pay it back, and charge him with acceptance of an illegal gratuity.

The importance of personal contact in a relationship with FDA cannot be overstated. Some of the most successful companies employ a regular FDA representative, who frequently drops off submissions in-person. In some divisions, that representative may not get past the document room, but in others he or she can develop a face-to-face relationship with a secretary or a consumer safety officer who will do their utmost to route the material to the right person or the right desk.

The FDA Website is a wonderful source of information. Go to <www.fda.gov> and click on "Special Information for Industry." Under the "Comprehensive List of Current FDA Guidance Documents," find one on-point from the last five years or so (some go back more than twenty years), and read it thoroughly; if questions remain, call the division responsible for it, as there is a good chance to be connected with the principal author of the document. Since the advent of prescription drug user fees, reviewers are held to tight timeframes for their work. Called-in questions do take away from the reviewer's time, so these calls should be brief.

E-mail communication saves the reviewer the trouble of rewriting questions in their responses. The FDA employee can use the time to focus on the write-up of an answer.

FDA advisory committee meetings are announced ahead of time on the FDA Website. Attend several meetings where products similar to your own are going to be discussed. You will learn the interests, concerns, and preferred manner of response for both FDA employees and advisory committee members.

The Center for Devices and Radiological Health operates a Division of Small Manufacturers Assistance. The other Centers have similar, but smaller, units to assist industry. Professional personnel are available in each of these units to help you find the right person, or at least the right division or office, that will handle your product.

When calling a reviewing division where you do not know anyone, the supervisory consumer safety officer is probably the first person to speak to. Tell him or her about your product; solicit advice; ask for a meeting to discuss protocols for the studies you are planning; and be prepared to wait. Waiting may be worth it however, when you realize it is a lot cheaper to change the protocol before the study is complete.

Under the Prescription Drug User Fee Act (PDUFA), the Center for Biologics Evaluation and Research (CBER) and the Center for Drug Evaluation and Research (CDER) have a goal of fourteen days from the request date for notifying the company of an actual meeting date. Meetings necessary for an otherwise stalled drug development program should occur within thirty calendar days of the agency receipt of the meeting request. Pre-IND, end of phase 1 (for Subpart E or Subpart H or similar products) or end of phase 2/pre-phase 3, and pre- NDA/PLA/BLA meetings should occur within sixty days of the request.

CDER's Office of Drug Evaluation IV has a formal pre-IND consultation program. They also have a Targeted Product Information (TPI) Document Program. The sponsor is encouraged to bring in early drafts of what they hope to get in final labeling. The TPI should summarize the studies that will supply the evidence for each major claim about the drug. These early drafts serve as a basis for discussion. Specific instructions for submitting a TPI are on the CDER Website.

At the meeting, FDA reviewers like to hear from people who are experts in their own fields. Thus, it is useful to bring experts in relevant scientific disciplines in addition to regulatory affairs-types. Lawyers often add an unnecessary layer of formality to a meeting.

Internet Grateful Med is a cost-free and fast way of searching for publications prepared by the person who has been assigned to review a particular product. Many FDA reviewers published as academics prior to coming to the agency, and some continue to publish using the one-half day per week allowed reviewers as "professional development time."

CDER presents an hour-long seminar on most Wednesday afternoons throughout the academic year. Videotapes of these seminars are kept in the eleventh floor library (Room 11B-45) of the Parklawn Building, and generally are available for onsite viewing. Most seminars also are open to the public. Topics frequently are listed in *News Along the Pike*, a CDER employee newsletter, published on the Internet, which can provide insight to items of current concern in the center.

C
H
A
P
T
E
R

26

Ronald M. Johnson

Quintiles Consulting

FDA Etiquette: Field Offices vs. Headquarters

The issue of etiquette frequently is raised when the topic of Food and Drug Administration (FDA) interactions is discussed. The reason for this is simple; failure to adhere to proper FDA etiquette can result in unwanted or unwarranted attention from FDA. FDA etiquette is more than "good manners"; it requires awareness and exercise of proper protocol. Good manners in business interactions are fairly well understood, and they do not pose a challenge for most companies. Knowing what constitutes good manners when dealing with FDA is a bit more challenging because it involves understanding the culture of FDA.

The Field Office/Headquarters Dynamic

Over the years there has been some friction between FDA components in "headquarters" and those in the field (i.e., those working outside of the Washington, D.C. beltway). Much of this tension may be explained simply as a function of FDA being a large, geographically-dispersed organization. Unfortunately, some of FDA's internal conflicts have been aired publicly. For example, FDA field investigators have testified before congressional oversight committees about the failures of FDA headquarters' components to protect the public health. The causes and extent of this internal conflict are too complicated to address here, but it is important for companies to understand this background when dealing with FDA. FDA has undertaken numerous initiatives to improve its inter-center relationships with mixed success.

When interfacing with FDA on inspectional findings or other matters in which the local FDA district office may be involved, a company must be careful not to alienate the district office by failing to follow proper protocol. The local field office may believe it has primary responsibility for FDA inspections and related compliance issues, but, in these situations, protocol calls for communications to be directed to the district office.

This process should be followed even if the company believes the source of the information may be an FDA office in headquarters; it is always wise to keep the district office in the loop. This may involve letting the district office interface with headquarters and basically lead the effort. It may result in the field office simply referring the company to a headquarters component. Communications with a headquarters component on these kinds of issues should be copied to the district office, and the district office should be notified of, and invited to, any meetings scheduled with headquarters.

Failure to recognize the district office or to include it in communications can lead to intra-agency resentments, that can, in turn, create distrust among multiple parties. Once, this distrust went so far that a district office believed a company and an FDA headquarters unit were covertly collaborating to minimize regulatory problems. When this happens, a company can be pulled into the power dynamic between the field and headquarters offices; the district may perceive that it has something to prove and the company inadvertently becomes the vehicle by which the district makes its point. This can have disastrous consequences because the district offices have great autonomy and are delegated significant authorities and powers. The last thing a company needs is to have an FDA investigator testifying before Congress about how FDA headquarters somehow failed to act on the company's unsafe product.

Of course, there are times when it is perfectly appropriate to deal with headquarters components without extending courtesies to the local district office. Communications regarding product approval submissions, general FDA information, or other issues that do not involve activities of the local office can, and should, be directed to the appropriate FDA office or component.

There also may be occasions when it becomes necessary for a company to go above a district office in the FDA hierarchy. Those occasions may involve a company's perception that the local office does not understand, or is not giving sufficient consideration, to the company's perspective on a particular enforcement matter. For example, the district office may be pressuring the company to initiate a recall, but the company has documentation that removal of its products may create a public health crisis.

There may be times when a company believes that the local district office is not being objective in assessing the company's compliance status. It could be that an investigator is not conducting him/herself appropriately. All of these may be legitimate reasons for seeking assistance from a level of FDA beyond the district office.

This escalation of communication, however, should be undertaken only after the local office has been given an opportunity to react to the company's concerns. There may be risks in going "over the head" of the local FDA office. In part because of human nature and in part because of the headquarters/field dynamic, the local office and its staff may feel challenged and, in turn, become defensive. These reactions may adversely affect the relationship between the company and the local office, but such a result may be a "cost" warranted by the situation. A company should not fail to upwardly pursue resolution of important issues that cannot be resolved at the district level.

Issues regarding conduct or demeanor of the district office or its staff should be addressed with management in the headquarters offices of FDA's Office of Regulatory Affairs. Scientific or health-related issues should be directed to the appropriate FDA Center. The FDA Ombudsman's office is another avenue of potential redress, particularly if efforts at FDA headquarters have not produced results.

C
H
A
P
T
E
R

27

Joseph Paul Hile

Phoenix Regulatory Associates, Ltd

Some Tips on FDA Etiquette II

For many readers, the word "etiquette" and the name "Emily Post" are synonymous. Over the years, Ms. Post has published books on etiquette for meal times, weddings, houseguests, invitations and letters, entertaining, and even business. In her book, *The New Emily Post's Etiquette*, she concludes that rules of etiquette "are derived from long experience; [and] their basis is always consideration for the feelings, beliefs, and sensibilities of others." If one were to apply this basic philosophy to relationships with the Food and Drug Administration (FDA), perhaps no further discussion of the subject would be necessary. Like Ms. Post with her books, however, a discussion on how to work with FDA would not be complete without some further delineation of the rules of etiquette, expanding on the courtesies appropriate for working with the agency.

Having sat on both sides of the table gives a person some advantages when considering how best to work with FDA; this author shares that perspective in the following set of suggested rules. Some overlapping with other chapters or sections of this book is inevitable, but thinking of the approaches as "rules of etiquette" may be different than from seeing them as "necessary burdens." Therefore, persons dealing with FDA are encouraged to follow these general principles of FDA etiquette to assist in enhancing their relationships with the agency.

Respect the FDA representatives as peers. Webster defines a peer as someone of equal standing with another. In dealing with FDA, that equality operates not necessarily as equal in knowledge and understanding of identical matters, but as equal in the business of ensuring that the public are provided safe, effective, wholesome, and properly-labeled products. You know your business well; give the FDA representatives credit for knowing their business well.

Be understanding of FDA's need to respond to a number of different sectors of the public. It is easy for persons in the regulated industry to focus on FDA–industry relations as the only agency concern. FDA employees, however, must not only consider their relationship with industry, but also must be conscious of FDA relationships with

Congress, consumer groups, the White House, and the Department of Health and Human Services (DHHS). It can be difficult for the agency to balance issues among these competing sectors, and being conscious of this difficulty for the agency is an important part of FDA etiquette.

Do not waste an FDA employee's time. If you have to meet, meet; if you have to call, call; if you have to write, fax, or e-mail, do so. But be certain that it is absolutely necessary before you act. Everyone complains of being too busy or having too much to do, yet it is popular to wrap all government employees into the same "deadwood" blanket. But remember, in addition to your matter on the agency's itinerary, there are always the competing industry petitions, Freedom of Information requests, congressional inquiries, and executive branch requirements that must be handled as part of the everyday routine. Another important aspect of this rule is to be prepared when you meet or talk on the telephone with FDA representatives. Regardless of the amount of time spent in preparation for a meeting by the FDA representatives, you must be rehearsed and ready to present your issues in full. In the same fashion, anticipate what an FDA representative will want to know before you pick up the telephone to ask for guidance. For the conscientious FDA employee (and there *is* a tradition of dedication in the agency), there is plenty to do each day without dealing with unnecessary requests for audiences or other interruptions from the industry.

Honor the chain of command. FDA employees understand that there will be times when an industry representative will feel compelled to go over the head of the person with whom he or she has been dealing; that is just part of conducting any kind of business. What often happens in FDA interactions, however, is that an exasperated top industry executive, instead of going to a person's supervisor, wants to jump directly to the top of FDA — to the Commissioner's Office or even to their congressperson. Two important rules of etiquette apply in these chain of command situations. First, if you decide to go up the chain of command, let the person you have been dealing with know what you are doing. This can be done easily, by providing the person a copy of any correspondence involved or by straightforwardly telling the person that you intend to contact his or her supervisor. This is the courteous, business-like thing to do. Second, be aware that, most often, neither the Commissioner nor the congressperson will want to respond to your request except they have already ascertained what FDA staff members have said about the matter. By going up the chain of command in an orderly manner, you will be viewed by everyone in the agency, and by the congressperson, as one who has followed the rules and exhausted all available avenues to resolve the matter before going to the top.

Be prompt in responding to calls or requests from FDA. Just as you may become angry and frustrated if your contact with FDA is not responded to in a timely manner, so will failure on your part to respond to an FDA request influence their attitude about you and your company. If you cannot immediately or fully respond, contact the FDA representatives and let them know when they can expect your reply; do not leave them waiting and wondering. If the matter is not of importance to you, you risk it becoming of little importance to the agency. Follow this rule, even if FDA does not. It is part of your obligation under the rules of FDA etiquette. In the same manner, do not leave an FDA investigator languishing in your front lobby when they appear unannounced for an inspection. As in all interpersonal relationships, first impressions are very important.

Do not expect a decision on every issue raised during a meeting. On key matters, FDA employees are mindful that a decision must represent "an agency position." Frequently an agency decision cannot be reached until the matter has been fully discussed and a position agreed upon by the involved parties. This process takes time, and must be outside the presence of industry representatives. Respect FDA's need to handle matters in this fashion. At the same time, as part of this rule, you must be certain you have given the agency all it needs in the way of information so it can reach a decision. Incomplete or vague information by industry will result in boilerplate responses by FDA.

Do not expect special treatment from an FDA representative. Increasingly, under today's policies, FDA is attempting to become helpful to industry by providing guidance on how best to meet its requirements. Further, except in the most egregious circumstances, FDA historically has given persons and companies opportunities to correct objectionable conditions before concluding that enforcement action is the only course of action left open to the agency. The rules of etiquette require, however, that one does not try to take advantage of these policies. Suggestion, or even hints, by individuals or companies that FDA provide them with some special treatment raises a red flag for FDA, with possible dire consequences. Playing the game by the rules is an integral part of FDA etiquette.

Use telephones calls to the FDA with discretion, recognizing that the answer you receive over the telephone may not be the agency's position on the matter. Further, do not go shopping within the agency for a best answer to your question. Proper FDA etiquette requires that one do their very best to identify the correct contact person within the agency on a given issue, and then, for that instance, be willing to live with the answer they receive. This further requires that one does his or her homework, and that the matter is presented clearly and completely to the FDA representative who is contacted. If you are not sure you have called the right person, do not be embarrassed to ask. But shopping around for an answer acceptable to you is like fishing without a license; if you get caught, you are in trouble.

Never directly offer to buy meals or pay for other services for FDA representatives. FDA employees are trained to refuse offers of payment for meals or other services. FDA may see such offers, regardless of their intent, as attempts by a company to influence an FDA decision or otherwise solicit special favors from the agency. Try to avoid such awkward situations if at all possible. Often, however, formal, and sometimes even informal, business situations make it difficult for an FDA employee not to accept such favors. For example, a manufacturing plant may be located far from commercial food service facilities; therefore the company provides its employees a meal at no cost to them (the employees). The FDA representative also may have to eat in the facility, if his or her business is to be completed in any reasonable time, and there are no procedures for accepting payment from the FDA employee. Professional meetings often include company-sponsored social events for all attendees, and these may be an integral part of the meeting program. In these situations, FDA etiquette requires that the company or meeting sponsor help the FDA employee by providing him or her with the documentation they need to report such events as being an unavoidable part of their FDA business responsibilities.

Total Quality Management (TQM) programs have become very popular within industry and government over the past several years. For the private sector especially, certain aspects of such programs focus on obligations to the customer. Companies are obligated to understand the customer's requirements, perform error-free work, and deliver the "product" on time, every time. Such objectives translate into "customer etiquette" for the companies within their TQM programs. If the regulated industry viewed FDA as a customer, and applied the TQM objectives, much concern over FDA etiquette would be mollified.

Elizabeth L. Post has carried on the work of her grandmother-in-law, by continuing to publish the Emily Post guidance on etiquette. In her *Revised Edition of Emily Post on Etiquette*, she concludes that "Good manners have always been based on common sense and thoughtfulness, and that hasn't changed." If industry follows the basic rules of common sense and thoughtfulness when interacting with FDA, then the general rules of etiquette will have been met.

Andrea E. Chamblee

Regulatory Consultant

28

Some Tips on FDA Etiquette III

I. Introduction

You drop the phone. Your brain fogs over — you do not even see the receiver dangling off its hook, or hear its harsh buzzing. You cannot comprehend the conversation you just had. What did the statement, "It is over" mean? Did you not anticipate every foreseeable need? Did you not eagerly do everything asked of you? Did you not readily fulfill any request, no matter the cost, no matter how unreasonable? How could you be rejected? Will the relationship end now? Like this?

No clear ideas escape, as you rack your brain, certain there must be a response that will win over someone so fickle. Perhaps you beg. Perhaps you feel so betrayed and angry, you scream. You know you should not say something cruel and hurtful; maybe you already did, but the outburst only deepened your predicament.

Now you may never be able to recover the relationship that was the envy of your peers. Should you ask for reconsideration? If you do, should you ask the person who is now your tormentor, or should you go to a higher authority?

It is senseless to file an appeal in matters of the heart. In commercial relationships, however, an appeal up the chain of command is a practical option. It is not unusual or unreasonable to seek a supervisor's intervention when baffled or offended by decisions at the staff level.

Many would-be suitors have brought their offerings to Food and Drug Administration (FDA) reviewers, only to be rebuffed. An applicant dismissed by FDA often feels more like a rejected suitor, without recourse, than like someone in a position to negotiate or to force a second opinion. Many applicants who deal with FDA take great pains not to offend agency staff. There are limited avenues of appeal, but there also is a fear, rarely spoken and even more rarely proved, that an applicant who steps on FDA toes will never be welcome again at "the dance."

Is it possible to deal with FDA without groveling? Is it possible to challenge FDA staff without permanently harming the relationship? Or is FDA so easily offended and vengeful that an applicant who asks too many questions will not receive timely and fair review?

Although it is not possible to cover everything that can cause disagreement between FDA and industry, there are two potential problems that always cost time and money no matter what office you deal with or what product you plan to sell. These problems also are the most difficult to correct. They are breaches of what might be called etiquette, and they can be severe enough to incite FDA to scrutinize every proposal you suggest and/or to refuse to communicate or cooperate in a meaningful way with the company.

After my ten years with FDA, the last five with the Commissioner's Office of the Chief Mediator and Ombudsman, I have seen hundreds of companies broken-hearted after a falling out with FDA. I have also heard FDA staff express their dissatisfaction with industry in meetings (and in hallways, stairwells, and bathrooms among themselves after meetings). Sometimes the public employees express their frustration with fellow FDA staff. Seeing both parties struggling in the process gave valuable insight into why such a relationship can go sour.

The good news is that by following some basic rules of etiquette, you can prevent an ugly divorce. If it already has happened, following these rules now can go a long way toward "making up." If pride stands in the way of an earnest attempt at reconciliation, let financial incentives inspire you to make a conciliatory gesture. After all, the price of a trial separation from FDA is expensive and arduous, even before you add the costs of frazzled nerves and squandered hours that could be spent free from the office.

The secrets to preventing a relationship from disintegrating during a conflict are the stock-in-trade of any counselor, be the focus on marriage, legal, or regulatory interactions. The circumstances surrounding a conflict may change, but a facilitator uses general precepts that enable quarreling sides to communicate, find common ground, identify principles underlying disagreements (preferably in a civil manner), and ultimately reach resolution. This section will explain some of those precepts and how to apply them when courting the agency. Although this discussion assumes that problems already have come up, you can certainly use these tools from the beginning to minimize the possibility that problems will emerge. With these rules in mind, you will be able to question decisions at FDA without losing face or losing ground.

II. Can This Marriage Be Saved?

Industry and FDA have different cultures, which often interfere with a happy collaboration. The parties work best, however, when each participant recognizes that collaboration, well done, can be the finest and fastest way to benefit patients. The noteworthy corollary is that collaboration, poorly done, sacrifices the very patients who depend most on the success of joint efforts.

It is tempting to portray the interests and sentiments of industry and FDA as polar opposites. Such a portrayal, however, is not necessarily true. Each consumer, including each person in FDA, makes an individual determination as to where to strike a balance of the respective roles/ability of government and manufacturers to protect the public health. More factors come into play when considering the roles for healthcare providers and for consumers who accept responsibility for their own health. Nevertheless, it can be irresistible to over-generalize when distinguishing between regulators and regulated industry. For example, FDA staff can agree that many applicants put more emphasis on cost than regulators do, and that many are naïve about FDA requirements. The expression of this perception may be interpreted as a sign that FDA staff care nothing about costs, and that they view the industry as a collective enemy. On the other hand, industry can agree that some FDA staff do not appreciate financial realities and marketing pressures. Instead of educating FDA to these realities, or recognizing where such pressures are tangential to the FDA mission, FDA staff are dismissed as "ivory tower" residents who build their careers out of keeping good treatments from patients. A view of FDA as the "health police" can change with something as simple as counting the smokers huddled outside the FDA buildings on a winter day. People at FDA get sick and their family members do, too, and they generally want good products available for their loved ones.

Even if neither side voices these disparaging preconceptions, each side seems to posture and brace for accusations, which raises defenses. Resist these preconceptions, and acknowledge the potential for a valuable exchange. I have witnessed many cases where FDA input not only improved products that would otherwise be outdated before product launch, but prevented liability nightmares from avoidable harms. On the other hand, there were at least an equal number of examples where industry's innovation, fortitude, exuberance, and financial strength delivered good products to sick patients against high odds. Instead of expecting the worst, industry should acknowledge, perhaps explicitly, that FDA is entitled to see evidence (more than mere testimonials) to demonstrate that the product actually is the good one that the sponsor says it is. And just as with humans found outside the Washington-area Beltway, FDA staff works best when asked for their cooperation in this endeavor without hostility.

III. How Industry Can Work With FDA

Even when people speak the same language, they do not always understand each other. Dialects are not the only barrier to understanding; technical vocabulary, institutional or corporate culture, regional customs (and even further subdivisions in these categories based on gender) can complicate our ability to understand each other. To paraphrase a title from a best-selling book, perhaps FDA is from Mars and industry is from Venus.

Cultural differences can fuel miscommunication and exacerbate conflict. Good diversity training has caught on because it can prevent miscommunication by bridging cultural differences, and by raising awareness that each side is affected by the different experiences they bring to the table. Those experiences affect presumptions and interpretations, the way we express ourselves, and the way we interpret the expressions of others. Industry can take the lead to make sure the parties are speaking the same language by using communication tools like feedback and clarification requests. It can also demonstrate a willingness to understand the cultural differences and to take the first step to declare a truce.

A. Prevailing Rules for Negotiating

There are basic "rules" for negotiating through any conflict, whether it is over a potential break-up or an application denial. You may not be able to list all the rules readily, but you probably learned them in kindergarten. When negotiating with FDA — or for that matter with your subordinates, your supervisor, or even your family members — you should use the rules of "fair fighting."

1. Apologize

There are many ways to react when things go awry. You are not alone if you are so invested in your products that you are not always able to see an unanswered question. You may have missed signs of trouble, or trivialized them. Maybe FDA deluged you, not with a flood of questions, but with a steady stream that seemed endless. Agency turnover and reassignments may have required you to manage an assembly line of reviewers, with each one insisting on changes until the project has become ponderous and unrecognizable. Maybe you are anguishing over the knowledge that failure to obtain agency clearance jeopardizes your job or your entire organization. You may react in ways that do not ingratiate you with FDA. Fortunately, many agency employees are sympathetic to the idea that this is a project close to your heart. This does not entitle a company to market a product without careful review, but it may mean that an inappropriate reaction is forgivable.

As in a romantic relationship, it is wise to apologize (even if you feel you have done nothing wrong). If you cannot stomach the humble pie, rephrase your apology to say you are sorry things went wrong, or sorry that a conversation ended so badly. It is not important to accept all the blame, but it is critical to demonstrate your willingness to move beyond acrimony. Of course, if you know you had taken out your frustrations on an individual at FDA, acknowledge your part. If you have not lost your cool, you can skip the apology, and move on to the part where you and FDA work together.

2. Do Not Play Hardball

Hardball negotiating for its own sake is not conducive to true negotiating. In fact, it is often so infuriating to the agency it can hurt your case. While you may catch someone off-guard the first time with hardball tactics, the next time the reviewer not only will be braced for battle, but so will others who have heard the war stories. The comrades will be lined up and ready for you.

Moreover, hardball negotiating is rarely necessary when you have a strong case, so FDA staff may jump to the conclusion that you do not have a principled argument, or that you fear what the examination might reveal. If there might be hidden adverse information, the agency will have a reason to fiercely scrutinize your motives and your application.

Close scrutiny can cause delays, and is often the basis of rumors of retaliation. It is difficult to object to the concept of careful scrutiny; that is precisely what FDA was created to do. Of course, this scrutiny should be even-handed. Where FDA can show the applicant has earned the agency's suspicions or lost its trust, FDA's easy retort is that it has learned from experience and that safety concerns do not leave room for FDA to be fooled a second time.

So, do not lose your cool. Have a plan of action to stem the tide of tempers rising. You may not recognize it in yourself, but you will in others around the table. Be sure the company team knows what to do in advance of such a reaction; it is not inappropriate to call a recess and caucus in another room.

3. Do Not Be Too Soft

Refraining from hardball negotiation does not require going soft. It is possible to be "hard on the problem, not on the people." This is the next step of good faith negotiation. Once you incorporate this tenet of good faith negotiation into your dealings with FDA, the character of the conflict can transform. In fact, the event becomes an opportunity for change and education. The team is attacking a problem instead of each other.

This may require you to change your presumption of how the encounter will proceed. If you begin by believing it is possible for FDA staff to be a welcome part of a team assigned to a problem-solving exercise, it is almost impossible to offend during the negotiations. Dealing with FDA can become an almost-enjoyable collaboration, an opportunity to resolve a potential problem with a product in advance. While mutually acceptable resolution may sound impossibly optimistic, at least you can relax knowing that discussion can ensue without the unpleasantness that characterizes some encounters with FDA.

4. Check Your Assumptions

Besides assuming that FDA ideas are unwelcome, there is another related source of tension that is pervasive in dealings between many public employees and regulated industry: the assumption that government workers are incompetent. Make sure this mindset does not control your encounters with FDA.

Be prepared, for example, to accept that a testy agency employee you encounter does not have a severe personality disorder. They may be having just a bad day. (It seems a foreign concept to some people outside the agency that FDA employees, like anyone else, struggle with life worries, e.g., sick parents or young children, that can interrupt a good night's sleep). Other callers may be downright abusive, which can temporarily affect the response you receive. Some workers receive death threats, especially when dealing with controversial products and issues like RU486 or alternative medicine. Whatever the reason for a lapse in courtesy, allow for the possibility that it is an aberration in conduct rather than a serious character flaw.

More often than being unproductive, FDA staff is overworked. Add to this that they lack resources to perform many of their duties efficiently, and that most individuals perform the related administrative tasks as well. Many federal employees have traded for these realities because there is less overtime required in the public sector, and they will have more time to attend to families or other personal demands. Treat them in a way that takes for granted that they are working hard, and they will appreciate it. Ask them about their working conditions, and even befriend reviewers where appropriate. Look for opportunities to take on some tasks that will speed the work on your application. Some duties cannot be delegated, but you can offer to fax invitations to your meetings, copy and distribute your meeting packages, and prepare meeting summaries.

This does not mean you should not report a difficult encounter to a supervisor, when appropriate. In that case, remember: you will have to trust that the supervisor has a more complete picture of the employee's performance and will put this encounter into perspective, and the supervisor cannot reveal whether any personnel action is taken. For your part, do not make the relationship worse by picking up where you left off at the next encounter. To do so gives the reviewer ammunition to explain away his or her conduct by blaming you for being the difficult one.

I remember shortly after the bombing of the federal building in Oklahoma, I was struggling to get a timely response from an FDA employee who had a child in FDA's day care center. Later I learned that after its own bomb scare, the center moved the children to an undisclosed location. For a confusing few hours, not even their parents had been told where the children had gone. There were even rumors that a bomb had been found on the site. I had no idea it was going on, and I pressed her for a response. Someone told me that after she had hung up, she began to cry. Of course, I was distraught myself once I realized my part. You must remember, as I had not that day, that FDA employees have their share of bad days. Sometimes because they work for the suspected New World Order, they have more than their share. (It is worth noting that for the past several years, security concerns in all government buildings have cost billions of dollars, aside from the distractions to everyone who works under those conditions).

Notwithstanding that incident, I was perhaps cursed with a reputation for defusing some of the angriest callers. Furious applicants and consumers were routed to me almost daily. For some of those people, FDA's actions had justified their anger. Even when that had been the case, however, the venting seemed to accomplish little. A tirade will delay the chance to provide help while it unfolds, and a reviewer who suffers through it may hesitate to return calls to that person the next time. Although most callers regain their composure after an initial outburst, those that do not are difficult to help even when FDA initially is in the wrong.

I related one particularly memorable caller to the deputy director of the Ombudsman's office. The caller had said that as FDA staff I was just another in the "bunch of brainless bureaucratic b* [expletive deleted]." "Too bad he didn't know I'm blond, too," I told my boss, admittedly somewhat snidely. "He could have used another 'b'-word." "Did you tell him how offensive it is to be called, you know, 'bureaucratic'?" he joked. I wish I had thought of that; a joke can be disarming. I had, however, just told the caller that I would call him back in an hour after he controlled his temper. Before he had a chance to object, I had hung up. I had to do that with three callers in almost five years; but when I did call back, I was prepared to forgive and forget the earlier incidents.

Another applicant complained to me that the reviewer would not spend time with her before issuing a non-approvable letter. She had hoped to preempt the letter with an informal discussion, and FDA often grants this courtesy. But FDA staff would not return her phone calls any more. I spoke to the exasperated reviewer, who admitted her animosity exhausted him. He said he delayed making calls to her because she was so unpleasant. After some thought, I decided to tell her the reason. "Oh!" she said, genuinely surprised. "Are other people pleasant?"

Yes some people are pleasant, without sacrificing principles or zealousness. Some people are not pleasant. The advantage for you is that so many people are hostile, if you can just avoid being one of them, FDA staff on the receiving end will be noticeably grateful. Applicants who stay mad never get to the substantive part of the discussion, or do so only after delay and after both sides are entrenched in their positions.

5. Ask Questions and Listen to the Answers

Instead of arguing over factual details, ask FDA reviewers what it is that concerns them. Your interest will surprise and delight them. Then, show that you have listened and use the information to formulate your response. If appropriate, accept the concerns suggested. If not, be prepared to explain why.

For example, in several cases that came before the Ombudsman, FDA review staff had asked for another study to see results from more patients. Before coming to the Ombudsman the companies would have argued for weeks over the specific number of additional subjects needed. When we were asked to intervene, I asked the review teams to explain the issues FDA had been trying to address. FDA responded that the study subjects may not have represented all the subpopulations that might use the product. Once that concern became clear, the teams could examine *all* the ways to respond to the issue, rather than just the single way a reviewer had suggested under tight deadlines. In those cases, for example, responses could show other data and evidence to demonstrate that additional risk to other populations was negligible, that labeling changes could address those groups, or that postmarketing studies could follow up on the groups.

6. Be Responsive

Do not make the common mistake of a response that does not address the issues. One common plea from applicants is they would not have conducted studies or prepared an application if the product were harmful — because they would have no desire to sell an unsafe product. This is a nonresponse that also suggests FDA review is superfluous. It is more important to show FDA that you care about safety, rather than just tell them; that is, do not just "talk the talk," but "walk the walk." Companies can better demonstrate their commitment to safety by answering the questions asked of them, or alternatively by demonstrating why those questions are irrelevant or unnecessary. Ignoring safety issues is not the answer.

Other applicants complain about the time in the queue when they are on their third (or more) cycle through the agency. While it might be fair to keep your place in line when an amendment is a small one, it is not helpful to suggest your application should be queued ahead of others that took the time and expense to prepare complete applications the first time. An exception can be made for a company that has submitted several times to meet changing data requests that were unclear at the outset, but the applicant must prove this exception is deserved.

Many applicants complain that the delay will force them out of business. This may be true — although it rarely seems to be in reality. As distressing as that can be when it is true, there are other companies in the queue who may also depend on FDA timeliness for their corporate survival. Again it is not fair to ask those applicants to wait, especially when they are bearing the same investment of time and costs to get products on markets, and may have made the investment in a better application.

In a handful of cases we worked on, the applications were clearly defective and the applicants demonstrated a lack understanding of basic FDA requirements. I remember a few where repackers intended to take products legally marketed for one indication and relabel them for other uses. When we explained the approval did not apply to a new indication, they objected. If their misunderstanding had been sincere, FDA staff was left very uncomfortable with the knowledge that such companies were trying to break into the medical device business. When company executives argued that FDA review would jeopardize the existence of their respective businesses, the response they evoked in FDA was probably not the one they had hoped for.

Being less than forthcoming wastes your time and shows a lack of respect for FDA. Outright dishonesty can evoke an expression of shock or sheepishness by the outside counsel or consultant sitting at the table. You will lose your own credibility, and will jeopardize the credibility of your counsel. Your representative has no obligation to let you mislead FDA, and may be unwilling to destroy a hard-fought reputation in the industry just for you. Furthermore, your lawyer may be *obligated* to correct you, or else be guilty of unethical practice. Do not be in a position where your own representatives have to apologize for your statements or omissions.

The diversion caused by "passive-aggression," avoidance or omissions also can delay a resolution of the underlying complaint at issue. In one case, an applicant was told to perform a compatibility study for its device in a dog study. The company agreed, although it had a legitimate complaint in that no other manufacturers in the device class had been asked to perform such a study. Instead of attacking the problem of this inequity, the manufacturer did the dog study — with one dog.

When the case came to the Ombudsman, the Center agreed that it would be fair to request compatibility testing evenly across the industry. The manufacturer won the battle, but it was a long battle that cost months of marketing, and the costs of the study, albeit small. More importantly, the company had jeopardized its credibility. If its later applications were examined very closely, surely that would feel like retaliation. The Division, however, believed that the company was manipulative and that its prior actions justified suspicion.

7. Be Prepared

If you do decide that the time has come to part with a reviewer, make a clean break. While some indiscretions may be forgiven, it is not enough to claim merely that your reviewer does not understand you or your product. Articulate a principled reason for someone up the chain of command to pay attention to your predicament. Too many applicants know only that they do not want to meet the FDA demands and that they want the product on the market. That is not an acceptable answer or a proper basis of complaint to FDA. Be prepared to suggest alternatives other than those suggested by the reviewer. Be able to explain why your alternative is reasonable, and why accepting it will not harm users. Also, be able to explain why your alternative will not sacrifice FDA's credibility before its constituencies, which include academic colleagues, healthcare professionals, consumers, and Congress.

Of course, unreasonable people do exist in the general population, and likewise FDA has its share. The FDA employees who seem unreasonable to you (however few they are) are likely to have exhibited this behavior within FDA as well. Their identities are not secret, as they can be just as controlling and obstreperous to people within their own ranks; others in the agency may have had to make up for their shortcomings and carry their loads. Sometimes an informal statement, as an aside to another FDA staff person, may be enough to have the project reassigned or the employee's power over it diminished, especially if your chosen confidante has witnessed some of the behavior in question.

I remember one meeting with industry that essentially had been "hijacked" by a particular FDAer. Not only was the company dismayed, but FDA staff were astounded when this individual espoused a position expressly rejected by the FDA majority and his own supervisor in advance of the meeting. This was not his first "protocol violation," and he was removed from the review team. Soon afterward other personnel action affected him.

B. When to Seek a Face-to-Face Meeting

The criteria for what constitutes a "personal" meeting have changed from one that is face-to-face to one that allows "real time" conversation, without some electronic intervenor such as voicemail or e-mail. Today a telephone meeting is personal by comparison. Although you cannot see facial expressions, at least you can listen to the other person's tone of voice for cues, and you can almost immediately correct unintentional offenses or flubs. Parties also can be face-to-face during a videoconference. On the other hand, sometimes your best interest dictates that you forego the time-saving, money-saving modern communication technologies for an actual visit to an FDA building. Personal visits also provide an opportunity to read body language and facial expressions that allow you to better identify miscommunication and to predict what is likely to be FDA's reaction afterward. Face-to-face meetings, however, also provide greater opportunities for *faux pas*.

1. Is a Meeting Necessary?
Face-to-face meetings will tend to be granted less often, as FDA staff must juggle so many duties and as meetings required under the Food and Drug Administration Modernization Act (FDAMA) increasingly take over staff time and conference rooms. Nevertheless, where credibility is an issue, a face-to-face meeting can be imperative, as long as it will improve the relationship.

Some meetings are contra-indicated. For example, meetings to demonstrate products under review are rarely necessary. The application should stand alone; if something goes horribly wrong later, FDA must be able to point to information in the file to explain what was relied upon to clear the product. Also, some records may be subject to Freedom of Information requests, and releasable information that is absent from the file is unlawful. If a product demonstration is needed, then the application probably is deficient.

2. Can You Be Too Well-Outfitted?
The first meeting I remember at FDA as a representative of the Commissioner was in 1988 at a two-day evidentiary hearing that began on a Thursday. To finish by the weekend, the subject of the hearing asked us to continue late into Friday night. During those two days, a limousine sat illegally parked outside FDA's Parklawn building. We

began to notice during the breaks that the limousine's passenger, was the doctor who was the subject of the hearing. He stood in the door to talk on a car phone, then an expensive and uncommon accessory. Into the night, the driver could be seen alternately pacing and leaning against the hood. My impression is that this conspicuous display of wealth did not help the doctor's case. A taxi may have been a wiser form of transportation to such a hearing.

Cars can no longer linger around federal buildings, but other errors abound. The "fashion police" will not ticket you for ostentatiousness, but extravagance of dress is still a bad idea. A nice watch, cuff links, and a well-fitted suit are accoutrements in consulting; FDA staff understand that careful attention to grooming details is a benefit, or perhaps a curse, of private practice. For interactions with government personnel, however, you would do well to stop there, without excess jewelry, big precious stones, or cologne. Avoid electronic distractions like the latest wireless PC embedded in the corner of your glasses. Tailor your tailoring so it is appropriate to the event.

3. Can You Have Too Many Invitees?

Attendees for a meeting should be carefully chosen and kept to a minimum. In selecting the attendees make sure that you have not only the right information in the room, but that you have a "choreographer" who will brief the others in advance.

Aside from having too many people in attendance, you should also pay attention to keeping less-than-helpful people away from the meeting setting. I remember one meeting where a doctor was being grilled on allegations that he spent more attention on his nurses than on his study subjects. One nurse replied indignantly that her interest in men in the workplace was strictly professional. During a break, I saw her speaking to an FDA attorney. She had lowered her head and raised her eyes at him coquettishly, and I had heard her giggling. When I inquired, the attorney recounted that the woman had asked about his marital status. Even though he had said he was married, she asked him to go out with her after the meeting. This inappropriate behavior may have been prevented, had better thought been extended as to the preferred attendees to that meeting.

More likely, blunders at meetings are less overt than that described above, but can inflict as much damage. Some people are excellent at what they do, but meetings with FDA may not be among those things they do well. It is true that some executives have enough clout and will not be dissuaded from attending. Nevertheless, all efforts should be made to keep the meeting attendees to a minimum without sacrificing information.

4. Advance Preparation

FDA staff will be attending an increasing number of required meetings. To have time to prepare, take an occasional day off, and still have time to perform actual review, FDA needs a package in advance of a meeting. Three to four weeks may seem unnecessarily long, but it allows time to circulate copies to the team members located in various agency buildings. Some divisions insist on more than four weeks for the package. Anything added later may not be read or even circulated. Prepare a package that can fax clearly, be e-mailed if appropriate, and can be taken on planes if necessary. If you add your contact information in the footer on all pages, you are more likely to find out if the package, or parts of it, get diverted in the shuffling, and if so, the package can be returned to you.

5. When to Arrive

It is increasingly important to arrive at meetings early, in plenty of time for you to go through the ubiquitous metal detectors and have your containers of meeting materials and baggage x-rayed. Add time to set up visual aides, and make additional copies of handouts to accommodate any unexpected attendees. You may be relieved when you find you allowed enough time to troupe to a nearby auxiliary office, as FDA occupies several buildings and has a complex campus. If you do arrive early, it is perfectly acceptable to ask any early-arriving FDA attendees to let you use the room to caucus in private.

6. Appearance of Impropriety

FDA staff use an abundance of caution when it comes to accepting gifts, and this may include situations that did not occur to you. On one hand, it is insulting to suggest that a public employee can compromise agency integrity and the public health for the price of a sandwich at lunch, or even a steak at dinner. Nevertheless, the prospect of an investigation is daunting, and most people avoid it at all costs.

The offer that most frequently makes FDA employees shudder is one to purchase a meal. Even though regulations are clear that under certain circumstances meals can be accepted, some staff go to extremes to ensure they receive no "free lunch." I have followed the lead of one colleague, who insisted on paying a few dollars for a small sandwich during a free open lunch that a company had on-site for its staff. One meeting that went hours longer than expected was interrupted when a company employee brought in a dozen doughnuts. FDA attendees agonized over whether they could accept any, until it was suggested that it would be all right to exchange one doughnut each for cups of coffee provided from an FDA staff person's own coffee supply.

If FDA personnel cannot be persuaded to accept a free meal, and a working lunch (or dinner) is needed, there are options other than fighting over the check. Each person can bring in his or her own meal. In that case, company personnel should not feast on a lavish spread while the FDA representative has a salmon-burger from the cafeteria. It may be agreeable for the group to go to one of the many mediocre restaurants that are located around government offices; the price at such an establishment will be within a public servant's budget and should be passable for someone perhaps more accustomed to finer dining.

Other gifts are also worrisome to government employees. One applicant stymied by FDA refusals to approve a submission let go with a string of epithets against one of my supervisors. He apologized later with several dozen roses. Unable to accept them, and unable to send them back before they withered, she placed them in a common area in the building. Although the regulations made it clear that her actions were acceptable under the circumstances, the obvious expense involved made her uneasy. A sincere apology would probably have been more effective.

IV. Conclusion

FDA staff can detect a company attitude that the agency is an annoyance to be undermined. This perception can persist even when that attitude is not really there. After many instances of being treated that way, many agency personnel just assume that is how applicants will feel about FDA's presence. Applicants would do well to treat FDAers at least as courteously as project team members within the company. The agency does not have the luxury of time for assisting every sponsor, but my experience has been that true retaliation is exceedingly rare. If your interactions confirm to FDA and the reviewer that you view them as nuisances, FDA staff may return the favor by not spending the extra time required to prepare for a thoughtful exchange as to what may be cheaper and faster alternatives to market. Instead, they will wait for your suggestions, and then consider them painstakingly slowly. If FDA reacts this way, it may be impossible for you to prove your retaliation case. Even if you convince someone your submissions are unwelcome, the reaction is hard to correct; most forces are powerless against an individual's reluctance to go the extra mile. As intangible as this may be, a company facing this obstacle has an expensive problem on its hands.

The current Ombudsman's office does not have the resources to solve every problem, and the new dispute resolution procedures in the Centers are not able to stop them from occurring. Therefore, companies have to be prepared to use to use good sense, good strategy, and impeccable etiquette in preventing and solving these problems.

James C. Morrison

Center for Drug Evaluation
and Research, FDA

CHAPTER 29

From FDA's Perspective

I. Introduction

As part of our transformation to a more transparent organization, we have provided
many opportunities for the industry to air complaints about the Food and Drug
Administration's (FDA's) Center for Drug Evaluation and Research (CDER). During a
recent meeting with industry representatives, the suggestion was made that I convey
what it is that most irritates the Center's staff about the industry. I conducted an informal, Center-wide e-mail poll. This chapter summarizes the results. The inquiry pro-
voked a wide spectrum of responses; some expressed appreciation for the opportunity
and then unloaded lists of grievances, but there were other comments that assessed the
industry as having its act together. Complaints are here grouped into four main categories: interactions, operational and submission quality, unrealistic expectations, and gaming the system.

II. Overly-Aggressive Interactions

By far the most common complaints of agency personnel involved what are perceived as overly-aggressive contacts by industry representatives. This type of behavior
includes: calling frequently regarding the status of a document or review; repeatedly
asking the same question looking for the desired answer (either asking the same person
one question in different forms or shopping around in different offices for the desired
answer); leaving a message for someone and then calling his or her supervisor shortly
thereafter to complain that calls are not being returned; failing to control anger, and
using inappropriate and demeaning statements to staff (almost always when a manager
is absent); insisting on an estimate of completion dates of reviews before anyone has
looked at the submission; asking for early warning of possible problems, and then de-
manding a meeting with the division to discuss the problems before they have had

supervisory review; and bypassing several levels in the supervisory chain to bring problems to senior management that could be solved at a lower level. Most CDER staff understand the time pressures that industry faces, and are sympathetic to the sense of urgency about products. These complaints stem from behavior that goes beyond normal angst. I always recommend to applicants that they communicate with the CDER project manager assigned to their application to determine what is reasonable in the way of status checks. Several status calls a day which does occur, are clearly excessive.

Most of the complaints are self-explanatory, but the difference between early warning about bad news and premature alarm deserves more discussion. Clearly, industry scientists want to learn of potential problems as soon as possible. But do applicants really want to know what concerns reviewers at every step? What will an applicant do with such detailed information? Unless everyone at CDER who needs to evaluate the potential problem has done so, the applicant runs the risk of getting an incomplete picture of the problem, or perhaps doing unnecessary work. On the other hand, if concerns can be allayed by pointing out information in the submission, early informal contact with the agency may save substantial time. Applicants should wait for at least a supervisory review before pushing for insights on potential problems; such issues should be broached by reviewers in the form of neutral questions to minimize alarm.

Other complaints about interactions with industry focused on administrative or protocol problems, such as contacting a reviewer directly without going through the project manager; bringing legal representatives and arguing legal issues at scientific meetings; and amending the agenda for a scheduled meeting at the last minute and sending in more data.

III. Operational and Submission Quality

Complaints about the quality of submissions and the science contained therein ranked just behind aggressive interactions. Agency personnel found fault with submitting poorly organized or sloppy documents (e.g., too much redundancy, poor pagination, unnecessary data such as printouts from lab equipment, inconsistent data, and repeated mistakes); ignoring advice on protocols and other input from previous meetings and correspondence; not stating in a cover letter what is in the attached submission; mixing important data in with routine submissions; not identifying when data have been submitted previously; and submitting MedWatch forms with missing data and no assessment or explanation.

The quality of submissions and data sent to CDER varies widely. Overall, the quality of submissions has been improving steadily. Attention to detail, especially in aspects that make submissions more understandable, is well worth the time entailed. If an applicant chooses not to follow the Center's advice on a protocol or suggestions provided in deficiency letters, it is wise to state that decision early in the submission, explain the reasons for the decision, and discuss plans with CDER. There may have been some miscommunication about what is expected and the reasons for the advice or suggestions.

IV. Unrealistic Expectations

Several complaints by FDA personnel regarding industry personnel behavior involved firms' requests for exceptions from stated policies and procedures or for special treatment, such as expedited review or moving up in the queue. These requests usually accompany appeals to the Center staff member's sense of fairness and equity, and they usually cite hardships that may have been created by CDER's past actions. It is not realistic to expect Center staff to bend or break established rules of procedure, or to change Center-wide priorities, to accommodate specific circumstances.

Were CDER to honor these requests, charges of favoritism and misfeasance would soon follow. If you feel you have suffered a grave injustice that needs to be addressed, I recommend that you talk with the director of the appropriate CDER division or contact me.

Another common complaint was that newcomers to the pharmaceutical industry sometimes expect CDER to function as a consulting service. Many in the Center have been approached by someone who claims to have discovered a great treatment for a disease and wants us to tell him or her how to get the product on the market. I always recommend that neophytes seek the services of a consultant.

The Center makes available much information about the drug review process, through the Internet and elsewhere, and it offers guidance to the industry in meetings. It is unrealistic, however, to expect that the limited time CDER staff members have would be sufficient to guide a company through the entire drug product development process. Companies should not expect extensive training in drug development from CDER anymore than one would expect training on how to build a space station from NASA.

Other examples of unrealistic expectations include:

- asking for a determination when there is clearly insufficient information on which to base a decision, and

- seeking immediate answers to complex regulatory issues at meetings or on the phone.

V. Gaming the System

The term "gaming the system" implies an intentional effort to subvert or misuse procedures and systems. Not all examples of the behaviors discussed below are intentional gaming strategies, but they often are perceived as such by Center staff.

From my experience, the vast majority of people who work in the regulated industry are honest and try to do the right thing. When their motives are questioned, they are understandably affronted. Certainly, industry representatives do try to improve their company's position, but they do not see themselves as gaming the system.

CDER staff must occasionally deal with those who seek to test legal and ethical limits. When agency personnel see behavior that can be construed as devious, they may well assume the worst — that the person, or the company itself, is gaming the system. By avoiding the following behaviors, companies can materially increase trust and improve interactions with the agency:

- deviating from an agreed-upon protocol design to achieve a more favorable result (e.g., changing inclusion and exclusion criteria or using different statistical methods);

- burying protocol changes or other key information in general correspondence and not discussing them with the reviewing division;

- exaggerating the consequences of failing to get whatever is being sought; staff so frequently hear that the company will fold if the requested accommodation is not made that they routinely ignore such claims;

- aiming to come as close to the regulatory line as possible or to do the absolute minimum work needed to fulfill regulatory requirements, then, when things do not work out (e.g., the study is underpowered), seeking relief from FDA's approval standards;

- complaining about a competitor's behavior and then asking to do the same thing if immediate regulatory action is not forthcoming;

- being less than forthright about safety issues with investigational or marketed drugs;

- asking CDER to delay an action to avoid adverse publicity, or to postpone bad news until after a shareholders' meeting or a critical financing decision.

The last two points above are particularly troubling to CDER staff. Nothing destroys working relationships and trust so much as appearing to be willing to trade public safety or corporate reputation for financial advantage. In the long run, strategies that attempt to hide information, even for a short time, cause much more damage than they can ever avoid.

One of the messages to take away from this survey of pet peeves is the wide range of behaviors and ethics to which CDER staff are exposed. It is well for industry representatives to keep in mind that Center staff are exposed to sufficient examples of untrustworthy behavior that it may color other interactions. Perhaps, then, CDER staff members should be forgiven when they seem generally suspicious.

The most difficult aspects of any type of law enforcement or regulatory work are how to recognize who is trustworthy and who is not — and to deal with each accordingly. It is a credit both to the regulated industry and to CDER staff that the vast majority of interactions between the Center and the regulated industry are positive, straightforward, and mutually respectful.

Whether you are a member of the regulated industry or a Center employee, you should be able to expect high standards of professionalism, courtesy, and respect in your interactions. I appreciate hearing about interactions that fail to meet those standards. You can contact this author by phone at (301)594-5298 or by e-mail at morrisonj@cder.fda.gov).

Author Affiliation Statements

Minnie V. Baylor-Henry, R.Ph., J.D., is Senior Director, Regulatory Affairs, The R.W. Johnson Pharmaceutical Research Institute, Raritan, NJ.

Kate C. Beardsley is a Partner, Buc & Beardsley, Washington, DC.

Anthony C. Celeste is President, AAC Consulting Group, Inc., Bethesda, MD.

Andrea E. Chamblee, Esq., is a Senior Regulatory Consultant in Silver Spring, MD.

Mark E. DuVal is Senior Counsel, 3M Pharmaceuticals Division, 3M Company, St. Paul, MN.

Bogdan Dziurzynski is Senior Vice President, Regulatory Affairs and Quality Assurance, MedImmune, Inc., Gaithersburg, MD.

Stacy L. Ehrlich is an Associate, Kleinfeld, Kaplan and Becker, Washington, DC.

Douglas B. Farquhar is a Member of Hyman, Phelps & McNamara, P.C., Washington, DC.

Joseph Paul Hile is a Senior Consultant and Chairman, Phoenix Regulatory Associates, Ltd., Sterling, VA.

Ronald M. Johnson is Executive Vice President, Quintiles Consulting, Rockville, MD.

Alan H. Kaplan is a Partner, Kleinfeld, Kaplan and Becker, Washington, DC.

Daniel A. Kracov is a Partner, Patton Boggs LLP, Washington, DC.

Steven M. Kowal is a Partner, Bell, Boyd & Lloyd, Chicago, IL.

Eugene I. Lambert is a Partner, Covington & Burling, Washington, DC.

Arthur N. Levine is a Partner, Arnold & Porter, Washington, DC.

Michael R. McConnell, R.Ph., is a Founder and Consultant, National Notification Center, Indianapolis, IN.

James C. Morrison is the Ombudsman, Center for Drug Evaluation and Research, Food and Drug Administration, Rockville, MD.

Jeannie Perron, D.V.M., is an Associate, Covington & Burling, Washington, DC.

Wayne L. Pines is President, Regulatory Services, APCO Associates Inc., Washington, DC.

Marjorie E. Powell is Assistant General Counsel, Pharmaceutical Research and Manufacturers of America, Washington, DC.

Peter H. Rheinstein, M.D., J.D., M.S., is Senior Vice-President for Medical and Clinical Affairs, Cell Works, Inc., Baltimore, MD.

Dvorah A. Richman is a Partner, King & Spalding, Washington, DC.

Janet L. "Lucy" Rose is President of Lucy Rose and Associates, Leesburg, VA.

Kathleen M. Sanzo is a Partner, Morgan Lewis & Bockius, LLP, Washington, DC.

Richard S. Silverman is a Partner, Hogan & Hartson L.L.P., Washington, DC.

Jennifer J. Spokes is an Attorney, Patton Boggs LLP, Washington, DC.

Marlene K. Tandy, M.D., J.D., is Associate General Counsel and Secretary, Health Industry Manufacturers Association, Washington, DC.

William W. Vodra is a Senior Partner, Arnold & Porter, Washington, DC.

David L. West, Ph.D., is Vice President, Quintiles Consulting, Rockville, MD.

Richard O. Wood is a Member, Bell, Boyd & Lloyd L.L.C., Chicago, IL.

Index

O

observations 169, 173
orphan drug 4
over-the-counter 7, 21, 25, 103
   active ingredients 8
   drugs 8
   monograph 7, 8, 104

P

patent extension 1
permanent injunction 136, 140
petition 113
Pharmaceutical Education and Research Institute 206
Pharmaceutical Research and Manufacturers of America 198, 200, 201
pharmacology 10
Phase II clinical testing 2
phased review 24
phased submission process 20
Photo-Dynamic Therapy 194
pivotal study 14
post-meeting 87, 88, 89
postmarket requirements 194
PowerPoint 68
pre-approval inspection 16, 151
pre-indictment 147, 148
pre-meeting 83, 84, 87, 89, 120
preclinical development 10
preliminary injunction 135, 139, 140
premarket approval 76, 194
   applications 29, 30, 31
premarket clearance 37
premarket notification 29, 30, 33, 40, 43
premarket review 191
preparation 143, 152, 222
prescription drug advertising 27
Prescription Drug Compliance and Surveillance Division 187
Prescription Drug Marketing Act 185
prescription drug samples 185, 189
Prescription Drug User Fee Act 5, 78, 101, 178, 208
prescription drugs 185
prescription-to-OTC 8
product approval decisions 73
product jurisdiction regulations 191, 192, 193, 194
production drugs 20
professional associations 197, 203
promotional labeling 27, 184
promotional material 177, 183
proposed guidance 199
proposed regulation 199
proprietary name 7
prosecution 149, 150
protocol 209
   design 230